Introduction to Data Mining and Soft Computing Techniques

INTRODUCTION TO DATA MINING AND SOFT COMPUTING TECHNIQUES

By

M. RAMAKRISHNA MURTHY

Associate Professor, Deptt. of Computer Science and Engineering,
GMR Institute of Technology, Rajam, Srikakulam
Andhra Pradesh

UNIVERSITY SCIENCE PRESS

(An Imprint of Laxmi Publications Pvt. Ltd.)

BANGALORE • CHENNAI • COCHIN • GUWAHATI • HYDERABAD
JALANDHAR • KOLKATA • LUCKNOW • MUMBAI • RANCHI • NEW DELHI
INDIA • USA • GHANA • KENYA

INTRODUCTION TO DATA MINING AND SOFT COMPUTING TECHNIQUES

Printed and bound in India
Typeset at Shubham Composer
First Edition: 2015
UDM-9738-195-DATA MIN SOFT COMP TECH-MUR
ISBN 978-93-83828-40-1
Price: ₹ 250.00

PUBLISHED IN INDIA BY

UNIVERSITY SCIENCE PRESS
(An Imprint of Laxmi Publications Pvt. Ltd.)
113, GOLDEN HOUSE, DARYAGANJ,
NEW DELHI - 110002, INDIA
Telephone : 91-11-4353 2500, 4353 2501
Fax : 91-11-2325 2572, 4353 2528
www.laxmipublications.com info@laxmipublications.com

Branches

Bangalore	080-26 75 69 30	
Chennai	044-24 34 47 26,	24 35 95 07
Cochin	0484-237 70 04,	405 13 03
Guwahati	0361-254 36 69,	251 38 81
Hyderabad	040-27 55 53 83,	27 55 53 93
Jalandhar	0181-222 12 72	
Kolkata	033-22 27 43 84	
Lucknow	0522-220 99 16	
Mumbai	022-24 91 54 15,	24 92 78 69
Ranchi	0651-220 44 64	

C—
Printed at : Repro Knowledgecast Limited, Thane

PREFACE

Data Mining and Softcomputing is the fastest growing technology for the business world. The collection of data, whether their origin is business or scientific experiment, has recently spread a tremendous interest in the area of knowledge discovery or data mining with help of softcomputing.

Data mining, also popularly referred to as Knowledge Discovery in Databases (KDD), is a process of finding value from volume. It is a multidisciplinary field, using ideas from database technology, machine learning, Artificial Intelligence, Neural networks, statistics, pattern recognition, information retrieval etc. Softcomputing is the useful technology to improve performance of the discovery process.

This book is of immense use for students of B.Tech(CSE), B.Tech(IT), MCA and M.Tech , software professionals, researchers and all others who are involved in this field.

This book is arranged into 11 chapters. At the end of each chapter summary of the chapter and review questions are provided and at the end of the book multiple choice questions of all chapters are given for the benefit of the students.

Chapter 1: This chapter introduces basic concepts of databases, foundations of data mining and evolution of data mining.

Chapter 2: In this chapter the topics covered include data mining process, architecture, functionalities and classification of data mining system. All the applications of Data mining are also covered.

Chapter 3: Data warehousing is the important concept related to the data mining. In this chapter data warehousing development and implementation technology, OLAP and OLTP technologies are covered.

Chapter 4: Data preprocessing is an essential part of work to improve the efficiency and ease of the data miming process. In this chapter data preprocessing issues are discussed like data cleaning, data integration, data transformation and data reduction.

Chapter 5: The primitives of data mining systems allow the users to interactively communicate with the data mining system during discovered in order to examine the findings from different angles or depth and direct the data mining process. In this chapter the above issues are discussed in easy manner and also emphasis is given on DMQL(Data Mining Query Language).

Chapter 6: In this chapter emphasis is given on association rule mining, which is a important functionality of data mining for market basket analysis. Apriori and FP-tree methods are discussed with interesting examples for easy understanding.

Chapter 7: This chapter has given basic idea of the classification techniques in data mining. The classification problem tends to occur in a wide variety of areas. This wide spread need for classification has led to the development of many different classification techniques.

Chapter 8: Cluster Analysis is emphasized in this chapter. Eight kinds of clustering algorithms have been discussed in easy and understandable manner and outlier analysis is introduced. At the end of the chapter comparison of all clustering algorithms in time and space complexity point of view is given.

Chapter 9: This chapter has given data mining techniques for complex types of data including spatial data, multimedia data, time series data, text data and the World Wide Web.

Chapter 10 and 11 present various softcomputing techniques. Particularly in the chapter 10 softcomputing techniques like evolutionary computing, genetic algorithms and machine learning are introduced. In chapter 11 basic concepts of artificial neural networks and its applications are discussed.

—Author

ACKNOWLEDGEMENTS

"Guru bramha guru Vishnu guru devo maheswara guru saksatu para bramha tasmai sri guravanmha .." Guru(Teacher) plays an important role in shaping future of every disciple. So it is my privilege to express my sincere, whole hearted gratitude to my beloved mentors Dr JVR Murty, Professor, JNTU-K, Kakinada, and Dr P.V.G.D Prasad Reddy, Registrar, Andhra University, Visakhapatnam for their motivation and encouragement without which this book would not have come to realization.

I wish to express my special thanks again to Dr JVR Murty Professor JNTU-K for his contribution towards chapter 5.

I thank Dr N.B.Venkateswarulu and Dr Suresh Satapati for their valuable suggestions for writing this book.

My sincere thanks to Dr G. Mallikarjuna Rao(GMR), chairman, GMR Group, Dr V. Raghunathan, CEO, GMRVF, Dr CLVRSV Prasad, Principal of GMRIT, Prof Shashi Kumar Totad, HOD, Department of CSE for providing encouraging environment for publishing activities in the college.

I also wish to express my sincere thanks to colleagues and friends Mr J. Vasudeva Rao, Mr Ch. Sreenu Babu, Mr Venkataramana.Attada, Mr P. Srinivasa Rao and all my colleagues in the department for their constant co-operation and encouragement.

My sweet wife & son Prasanna Jyothi & Venkata Sai Prabash were so patient with my late nights, and I wish to thank them for their support in writing this book.

1 deeply express my heartful thanks to the publisher for publishing this book in such a beautiful shape and well in time.

—Author

CONTENTS

1

INTRODUCTION

1.1 OVERVIEW

Globalization changes the business scenario entirely around the globe. To survive and grow in this highly competitive business world, the management of every organization has to meet certain goals. Those are like:

- Predict future business trends
- Respond quickly to the customer demands
- Quick react to the market opportunities and threats
- Predict pulse of the customers
- Market analysis and financial forecasting.

It is absolutely difficult to even attempt to achieve these goals, if the management can not aware about technical growth in the relational databases, data warehouse, data mining concepts and techniques which we will discuss in this book.

A question that naturally arises is whether the enormous data is generated and stored as archives can be used for improving the efficiency of business performance.

In the domain of scientific computing, the major problem is to infer some valuable information from the observed data. The use of computing technology has helped researches to collect very large volumes of data. The development of other scientific disciplines helped the community to collect such large volumes of data effortlessly. Some typical examples are remote-sensing data, as satellite is streaming in an enormous amount of remote sensing data every day. In the area of health science, the repository of protein data and genome data are an invaluable source of scientific experiments. On the other side, we are drowning in oceans of text data and data of other media that are generated from the web.

The collection of data, whether their origin is business enterprise or scientific experiment, has recently spurred a tremendous interest in the area of knowledge discovery and data mining. Statisticians and data miners now have faster analysis tools that can help sift and analyze the stockpiles of data, turning up valuable and often surprising information. As result, a new discipline in Computer Science, Data Mining, gradually evolved. Data mining is the exploration and analysis of large data sets, in order to discover meaningful patterns and rules. The key idea is to find effective ways to combine the computer's power to process data with the human eye's ability to detect patterns.

So let us aware of relational database, data warehouse briefly in this introductory chapter, and detail discussion in the coming chapters.

1.2 DATABASES

Computerization started in 1960's, database and information technology has been evolving systematically from primitive file processing systems to sophisticated and powerful database systems. The research and development in database systems since the 1970s has progressed from early hierarchical and network database systems to the development of relational database systems.

The relational model is today the primary data model for commercial data-processing applications. It has attained its primary position because of its simplicity, which eases the job of the programmer, compared to earlier data models such as the network model and the hierarchical model.

A **Database Management System (DBMS)** is a collection of **interrelated** data and a set of programs to access those data. The collection of data, usually referred to as the **database**, contains information relevant to an enterprise. The primary goal of the DBMS is to provide a way to store and retrieve database information that is both convenient and efficient.

The relational database consists of a collection of tables, each of which is assigned a unique name. Each table consists of a set of attributes (columns or fields) and usually stores an object identified by a unique key and described by a set of attribute values. A semantic data model, such as an **entity-relational (ER)** data model, which models the database as a set of entities and their relationships, is often constructed for relational databases.

1.2.1 Problems with DBMS

Almost every organization is using DBMS for its day-to-day operations. But now organizations are looking for data warehouse because organizations data is increased enormously. So that DBMS can not fulfill industry needs. Here is a list of some problems/issues:

- If an organization has multiple offices, each office will develop its own database. If the development is not centrally controlled and no coding guidelines are followed across the different branches of the organization, it is difficult to integrate the databases to obtain consolidated information. Note that for databases to be integrated, the table names and even the field names have to be the same.
- As RDBMS is for operational data, historical data is not preserved. It is generally kept only for archival purposes in a backup media.

Because of the above reasons we are looking for another break through of technology to handle huge amount of transaction and historical data, which is exactly the data warehouse.

1.3 DATA WAREHOUSE

In today's competitive business environment, information is power. To get the right information at the right time, for by the decision makers, is the key to success. A data warehouse has emerged as recognition of the value and role of information. It is the means for this strategic data usage. A data warehouse is not the same as a decision support system. Rather, a data warehouse is a platform with integrated data of improved quality to support many decision support system and management information system applications and processes within an enterprise. Data warehouse improves the productivity of corporate decision makers through consolidation, conversion, transformation, and integration of operational data, and provides a consistent view of an enterprise.

Data warehousing provides architecture and tools for business executive to systematically organize, understand, and use their data to make strategic decisions. The important requirement of a data warehouse is that it is an on-line query analysis based on historical data for decision support rather than on-line transaction processing of operational data. Hence, On-Line Transaction Processing (OLTP) refers to operational database On-Line Analytical Processing (OLAP) refers to warehousing data which contains historical data which is contains historical data that is derived from transaction data.

We shall discuss the detailed technical study about data warehouse in coming chapter.

Basically it is important to differentiate the terms *data, information and knowledge* before we start study of data mining and data warehousing.

Data: Data is unprocessed/raw facts collected during a business transaction.

Information: Information processed data that provides the analysis of the collected data.

Knowledge: Knowledge is processed information that is used for decision-making and creativity.

1.4 THE FOUNDATIONS OF DATA MINING

Data mining techniques are the result of a long process of research and product development. This evolution began when business data was first stored on computers, continued with improvements in data access, and more recently, generated technologies that allow users to navigate through their data in real time. Data mining takes this evolutionary process beyond retrospective data access and navigation to prospective and proactive information delivery. Data mining is ready for application in the business community because it is supported by three technologies that are now sufficiently mature:

- Massive data collection
- Powerful multiprocessor computers
- Data mining algorithms

Commercial databases are growing at unprecedented rates. A recent META Group survey of data warehouse projects found that 19% of respondents are beyond the 50 gigabyte level, while 59% expect to be there by second quarter of 1996. In some industries, such as retail, these numbers can be much larger. The accompanying need for improved computational engines can now be met in a cost-effective manner with parallel multiprocessor computer technology. Data mining algorithms embody techniques that have existed for at least 10 years, but have only recently been implemented as mature, reliable, understandable tools that consistently outperform older statistical methods.

In the evolution from business data to business information, each new step has built upon the previous one. For example, dynamic data access is critical for drill-through in data navigation applications, and the ability to store large databases is critical to data mining. From the user's point of view, the four steps listed in Table 1.1 were revolutionary because they allowed new business questions to be answered accurately and quickly.

Table 1.1 Steps in the Evolution of Data Mining

Evolutionary Step	*Business Question*	*Enabling Technologies*	*Product Providers*	*Characteristics*
Data Collection (1960s)	"What was my total revenue in the last five years?"	Computers, tapes, disks	IBM, CDC	Retrospective, static data delivery
Data Access (1980s)	"What were unit sales in New Delhi last March?"	Relational databases (RDBMS), Structured Query Language (SQL), ODBC	Oracle, Sybase, Informix, IBM, Microsoft	Retrospective, dynamic data delivery at record level
Data Warehousing & Decision Support (1990s)	"What were unit sales in New Delhi last March? Drill down to Hyderbad"	On-line analytic processing (OLAP), multidimensional databases, data warehouses	Pilot, Comshare, Arbor, Cognos, Microstrategy	Retrospective, dynamic data delivery at multiple levels
Data Mining (Emerging Today)	"What's likely to happen to Hyderbad unit sales next month? Why?"	Advanced algorithms, multiprocessor computers, massive databases	Pilot, Lockheed, IBM, SGI, numerous startups (nascent industry)	Prospective, proactive information delivery

The core components of data mining technology have been under development for decades, in research areas such as statistics, artificial intelligence, and machine learning. Today, the maturity of these techniques, coupled with high-performance relational database engines and broad data integration efforts, make these technologies practical for current data warehouse environments.

SUMMARY

- A **database management system (DBMS)** is a collection of **interrelated** data and a set of programs to access those data. The collection of data, usually referred to as the **database**, contains information relevant to an enterprise.
- Database technology has evolved from primitive file processing to the development of database management systems with query and transaction processing. Further progress has led to the increasing demand for efficient and effective advanced data analysis tools. This need is a result of the explosive growth in data collected from applications, including business and management, government administration, science and engineering, and environmental control.
- The primary goal of the DBMS is to provide a way to store and retrieve database information that is both convenient and efficient.
- The relational database consists of a collection of tables, each of which is assigned a unique name. Each table consists of a set of attributes (columns or fields) and usually stores an object identified by a unique key and described by a set of attribute values.
- Data warehouse improves the productivity of corporate decision makers through consolidation, conversion, transformation, and integration of operational data, and provides a consistent view of an enterprise.

- The important requirement of a data warehouse is that it is an on-line query analysis based on historical data for decision support rather than on-line transaction processing of operational data. Hence, On-Line Transaction Processing (OLTP) refers to operational database On-Line Analytical Processing (OLAP) refers to warehousing data which contains historical data which is contains historical data that is derived from transaction data.

REVIEW QUESTIONS

1. Define database and write few problems with database.
2. Write the differences between data, information and knowledge.
3. Write about briefly about data warehouse.
4. Discuss foundations of data mining.
5. How is a data warehouse different from a database? How they are similar?

2

DATA MINING

2.1 WHAT IS DATA MINING?

Data mining or knowledge discovery in databases (KDD) is a collection of exploration techniques based on advanced analytical methods and tools for handling a large amount of information. The techniques can find novel patterns that may assist an enterprise in understanding the business better and in forecasting. Many data mining techniques are closely related to some of the machine learning techniques that have been developed over the last 40 years. Others are related to techniques that have been developed in statistics, sometimes called exploratory data analysis.

Data mining is an attempt at providing some of the intelligence that lets a manager understands his/her business better. In conventional analysis, a manager may have a question or hypothesis or perhaps just a hunch and be interested in proving or disproving it. If the manager is having series of hypotheses, the process of proving or disproving them is likely to be time consuming and expensive. In data mining, the responsibility of the manager does not disappear entirely, but much of the work shifted to the data mining software, thereby reducing the analysis effort required of the manager.

As we mentioned earlier conventional database systems are often designed for day-to-day running of an organization and are called Online Transaction Processing (OLTP) system. These systems are designed to capture business transactions online and are optimized for high throughput, a high level of availability and in some cases high security of information. Since the operation of an enterprise depends on the running of such operational OLTP systems, high availability is essential.

2.1.1 Data Mining: Definitions

Data mining, the extraction of the hidden predictive information from large databases is a powerful new technology with great potential to analyze important information in the data warehouse. Data mining scours databases for hidden patterns, finding predictive information that experts may miss, as it goes beyond their expectations. When implemented on a high performance client/sever or parallel processing computers, data mining tools can analyze massive databases to deliver answers to questions such as which clients are most likely to respond to the next promotional mailing.

Data mining and knowledge discovery in the databases is a new interdisciplinary field, merging ideas from statistics, machine learning, databases and parallel computing. Researchers have defined the term "data mining" in many ways.

1. *Data mining is non-trivial process of identifying valid, novel, potentially useful ultimately understandable patters of data.*

   The term data mining refers to the finding of relevant and useful information from databases.

2. *Data mining refers to using a variety of techniques to identify nuggets of information or decision-making knowledge in the database and extracting these in such a way that they can be put to use in areas such as decision support, prediction, forecasting and estimation. The data is often voluminous, but it has low value and no direct use can be made of it. It is the hidden information in the data that is useful.*

   Data mining is a process of finding value from volume. In any enterprise, the amount of transaction data generated during day-to-day operations is massive in volume. Although these transactions record every instance of any activity, it is of little use in decision making. Data mining attempts to extract smaller pieces of valuable information from this massive database.

3. *Data mining is the process of discovering meaningful, new correlation patterns and trends by sifting through large amount of data stored in repositories, using pattern recognition techniques as well as statistical and mathematical techniques.*

   One important aspect of data mining is that it scans through a large volume of data to discover patterns and correlations between attributes. Thus, though there are techniques like clustering, decision trees etc., existing in different disciplines, these are not readily applicable to data mining as they are not designed to handle large amounts of data. Thus, in order to apply statistical and mathematical tools, we have to modify these techniques to be able efficiency sift through large amounts of data stored in the secondary memory.

2.2 DATA MINING PROCESS

Many people treat data mining as a synonym for another popularly used term, *Knowledge Discovery in Databases, or KDD*. Alternatively, others view data mining as simply an essential step in the process of knowledge discovery in databases. Knowledge discovery as a process is shown in the Fig. 2.1 and consists of an iterative sequence of the following steps:

1. **Data cleaning** (to remove noise and inconsistent data).
2. **Data integration** (where multiple data sources may be combined).

   A popular trend in the information industry is to perform data cleaning and data integration as a preprocessing step where the resulting data are stored in a data warehouse.
3. **Data selection** (where data relevant to the analysis task are retrieved from the database).
4. **Data transformation** (where data are transformed or consolidated into forms appropriate for mining by performing summary or aggregation operations. For instance).

   Sometimes data transformation and consolidation are performed before the data selection process particularly in the case of data warehousing.
5. **Data mining** (an essential process where intelligent methods are applied in order to extract data patterns).

6. **Pattern evaluation** (to identify the truly interesting patterns representing knowledge based on some interesting measures).
7. **Knowledge presentation** (Where visualization and knowledge representation techniques are used to present the mined knowledge to the user).

The data mining step may interact with the user or a knowledge base. The interesting patterns are presented to the user, and may be stored as new knowledge in the knowledge base.

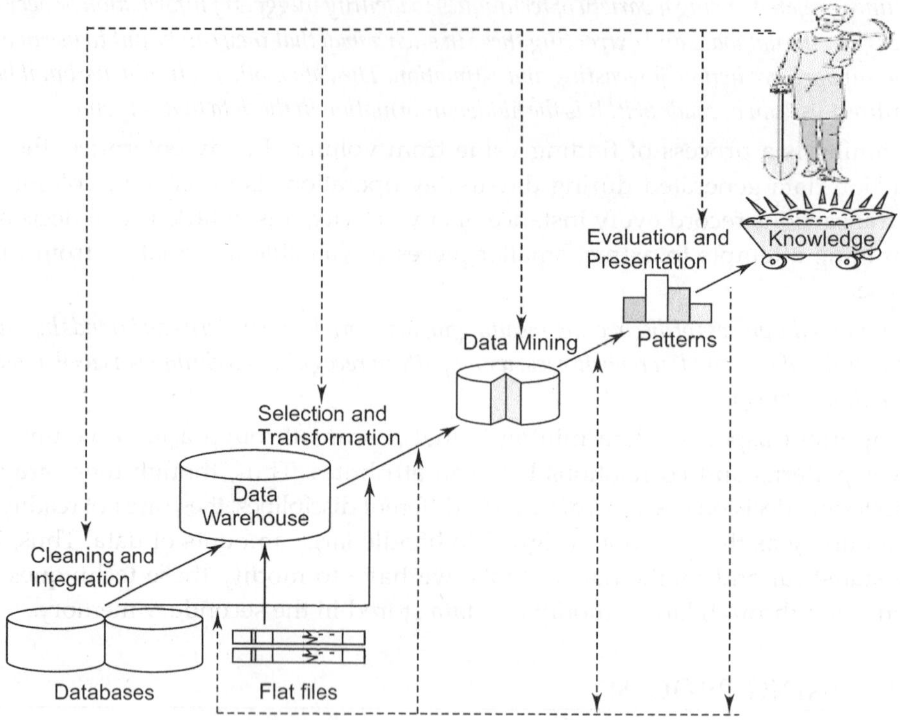

Fig. 2.1 Data mining stages

2.3 DATA MINING ARCHITECTURE

The data mining step may interact with the user or a knowledge base. The interesting patterns are presented to the user, and may be stored as new knowledge in the knowledge base. Note that according to this view, data mining is only one step in the entire process.

The architecture of typical data mining system may have the following components

- **Database, data warehouse, or other information repository:** This is one or a set of database, data warehouses, spreadsheets, or other kinds of information repositories. Data cleaning and data integration techniques may be performed on the data.
- **Database or data warehouse server:** The database or data warehouse server is responsible for fetching the relevant data, based on the user's data mining request.
- **Knowledge base:** This is the domain knowledge that is used to guide the search, or evaluate the interesting of resulting patterns. Such knowledge can include concept hierarchies, used to organize attributes or attribute values into different levels of abstractions.

- **Data mining engine:** This is essential to the data mining system and ideally consists of a set of functional modules for tasks such a characterization, association, classification, cluster analysis, and evolution and deviation analysis.
- **Pattern evaluation module:** This is components typically employs interestingness measure and interacts with the data mining modules so as to focus the search towards interesting patterns.
- **Graphical user interface:** This module communicates between users and the data mining system, allowing the user to interact with the system.

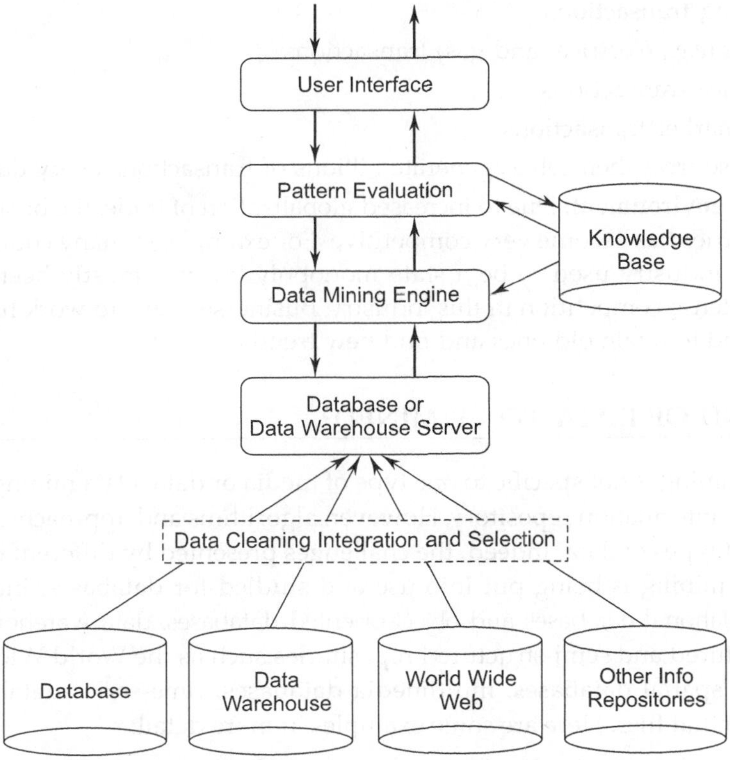

Fig. 2.2 Architecture data mining system

2.4 WHY DATA MINING NOW?

Data is growing rapidly in the last few years for a number of reasons. Use that data properly to growth of business. So apply data mining techniques to discover the knowledge from the databases. The following are might be the good reasons for the use data mining.

1. **Growth in OLTP data:** The first database systems were implemented in the 1960s and 1970s. Many enterprises therefore have more than 30 years of experience in using database systems and they have accumulated large amounts of data during that time. Also as noted earlier, other technological developments have also resulted in growth, in some cases drastic growth, in accumulated data.
2. **Growth in data due to cards:** The growing use of credit cards and loyalty cards is an important area of data growth.

3. **Growth in data due to the web:** E-commerce development have resulted in information about visitors to web sites being captured, once again resulting in mountains of data for some companies.
4. **Growth in data due to other sources:** There are many other sources of data. Some of them are:
   - Telephone transactions
   - Medical transactions
   - Banking transactions
   - Motor vehicle transactions
   - Shopping transactions
   - Utilities (*e.g.*, electrical and gas) transactions
   - Insurance transactions
   - Stock market transactions

   Again these sources themselves generate billions of transactions every day.
5. **Competitive environment:** Due to increased globalization of trade, the business environment is most countries has become very competitive. For example, in many countries the telecommunications industry used to be a state monopoly but has mostly been privatized now, leading to intense competition in this industry. Businesses have to work harder to find new customers and to retain old ones and find new trends.

2.5 WHAT KIND OF DATA TO BE MINED?

In principle, data mining is not specific to one type of media or data. Data mining should be applicable to any kind of information repository. However, algorithms and approaches may differ when applied to different types of data. Indeed, the challenges presented by different types of data vary significantly. Data mining is being put into use and studied for databases, including relational databases, object-relational databases and object-oriented databases, data warehouses, transactional databases, unstructured and semi-structured repositories such as the World Wide Web, advanced databases such as spatial databases, multimedia databases, time-series databases and textual databases, and even flat files. Here are some examples in more detail:

- **Flat files:** Flat files are actually the most common data source for data mining algorithms, especially at the research level. Flat files are simple data files in text or binary format with a structure known by the data mining algorithm to be applied. The data in these files can be transactions, time-series data, scientific measurements, etc.
- **Relational databases:** Briefly, a relational database consists of a set of tables containing either values of entity attributes, or values of attributes from entity relationships. Tables have columns and rows, where columns represent attributes and rows represent tuples. A tuple in a relational table corresponds to either an object or a relationship between objects and is identified by a set of attribute values representing a unique key.

  Data mining algorithms using relational databases can be more versatile than data mining algorithms specifically written for flat files, since they can take advantage of the structure inherent to relational databases. While data mining can benefit from SQL for data selection, transformation and consolidation, it goes beyond what SQL could provide, such as predicting, comparing, detecting deviations, etc.

- **Data warehouses:** A data warehouse as a storehouse is a repository of data collected from multiple data sources (often heterogeneous) and is intended to be used as a whole under the same unified schema. A data warehouse gives the option to analyze data from different sources under the same roof.

  We will discuss more details about data warehouse incoming chapters

- **Transaction databases:** A transaction database is a set of records representing transactions, each with a time stamp, an identifier and a set of items. Associated with the transaction files could also be descriptive data for the items. Since relational databases do not allow nested tables (*i.e.*, a set as attribute value), transactions are usually stored in flat files or stored in two normalized transaction tables, one for the transactions and one for the transaction items. One typical data mining analysis on such data is the so-called market basket analysis or association rules in which associations between items occurring together or in sequence are studied.

- **Multimedia databases:** Multimedia databases include video, images, and audio and text media. They can be stored on extended object-relational or object-oriented databases, or simply on a file system. Multimedia is characterized by its high dimensionality, which makes data mining even more challenging. Data mining from multimedia repositories may require computer vision, computer graphics, image interpretation, and natural language processing methodologies.

- **Spatial databases:** Spatial databases contain spatial-related information. Such databases include geographic (map) databases, VLSI chip design databases, and medical and satellite image databases. Spatial data may be represented in a raster format, consisting of n-dimensional bit maps or pixel maps. For example, *a*2-D satellite image may be represented as raster data, where each pixel registers the rainfall in a given area. Maps can be represented in vector format, where roads, bridges, buildings and lakes are represented as unions of basic geometric constructs, such as points, lines, polygons, and the partitions and networks formed by these shapes.

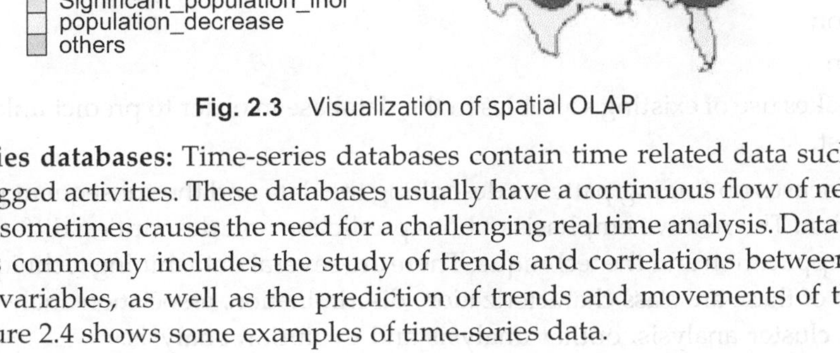

Fig. 2.3 Visualization of spatial OLAP

- **Time-series databases:** Time-series databases contain time related data such stock market data or logged activities. These databases usually have a continuous flow of new data coming in, which sometimes causes the need for a challenging real time analysis. Data mining in such databases commonly includes the study of trends and correlations between evolutions of different variables, as well as the prediction of trends and movements of the variables in time. Figure 2.4 shows some examples of time-series data.

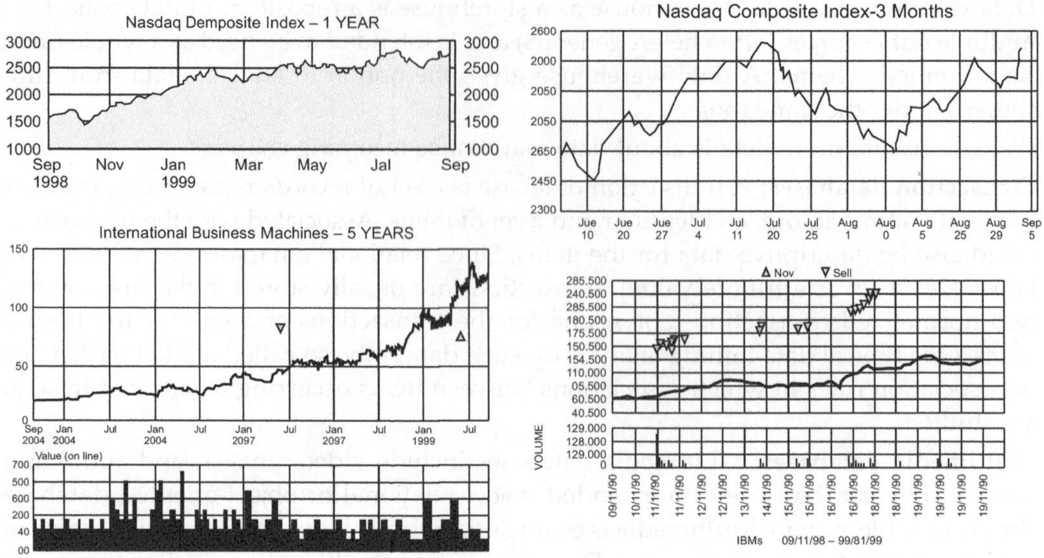

Fig. 2.4 Examples of time-series data

- **World wide web:** The World Wide Web is the most heterogeneous and dynamic repository available. A very large number of authors and publishers are continuously contributing to its growth and metamorphosis, and a massive number of users are accessing its resources daily. Data in the World Wide Web is organized in inter-connected documents. These documents can be text, audio, video, raw data, and even applications. Conceptually, the World Wide Web is comprised of three major components: The content of the Web, which encompasses documents available; the structure of the Web, which covers the hyperlinks and the relationships between documents; and the usage of the web, describing how and when the resources are accessed. A fourth dimension can be added relating the dynamic nature or evolution of the documents. Data mining in the World Wide Web, or web mining, tries to address all these issues and is often divided into web content mining, web structure mining and web usage mining.

2.6 DATA MINING FUNCTIONALITIES

Data mining functionalities are used to specify the kind of patterns to be found in data mining tasks. In general, data mining tasks can be classified into two categories:

- Description
- Prediction

Prediction makes use of existing variables in the database in order to predict unknown or future values of interest.

Description focuses on finding patterns describing the data and the subsequent presentation for user interpretation. The relative emphasis of both prediction and description differ with respect to the underlying application and the technique. There are several data mining techniques fulfill these objectives. Some of these are class characterization, discrimination, association analysis, classification and prediction, cluster analysis, outlier analysis and evolution analysis.

Another approach of study of Data mining techniques is to classify into:

- User-guided or verification -driven data mining (supervised)
- Discovery-driven or automatic discovery of rules (Unsupervised)

Most of the techniques of data mining have elements of both the models.

2.6.1 Verification Model (Supervised)

In the process of data mining, the user makes hypothesis and tests the hypothesis on the data to verify its validity. The emphasis is on the user who is responsible for formulating the hypothesis and issuing the query on the data to affirm or negate the hypothesis.

2.6.2 Discovery Model (Unsupervised)

The discovery model differs in its emphasis, in that it is the system automatically discovering important information hidden in the data. The data is sifted in search of frequently occurring patterns, trends and generalization about the data without intervention or guidance from the user.

2.6.3 Data Characterization

Data characterization is a summarization of the general characteristics or features of a target class of data. The data corresponding to the user-specified class are typically collected by a database query. For example, to study the characteristics of software products whose sales increased by 10% in the last year, the data related to such products can be collected by executing in SQL query.

There are several methods for effective data summarization and characterization. For instance, the data cube-based OLAP roll-up operation can be used to perform user-controlled data summarization along a specified dimension. These concepts will discuss in next chapters detailed.

The output of data characterization can be presented in various forms like pie charts, bar charts, curves, multidimensional data cubes, and multidimensional tables, including cross tabs. The resulting descriptions can also be presented as generalized or in rule form(called characteristic rules).

2.6.4 Data Discrimination

Data discrimination is a comparison of the general features of target class data objects with the general features of objects from one or a set of contrasting classes. The target and contrasting classes can be specified by the user, and the corresponding data objects retrieved through database queries.

The forms of output presentation are similar to those for characteristic descriptions, although discrimination descriptions should include comparative measures that help distinguish between the target and contrasting classes. Discrimination descriptions express in rule form is referred to as discriminate rules. The user should be able to manipulate the output for characteristic and discriminate descriptions.

Other data mining functionalities are, association analysis, cluster analysis classification and other. These functionalities are discussed in coming chapters.

2.7 CLASSIFICATION OF DATA MINING SYSTEMS

Data mining is an interdisciplinary field, the confluence of a set of discipline include database systems, statistics, machine learning, visualization, and information science. Moreover, depending on the data mining approach used, techniques from other disciplines may be applied, such as neural networks, fuzzy and/or rough set theory, knowledge representation, inductive logic programming, or high performance computing. Depending on the kind of data to be mined or on the given data mining application, the data mining system may also integrate techniques from spatial data analysis, information retrieval, pattern recognition, image analysis, signal processing, computer graphics, web technology, economics, business, bioinformatics, or psychology.

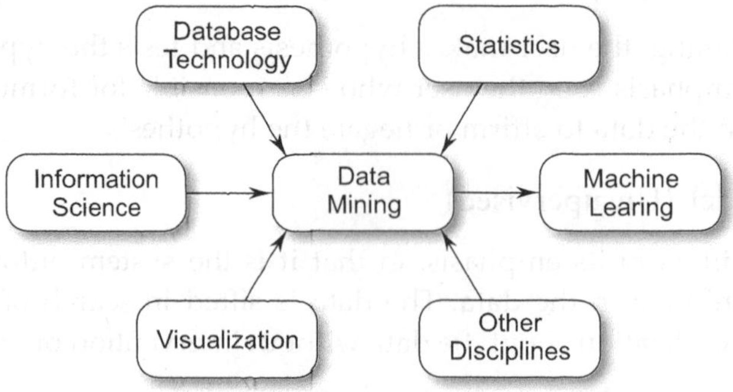

Fig. 2.5 Influence of interdisciplinary fields to data mining

Because of the diversity of disciplines contributing to data mining, data mining research is expected to generate a large variety of data mining systems. Therefore, it is necessary to provide a clear classification of data mining systems. Such a classification may help potential users distinguish data mining systems and identify those that best match their needs. Data mining systems can be categorized according to various criteria, as follows.

Classification according to the kind of database mined

The data mining systems can be classified according to the kind of databases mined. Database systems themselves can be classified according to different criteria (such as data models, or the type of data or applications involved), each of which may require its own data mining technique. Data mining systems can therefore be classified accordingly.

For instance, if classifying according to data models, we may have a relational, transactional, object-oriented, object-relational, or data warehouse mining system. If classifying according to the special types of data handled, we may have a spatial, time-series, text, or multimedia data mining system, or a World Wide Web mining system.

Classification according to the kinds of knowledge mined

Data mining systems can be categorized according to the kinds of knowledge they mine, that is based on data mining functionalities, such as characterization, discrimination, association, classification, clustering, outlier analysis, and evolutions analysis. A comprehensive data mining system usually provides multiple and/or integrated data mining functionalities.

Moreover, data mining systems can be distinguished based on the granularity or levels of abstraction of the knowledge mined, including generalized knowledge (at a high level of abstraction), primitive-level knowledge (at a raw data level) or knowledge at multiple levels (considering several levels of abstraction). An advanced data mining system should facilitate the discovery of knowledge at multiple levels of abstraction.

Data mining systems can also be categorized as those that mine data regularities (commonly occurring patterns) verses those that mine data irregularities (such as exceptions, outliers). In general, concept description, association analysis, classification, prediction, and clustering mine data regularities, rejecting outliers as noise. These methods may also help to detect outliers.

Classification according to the kind of techniques utilized

Data mining system can be categorized according to the underlying data mining techniques employed. These techniques can be described according to the degree of user interaction involved(*e.g.*, autonomous systems, interactive exploratory systems, query driven systems) or the methods of data analysis employed(*e.g.*, database oriented or data warehouse-oriented techniques, machine learning statistics, visualization, pattern recognition, neural networks, and so on). A sophisticated data mining system will often adopt multiple data mining techniques or work out an effective, integrated technique that combines the merits of a few individual approaches.

Classification according to the application adapted

Data mining systems can also be categorized according to the applications they adapt. For example, there could be data mining systems tailored specifically for finance, telecommunications, DNA, stock markets, e-mail, and so on. Different applications often require the integration of application-specific methods. Therefore, a generic, all-purpose data mining system may fit domain-specific mining tasks.

2.7.1 Supervised Learning

Supervised learning means learning from examples, where a training set is given which acts as examples for the classes. The system finds a description of each class. Once the description has been formulated, it is used to predict the class of previously unseen objects. This is similar to discriminate analysis which occurs in statistics.

2.7.2 Unsupervised Learning

Unsupervised learning is learning from observation and discovery. In this mode of learning, there is no training set or prior knowledge of the classes. The system analyzes the given set of data to observe similarities emerging out of the subsets of the data. The outcome is a set of class descriptions, one for each class, discovered in the environment. This is similar to cluster analysis in statistics.

Data mining and the part of machine learning dealing with learning from examples, and overlap in the algorithms used and the problems addressed. Data mining is concerned with finding understandable knowledge, while machine learning is concerned with improving the performance of an intelligent system or agent for problem-solving tasks. When integrating machine learning techniques into database systems, some of the databases require more efficient learning algorithms because realistic databases are normally very large and noisy.

2.8 ISSUES IN DATA MINING

Data mining algorithms embody techniques that have sometimes existed for many years, but have only lately been applied as reliable and scalable tools that time and again outperform older classical statistical methods. While data mining is still in its infancy, it is becoming a trend and ubiquitous.

Before data mining develops into a conventional, mature and trusted discipline, many still pending issues have to be addressed. Some of these issues are addressed below. Note that these issues are not exclusive and are not ordered in any way.

Security and social issues: Security is an important issue with any data collection that is shared and/or is intended to be used for strategic decision-making. In addition, when data is collected for customer profiling, user behavior understanding, correlating personal data with other information, etc., large amounts of sensitive and private information about individuals or companies is gathered and stored. This becomes controversial given the confidential nature of some of this data and the potential illegal access to the information. Moreover, data mining could disclose new implicit knowledge about individuals or groups that could be against privacy policies, especially if there is potential dissemination of discovered information. Another issue that arises from this concern is the appropriate use of data mining. Due to the value of data, databases of all sorts of content are regularly sold, and because of the competitive advantage that can be attained from implicit knowledge discovered, some important information could be withheld, while other information could be widely distributed and used without control.

User interface issues: The knowledge discovered by data mining tools is useful as long as it is interesting, and above all understandable by the user. Good data visualization eases the interpretation of data mining results, as well as helps users better understand their needs. Many data exploratory analysis tasks are significantly facilitated by the ability to see data in an appropriate visual presentation. There are many visualization ideas and proposals for effective data graphical presentation. However, there is still much research to accomplish in order to obtain good visualization tools for large datasets that could be used to display and manipulate mined knowledge. The major issues related to user interfaces and visualization are "screen real-estate", information rendering, and interaction. Interactivity with the data and data mining results is crucial since it provides means for the user to focus and refine the mining tasks, as well as to picture the discovered knowledge from different angles and at different conceptual levels.

Mining methodology issues: These issues pertain to the data mining approaches applied and their limitations. Topics such as versatility of the mining approaches, the diversity of data available, the dimensionality of the domain, the broad analysis needs (when known), the assessment of the knowledge discovered, the exploitation of background knowledge and metadata, the control and handling of noise in data, etc., are all examples that can dictate mining methodology choices. For instance, it is often desirable to have different data mining methods available since different approaches may perform differently depending upon the data at hand. Moreover, different approaches may suit and solve user's needs differently.

Most algorithms assume the data to be noise-free. This is of course a strong assumption. Most datasets contain exceptions, invalid or incomplete information, etc., which may complicate, if not obscure, the analysis process and in many cases compromise the accuracy of the results. As a consequence, data preprocessing (data cleaning and transformation) becomes vital. It is often seen as lost time, but data cleaning, as time consuming and frustrating as it may be, is one of the most important phases in the knowledge discovery process. Data mining techniques should be able to handle noise in data or incomplete information.

More than the size of data, the size of the search space is even more decisive for data mining techniques. The size of the search space is often depending upon the number of dimensions in the domain space. The search space usually grows exponentially when the number of dimensions increases. This is known as the *curse of dimensionality*. This "curse" affects so badly the performance of some data mining approaches that it is becoming one of the most urgent issues to solve.

Performance issues: Many artificial intelligence and statistical methods exist for data analysis and interpretation. However, these methods were often not designed for the very large data sets data mining is dealing with today. Terabyte sizes are common. This raises the issues of scalability and efficiency of the data mining methods when processing considerably large data. Algorithms with exponential and even medium-order polynomial complexity cannot be of practical use for data mining. Linear algorithms are usually the norm. In same theme, sampling can be used for mining instead of the whole dataset. However, concerns such as completeness and choice of samples may arise.

Other topics in the issue of performance are *incremental updating,* and parallel programming. There is no doubt that parallelism can help solve the size problem if the dataset can be subdivided and the results can be merged later. Incremental updating is important for merging results from parallel mining, or updating data mining results when new data becomes available without having to re-analyze the complete dataset.

Data source issues: There are many issues related to the data sources, some are practical such as the diversity of data types, while others are philosophical like the data glut problem. We certainly have an excess of data since we already have more data than we can handle and we are still collecting data at an even higher rate. If the spread of database management systems has helped increase the gathering of information, the advent of data mining is certainly encouraging more data harvesting. The current practice is to collect as much data as possible now and process it, or try to process it, later. The concern is whether we are collecting the right data at the appropriate amount, whether we know what we want to do with it, and whether we distinguish between what data is important and what data is insignificant. Regarding the practical issues related to data sources, there is the subject of heterogeneous databases and the focus on diverse complex data types.

We are storing different types of data in a variety of repositories. It is difficult to expect a data mining system to effectively and efficiently achieve good mining results on all kinds of data and sources. Different kinds of data and sources may require distinct algorithms and methodologies. Currently, there is a focus on relational databases and data warehouses, but other approaches need to be pioneered for other specific complex data types.

A versatile data mining tool, for all sorts of data, may not be realistic. Moreover, the proliferation of heterogeneous data sources, at structural and semantic levels, poses important challenges not only to the database community but also to the data mining community.

2.9 DATA MINING CHALLENGES

Data mining systems rely on databases to supply the raw data for input and this raises problems in that databases tend be dynamic, incomplete, noisy, and large. Other problems arise as a result of the adequacy and relevance of the information stored.

2.9.1 Limited Information

A database is often designed for purposes different from data mining and sometimes the properties or attributes that would simplify the learning task are not present nor can they be requested from the real world. Inconclusive data causes problems because if some attributes essential to knowledge about the application domain are not present in the data it may be impossible to discover significant knowledge about a given domain. For example cannot diagnose malaria from a patient database if that database does not contain the patients red blood cell count.

2.9.2 Noise and Missing Values

Databases are usually contaminated by errors so it cannot be assumed that the data they contain is entirely correct. Attributes which rely on subjective or measurement judgments can give rise to errors such that some examples may even be miss-classified. Errors in either the values of attributes or class information are known as noise. Obviously where possible it is desirable to eliminate noise from the classification information as this affects the overall accuracy of the generated rules.

Missing data can be treated by discovery systems in a number of ways such as;

- simply disregard missing values
- omit the corresponding records
- infer missing values from known values
- treat missing data as a special value to be included additionally in the attribute domain
- or average over the missing values using Bayesian techniques.

Noisy data in the sense of being imprecise is characteristic of all data collection and typically fit a regular statistical distribution such as Gaussian while wrong values are data entry errors. Statistical methods can treat problems of noisy data, and separate different types of noise.

2.9.3 Uncertainty

Uncertainty refers to the severity of the error and the degree of noise in the data. Data precision is an important consideration in a discovery system.

2.9.4 Size, Updates, and Irrelevant Fields

Databases tend to be large and dynamic in that their contents are ever-changing as information is added, modified or removed. The problem with this from the data mining perspective is how to ensure that the rules are up-to-date and consistent with the most current information. Also the learning system has to be time-sensitive as some data values vary over time and the discovery system is affected by the 'timeliness' of the data.

Another issue is the relevance or irrelevance of the fields in the database to the current focus of discovery for example post codes are fundamental to any studies trying to establish a geographical connection to an item of interest such as the sales of a product.

2.10 DATA MINING APPLICATIONS

Data mining is being used for a wide variety of applications.

1. **Prediction and description:** Data mining may be used to answer questions like "would this customer buy a product or not "Data mining techniques may also be used for sales forecasting and analysis. Usually the techniques involve selecting some or all the attributes of the objects in a database to predict other variables of interest.
2. **Relationship market:** Data mining can help in analysis customer profiles, discovering sales triggers, and in identifying critical issues that determine client loyalty and help in improving customer retention. This also includes analysis to identify customers suitable for cross selling other products.
3. **Customer profiling:** It is the process of using the relevant and available information to describe the characteristics of a group of customers and to identity their discriminators from other customers or ordinary consumers and drivers for their purchasing decisions.

4. **Outliers identification and detecting fraud:** There are many uses of data mining in identifying outliers, fraud or unusual cases. These might be as simple as identifying unusual expense claims by staff, identifying anomalies in expenditure between similar units of an enterprise, perhaps during auditing, or identifying fraud.
5. **Business and E-commerce:** Modern business processes are consolidating with millions of customers and billions of their transactions. Business enterprises require necessary information for their effective functioning in today's competitive world. Now a day people does not have the enough time to shop personally, their purchasing is mostly on web, then here also data mining provide its prominent role.

Here listed some more application areas of data mining:

- Ad revenue forecasting
- Churn (turnover) management
- Claims processing
- Credit risk analysis
- Cross-marketing
- Customer retention
- Exception reports
- Food-service menu analysis
- Fraud detection
- Government policy setting
- Hiring profiles
- Market basket analysis
- Medical management
- Member enrollment
- New product development
- Pharmaceutical research
- Process control
- Quality control
- Shelf management/store management
- Student recruiting and retention
- Targeted marketing
- Warranty analysis

SUMMARY

- Data mining is the task of discovering interesting patterns from large amounts of data, where the data can be stored in databases, data warehouses, or other information repositories. It is a young interdisciplinary field, drawing from areas such as database systems, data warehousing, statistics, machine learning, data visualization, information retrieval, and high-performance computing. Other contributing areas include neural networks, pattern recognition, spatial data analysis, image databases, signal processing, and many application fields, such as business, economics, and bioinformatics.
- Data mining is a process of finding value from volume. Data mining attempts to extract smaller pieces of valuable information form this massive database.

- Data mining is an interdisciplinary field, the confluence of a set of discipline include database systems, statistics, machine learning, visualization, and information science.
- A knowledge discovery process includes data cleaning, data integration, data selection, data transformation, data mining, pattern evaluation, and knowledge presentation.
- Data patterns can be mined from many different kinds of databases, such as relational databases, data warehouses, and transactional, and object-relational databases. Interesting data patterns can also be extracted from other kinds of information repositories, including spatial, time-series, sequence, text, multimedia, and legacy databases, data streams, and the World Wide Web.
- Data mining functionalities include the discovery of concept/class descriptions, associations and correlations, classification, prediction, clustering, trend analysis, outlier and deviation analysis, and similarity analysis. Characterization and discrimination are forms of data summarization.
- Data mining systems can be classified according to the kinds of databases mined, the kinds of knowledge mined, the techniques used, or the applications adapted.
- Data mining system have challenges with noisy and missing information, uncertainty, size, updates, irrelevant fields and limited information.
- Data mining is being used for a wide variety of all business and scientific applications.

REVIEW QUESTIONS

1. What is data mining?
2. Discuss different data mining tasks.
3. Discuss data mining techniques.
4. Explain data mining as a step in the process of knowledge discovery.
5. Draw and explain the architecture for on-line analytical mining.
6. Draw and explain the architecture of typical data mining system.
7. Define spatial database, multimedia database, time-series database, sequence database, and text database.
8. Explain the major issues in data mining.

3

DATA WAREHOUSE

3.1 DATA WAREHOUSING

Data mining potential can be enhanced if the appropriate data has been collected and stored in a data warehouse. A data warehouse is a relational database management system (RDMS) designed specifically to meet the needs of transaction processing systems. It can be loosely defined as any centralized data repository which can be queried for business benefit but this will be more clearly defined later. Data warehousing is a new powerful technique making it possible to extract archived operational data and overcome inconsistencies between different legacy data formats. As well as integrating data throughout an enterprise, regardless of location, format, or communication requirements it is possible to incorporate additional or expert information.

In other words the data warehouse provides data that is already transformed and summarized, therefore making it an appropriate environment for more efficient DSS and EIS applications.

According to W.H Inmon, a leading architect and guru in the construction of data warehouse systems.

"A data warehouse is a subject-oriented, integrated, time-variant, and nonvolatile collection of data in support of management's decision making process".

This short, but comprehensive definition presents the major features of a data warehouse. The four keywords, subject-oriented, integrated, time-variant and nonvolatile, distinguish data warehouse from other data repository system, such as relational database systems, transaction processing systems, and file system. Let's take closer look at each of these key words in the definition.

- **Subject-oriented:** data are organized according to subject instead of application *e.g.*, an insurance company using a data warehouse would organize their data by customer, premium, and claim, instead of by different products (auto, life, etc.). The data organized by subject contain only the information necessary for decision support processing.
- **Integrated:** A data warehouse is usually constructed by integrating multiple heterogeneous sources, such as relational databases, flat files and on-line transaction records. Data cleaning and data integration techniques are applied to ensure consistency in naming conventions, encodings structures, attribute measures, and so on.

- **Time-variant:** The data warehouse provides information from historical perspective (*e.g.*, the past 5-10 years). Every key structure in the data warehouse contains, either implicitly or explicitly, an element of time.
- **Non-volatile:** Data are not updated or changed in any way once they enter the data warehouse, but are only loaded and accessed.

The first phase in data warehousing is to "insulate" your current operational information, *i.e.*, to preserve the security and integrity of mission-critical OLTP applications, while giving you access to the broadest possible base of data. The resulting database or data warehouse may consume hundreds of gigabytes - or even terabytes - of disk space, what is required then are efficient techniques for storing and retrieving massive amounts of information. Increasingly, large organizations have found that only parallel processing systems offer sufficient bandwidth.

The data warehouse thus retrieves data from a variety of heterogeneous operational databases. The data is then transformed and delivered to the data warehouse/store based on a selected model (or mapping definition). The data transformation and movement processes are executed whenever an update to the warehouse data is required so there should some form of automation to manage and execute these functions. The information that describes the model and definition of the source data elements is called "metadata". The metadata is the means by which the end-user finds and understands the data in the warehouse and is an important part of the warehouse. The metadata should at the very least contain;

- The structure of the data;
- The algorithm used for summarization;
- And the mapping from the operational environment to the data warehouse.

Data cleaning is an important aspect of creating an efficient data warehouse in that it is the removal of certain aspects of operational data, such as low-level transaction information, which slow down the query times. The cleansing stage has to be as dynamic as possible to accommodate all types of queries even those which may require low-level information. Data should be extracted from production sources at regular intervals and pooled centrally but the cleansing process has to remove duplication and reconcile differences between various styles of data collection.

Once the data has been cleaned it is then transferred to the data warehouse which typically is a large database on a high performance box SMP, Symmetric Multi-Processing or MPP, Massively Parallel Processing. Number-crunching power is another important aspect of data warehousing because of the complexity involved in processing ad hoc queries and because of the vast quantities of data that the organization want to use in the warehouse. A data warehouse can be used in different ways for example it can be used as a central store against which the queries are run or it can be used to like a data mart. Data marts which are small warehouses can be established to provide subsets of the main store and summarized information depending on the requirements of a specific group/department. The central store approach generally uses very simple data structures with very little assumptions about the relationships between data whereas marts often use multidimensional databases which can speed up query processing as they can have data structures which are reflect the most likely questions.

Many vendors have products that provide one or more of the above described data warehouse functions. However, it can take a significant amount of work and specialized programming to provide the interoperability needed between products from multiple vendors to enable them to perform the required data warehouse processes. A typical implementation usually involves a mixture of products from a variety of suppliers.

Another approach to data warehousing is Parsaye's Sandwich Paradigm put forward by Dr. Kamran Parsaye, CEO of Information Discovery, Hermosa Beach, CA. This paradigm or philosophy encourages acceptance of the probability that the first iteration of a data-warehousing effort will require considerable revision. The Sandwich Paradigm advocates the following approach:

- pre-mine the data to determine what formats and data are needed to support a data-mining application;
- build a prototype mini-data warehouse *i.e.*, the meat of the sandwich, with most of the features envisaged for the end product;
- revise the strategies as necessary;
- build the final warehouse.

Data warehousing provides an interesting alternative to the traditional approach of heterogeneous database integration. Rather than using a query-driven approach, data warehousing employs an update-driven approach in which information from multiple, heterogeneous sources is integrated in advance and stored in a warehouse for direct querying and analysis. Unlike online transaction processing databases, data warehouses do not contain the most current information. However, a data warehouse brings high performance to the integrated heterogeneous database system since data are copied, preprocessed, integrated, annotated, summarized, and restructured into one semantic data store.

Furthermore query processing in data warehouses does not interface with the processing at local sources. Moreover, data warehouse can store and integrate historical information and support complex multidimensional queries. As a result, data warehouse has become very popular in industry.

3.2 DIFFERENCE BETWEEN OPERATIONAL DATABASE SYSTEMS AND DATA WAREHOUSES

A database which is built for on-line transaction processing, OLTP, is generally regarded as unsuitable for data warehousing as they have been designed with a different set of needs in mind *i.e.*, maximizing transaction capacity and typically having hundreds of tables in order not to lock out users etc. Data warehouses are interested in query processing as opposed to transaction processing.

OLTP systems cannot be repositories of facts and historical data for business analysis. They cannot quickly answer ad hoc queries and rapid retrieval is almost impossible. The data is inconsistent and changing, duplicate entries exist, entries can be missing and there is an absence of historical data which is necessary to analyze trends. Basically OLTP offers large amounts of raw data which is not easily understood. The data warehouse offers the potential to retrieve and analyze information quickly and easily.

Let us first aware of operational database and data warehouse then go for difference between these two.

3.2.1 Operational Database

Day-to-day transactions of an organizations is called operational database, such as purchasing, inventory, manufacturing, banking, payroll, registration, and accounting.

The major task of on-line operational database systems is to perform on-line transaction and query processing. These systems are called **on-line transaction processing (OLTP)** systems.

3.2.2 Data Warehouse

Data warehouse systems, on the other hand, serve users or knowledge workers in the role of data analysis and decision making. Such systems can organize and present data in various formats in order to accommodate the diverse needs of the different users. These systems are known as **on-line analytical processing (OLAP)** systems.

The major distinguishing features between OLTP and OLAP are listed below

Users and system orientation

- An OLTP system is customer-oriented and is used for transaction and query processing by clerks, clients, and information technology professionals.
- An OLAP system is market-oriented and is used for data analysis by knowledge workers, including managers, executives, and analysts.

Data contents

- An OLTP system manages current data that, typically, are too detailed to be easily used for decision-making.
- An OLAP system manages large amounts of historical data, provides facilities for summarization and aggregation, and stores and manages information at different levels of granularity. These features make the data easier to use in informed decision making.

Database design

- An OLTP system usually adopts an entity-relationship (ER) data model and an application-oriented database design.
- An OLAP system typically adopts either a star or snowflake model

View

- An OLTP system focuses mainly on the current data within an enterprise or department, without referring to historical data or data in different organizations.
- An OLAP system often spans multiple versions of a database schema, due to the evolutionary process of an organization. OLAP system also deals with information that originates from different organizations, integrating information from many data stores. Because of their huge volume, OLAP data are stored on multiple storage media

Access patterns

- The access patterns of an OLTP system consist mainly of short, atomic transactions. Such systems require concurrency control and recovery mechanisms.
- OLAP systems are mostly read only operations, because of data warehouse store historical rather than up-to-data information.

Other similarities and differences between OLTP and OLAP systems are listed on Table 3.1.

Table 3.1 Difference between OLAP and OLTP

	OLTP	*OLAP*
SIMILARITY		
Data	Integrated Data Subject-oriented	Integrated Data Subject-oriented
DIFFERENCES		
Characteristic	Operational processing	Information processing
Orientation	Transactional	Analysis
Function	Day-to-day operations	Decision support
Database design	ER-model	Star/snowflake schemas
Access	Read/write	Mostly read/aggregate
Users	Database professionals	Knowledge workers
Access frequency	High	Medium to low
Data content	Current values	Summarized, archive, derived
Data organization	By application	By subject
Database size	100 MB to GB	100 GB to TB

3.3 MULTIDIMENSIONAL DATA MODEL

The data warehouse and OLAP tools are based on a multidimensional data model. This model views data in the form of a data cube. The multidimensional data model is an integral part of On-Line Analytical Processing, or OLAP. Because OLAP is on-line, it must provide answers quickly; analysts pose iterative queries during interactive sessions, not in batch jobs that run overnight. And because OLAP is also analytic, the queries are complex. The multidimensional data model is designed to solve complex queries in real time.

The multidimensional data model is composed of logical cubes, measures, dimensions, hierarchies, levels, and attributes. The simplicity of the model is inherent because it defines objects that represent real-world business entities. Analysts know which business measures they are interested in examining, which dimensions and attributes make the data meaningful, and how the dimensions of their business are organized into levels and hierarchies.

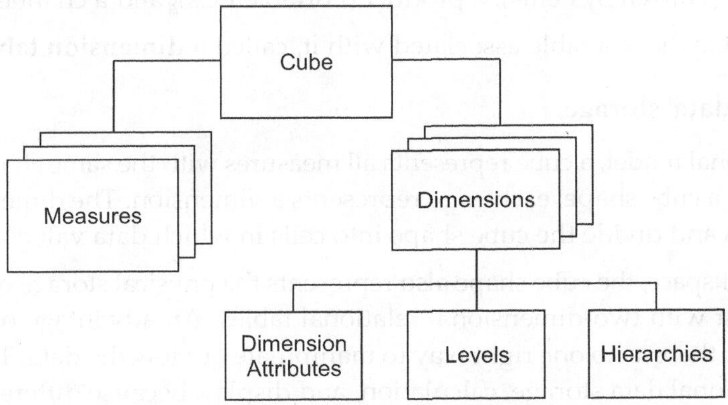

Fig. 3.1 Shows the relationships among the logical objects

3.3.1 Data from Relational Tables and Spreadsheets to Data Cubes

Cubes

Logical cubes provide a means of organizing measures that have the same shape, that is, they have the exact same dimensions. Measures in the same cube have the same relationships to other logical objects and can easily be analyzed and displayed together.

Measures

Measures populate the cells of a logical cube with the facts collected about business operations. Measures are organized by dimensions, which typically include a Time dimension.

An analytic database contains snapshots of historical data, derived from data in a legacy system, transactional database, syndicated sources, or other data sources. Three years of historical data is generally considered to be appropriate for analytic applications.

Measures are static and consistent while analysts are using them to inform their decisions. They are updated in a batch window at regular intervals: weekly, daily, or periodically throughout the day. Many applications refresh their data by adding periods to the time dimension of a measure, and may also roll off an equal number of the oldest time periods. Each update provides a fixed historical record of a particular business activity for that interval. Other applications do a full rebuild of their data rather than performing incremental updates.

A critical decision in defining a measure is the lowest level of detail (sometimes called the grain). Users may never view this **base level data**, but it determines the types of analysis that can be performed.

Dimensions

Dimensions contain a set of unique values that identify and categorize data. They form the edges of a logical cube, and thus of the measures within the cube. Because measures are typically multidimensional, a single value in a measure must be qualified by a member of each dimension to be meaningful.

For example, the Sales measure has four dimensions: Time, Customer, Product, and Channel. A particular Sales value (43,613.50) only has meaning when it is qualified by a specific time period (Feb-01), a customer (Warren Systems), a product (Portable PCs), and a channel (Catalog).

Each dimension may have a table associated with it, called a **dimension table.**

Multidimensional data storage

In the multidimensional model, a cube represents all measures with the same shape, that is, the exact same dimensions. In a cube shape, each edge represents a dimension. The dimension members are aligned on the edges and divide the cube shape into cells in which data values are stored.

In an analytic workspace, the cube shape also represents the physical storage of multidimensional measures, in contrast with two-dimensional relational tables. An advantage of the cube shape is that it can be rotated: there is no one right way to manipulate or view the data. This is an important part of multidimensional data storage, calculation, and display, because different analysts need to view the data in different ways. For example, if you are the Sales Manager for the particular area, then you need to look at the data differently from a product manager or a financial analyst.

Assume that a company collects data on sales. The company maintains records that quantify how many of each product was sold in a particular sales region during a specific time period. You can visualize the sales measure as the cube shown in Fig. 3.2.

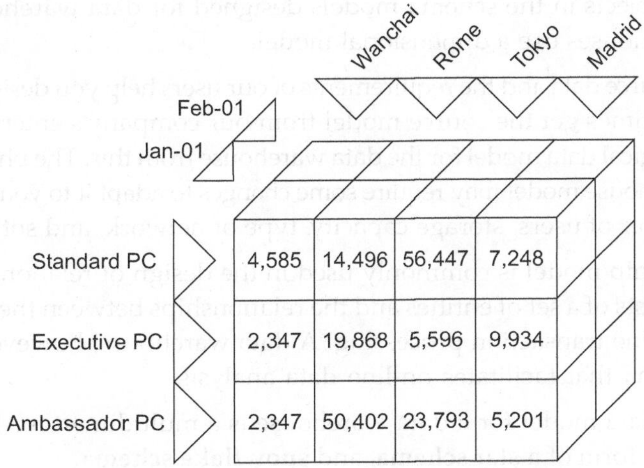

Fig. 3.2 Comparisons of Product Sales by City

Figure 3.2 shows compares the sales of various products in different cities for January 2001 (shown) and February 2001 (not shown). This view of the data might be used to identify products that are performing poorly in certain markets.

Figure 3.3 shows sales of various products during a four-month period in Rome (shown) and Tokya (not shown). This view of the data is the basis for trend analysis.

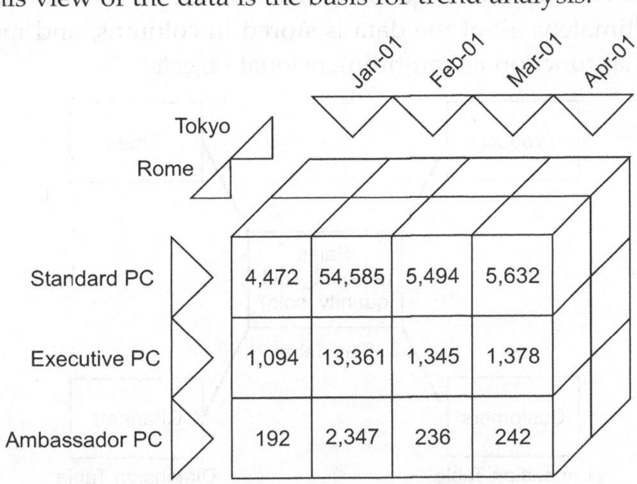

Fig. 3.3 Comparisons of Product Sales by Month

A cube shape is three dimensional. Of course, measures can have many more than three dimensions, but three dimensions are the maximum number that can be represented pictorially. Additional dimensions are pictured with additional cube shapes.

3.4 SCHEMAS FOR DATA WAREHOUSE

A schema is a collection of database objects, including tables, views, indexes, and synonyms. We can arrange schema objects in the schema models designed for data warehousing in a variety of ways. Most data warehouses use a dimensional model.

The model of our source data and the requirements of our users help you design the data warehouse schema. We can sometimes get the source model from our company's enterprise data model and reverse-engineer the logical data model for the data warehouse from this. The physical implementation of the logical data warehouse model may require some changes to adapt it to your system parameters—size of machine, number of users, storage capacity, type of network, and software.

The entity relationship model is commonly used in the design of relational databases, where a database schema consists of a set of entities and the relationships between them. Such a data model is appropriate for on-line transaction processing. A data warehouse, however, requires a concise, subject-oriented schema that facilitates on-line data analysis.

The most popular data model for a data warehouse is a multidimensional data model. Such a model can exists in the form of a **star schema**, and **snowflake schema.**

3.4.1 Star Schema

The star schema is a simplest data warehouse schema. It is called a star schema because the diagram resembles a star, with points radiating from a center. The center of the star consists of one or more fact tables and the points of the star are the dimension tables, as shown in Fig. 3.4.

A star schema is a convention for organizing the data into dimension tables, fact tables, and materialized views. Ultimately, all of the data is stored in columns, and metadata is required to identify the columns that function as multidimensional objects.

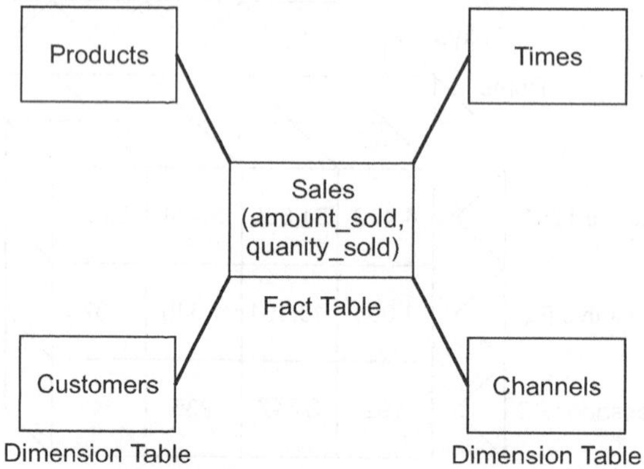

Fig. 3.4 Star Schema

The most natural way to model a data warehouse is as a star schema, only one join establishes the relationship between the fact table and any one of the dimension tables.

A star schema optimizes performance by keeping queries simple and providing fast response time. All the information about each level is stored in one row.

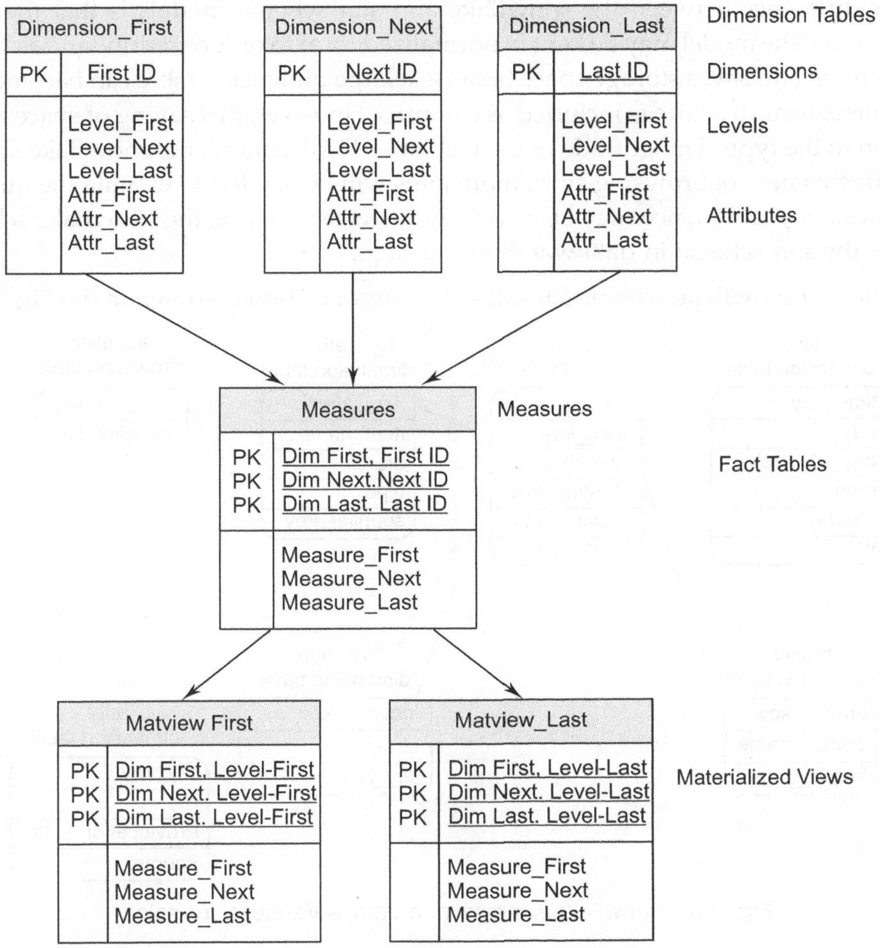

Fig. 3.5 Diagram of a star schema

Dimension tables

A star schema stores all of the information about a dimension in a single table. Each level of a hierarchy is represented by a column or column set in the dimension table. A dimension object can be used to define the hierarchical relationship between two columns (or column sets) that represent two levels of a hierarchy; without a dimension object, the hierarchical relationships are defined only in metadata. Attributes are stored in columns of the dimension tables.

Fact tables

Measures are stored in fact tables. Fact tables contain a composite primary key, which is composed of several foreign keys (one for each dimension table) and a column for each measure that uses these dimensions.

3.4.2 Snowflake Schema

The snowflake schema is a variant of the star schema model, where some dimension tables are normalized, there by further splitting the data into additional tables.

The major difference between the snowflake and star schema models is that the dimension tables of the snowflake model may be kept in normalized form to reduce redundancies. Such a table is easy to maintain and saves storage space because a large dimension table can become enormous when the dimensional structure is included as columns. However, this saving of space is negligible in comparison to the typical magnitude of the fact table. Furthermore, the snowflake structure can reduce the effectiveness of browsing since more joins will be needed to execute the query. Consequently, the system performance may be adversely impacted. Hence, the snowflake schema is not as popular as the star schema in data warehouse design.

An example of a snowflake schema for sales of an organization is shown in the Fig. 3.6.

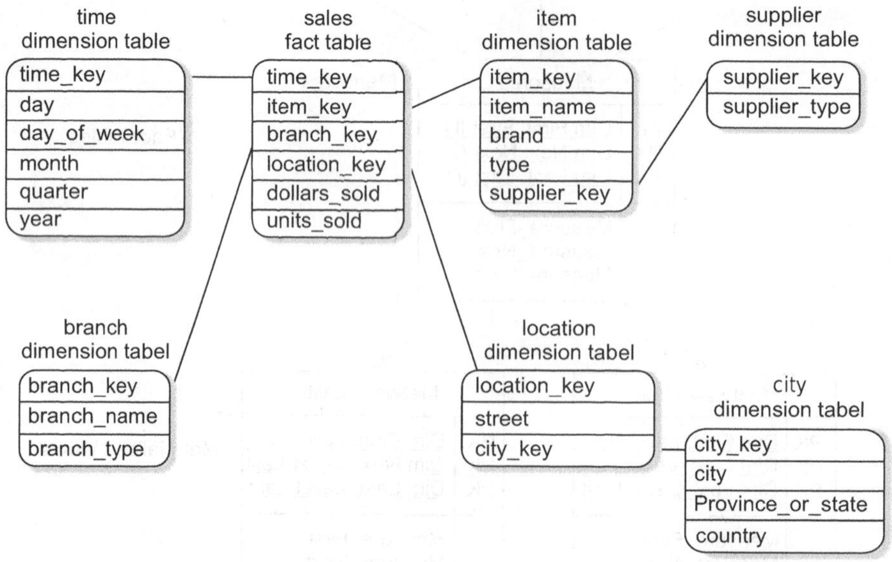

Fig. 3.6 Snowflake schema of a data warehouse for sales

3.5 CONCEPT HIERARCHIES

A **concept hierarchy** defines a sequence of mappings from a set of low-level concepts to higher-level, more general concepts.

Hierarchies are logical structures that use ordered levels as a means of organizing data. A hierarchy can be used to define data aggregation. For example, in a time dimension, a hierarchy might aggregate data from the *month* level to the *quarter* level to the *year* level. A hierarchy can also be used to define a navigational drill path and to establish a family structure.

Within a hierarchy, each level is logically connected to the levels above and below it. Data values at lower levels aggregate into the data values at higher levels. A dimension can be composed of more than one hierarchy. For example, in the product dimension, there might be two hierarchies—one for product categories and one for product suppliers.

Dimension hierarchies also group levels from general to granular. Query tools use hierarchies to enable you to drill down into our data to view different levels of granularity. This is one of the key benefits of a data warehouse.

Hierarchies impose a family structure on dimension values. For a particular level value, a value at the next higher level is its parent, and values at the next lower level are its children. These familial relationships enable analysts to access data quickly.

3.5.1 Levels

A level represents a position in a hierarchy. For example, a *time* dimension might have a hierarchy that represents data at the *month, quarter,* and *year* levels. Levels range from general to specific, with the root level as the highest or most general level. The levels in a dimension are organized into one or more hierarchies.

Level relationships

Level relationships specify top-to-bottom ordering of levels from most general (the root) to most specific information. They define the parent-child relationship between the levels in a hierarchy.

Hierarchies are also essential components in enabling more complex rewrites. For example, the database can aggregate existing sales revenue on a quarterly base to a yearly aggregation when the dimensional dependencies between quarter and year are known.

Dimension hierarchy

Figure 3.7 illustrates a dimension hierarchy based on customers. It shows location is the dimension and it shows the concept hierarchy of that dimension.

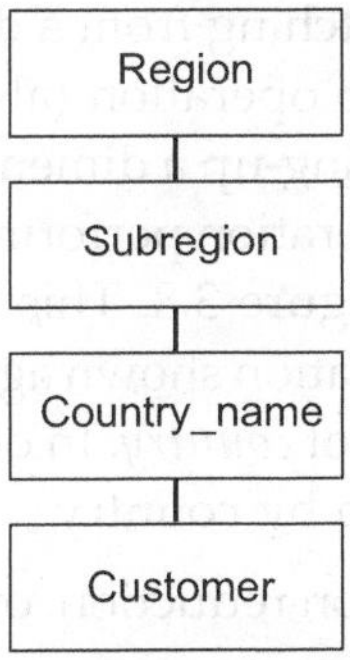

Fig. 3.7 Typical Levels in a dimension hierarchy

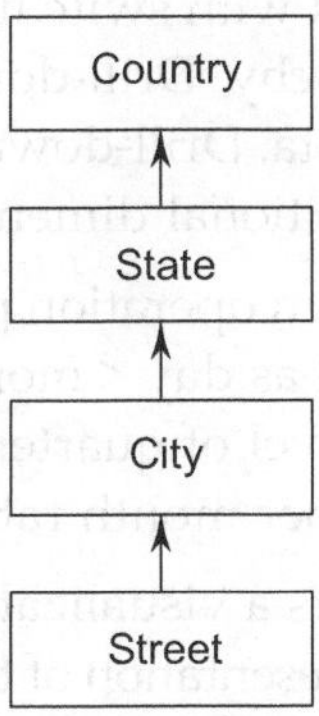

Fig. 3.8 Hierarchy for location

3.6 OLAP OPERATIONS

Once we model our data warehouse in the form of a multidimensional data model, it is necessary to explore the different analytical tools with which to perform the complex analysis of data. These data analysis tools are called OLAP (On-Line Analytical Processing). OLAP is mainly used to access the live data online and to analyze it. OLAP tools are designed in order to accomplish such analyses on very large databases. Hence, OLAP provides a user-friendly environment for interactive data analysis. Whilst data warehousing is primarily targeted at providing consolidated data for further analysis, OLAP provides the means to analyze those data in an application-oriented manner.

In the multidimensional model, data are organized into multiple dimensions, and each dimension contains multiple levels of abstraction defined by concept hierarchies. Such organization provides users with the flexibility to view data from different perspectives. A number of OLAP data cube operations exist to materialize these different views, allowing interactive querying and analysis of the data at hand. Hence, OLAP provides a user-friendly environment for interactive data analysis.

Slice & Dice These operations are used for reducing the data cube by one or more dimensions. The slice operation performs a selection on one dimension of the give cube, resulting in a subcube. Figure 3.9 shows a slice operation where the sales data are selected form the central cube for the dimension *time* using the criterion time="Q1".

The *dice* operation defines a sub cube by performing a selection on two or more dimensions. Figure 3.9 shows a dice operation on the central cube based on the dimensions

Drill-up: This operation deals with switching from a detailed to an aggregated level with in the same classification hierarchy. The Drill-up operation (also called the roll-up operation) performs aggregation on a data cube, either by climbing-up a dimension hierarchy or by dimension reduction. Figure 3.9 shows the result of a drill-up operation performed on the central cube by climbing up the concept hierarchy for location given in Figure 3.8. This hierarchy was defined as the total order *street< city < state < country*. The roll-up operation shown aggregates the data by ascending the *location* hierarchy from the level of city to the level of *country*. In other words, rather than grouping the data by city, the resulting cube groups the data by country.

When drill-up is performed by dimension reduction, one or more dimensions are removed from the given cube.

Drill-down: This operation is concerned with switching from an aggregated to a more detailed level within the same classification hierarchy. Drill-down is the reverse of roll-up. It navigates form less detailed data to more detailed data. Drill-down can be realized by either stepping down a dimension hierarchy or introducing additional dimensions.

Figure 3.9 shows the result of a drill-down operation performed on the central cube by stepping down a concept hierarchy for *time* defined as day < month <quarter < year. Drill-down occurs by descending the time hierarchy from the level of quarter to the more detailed level of *month*. The resulting data cube details the total sales per month rather than summarized by quarter.

Pivot (rotate): Pivot (also called rotate) is a visualization operation which rotates the data axes in view in order to provide an alternative presentation of the data. Figure 3.9 shows a pivot operation where the item and location axes in a 2-D slice are rotated. Other examples include rotating the axes in a 3-D cube, or transforming a 3-D cube into a series of 2-D planes.

Other OLAP operations may include ranking the top-N or bottom-N in lists, as well as computing moving averages, growth rates, interests, and internal rates of return, depreciation, currency conversions, and statistical functions. The results of these operations are typically visualized in a cross-tabular for, *i.e.*, mapped to a grid-oriented, two-dimensional layout structure.

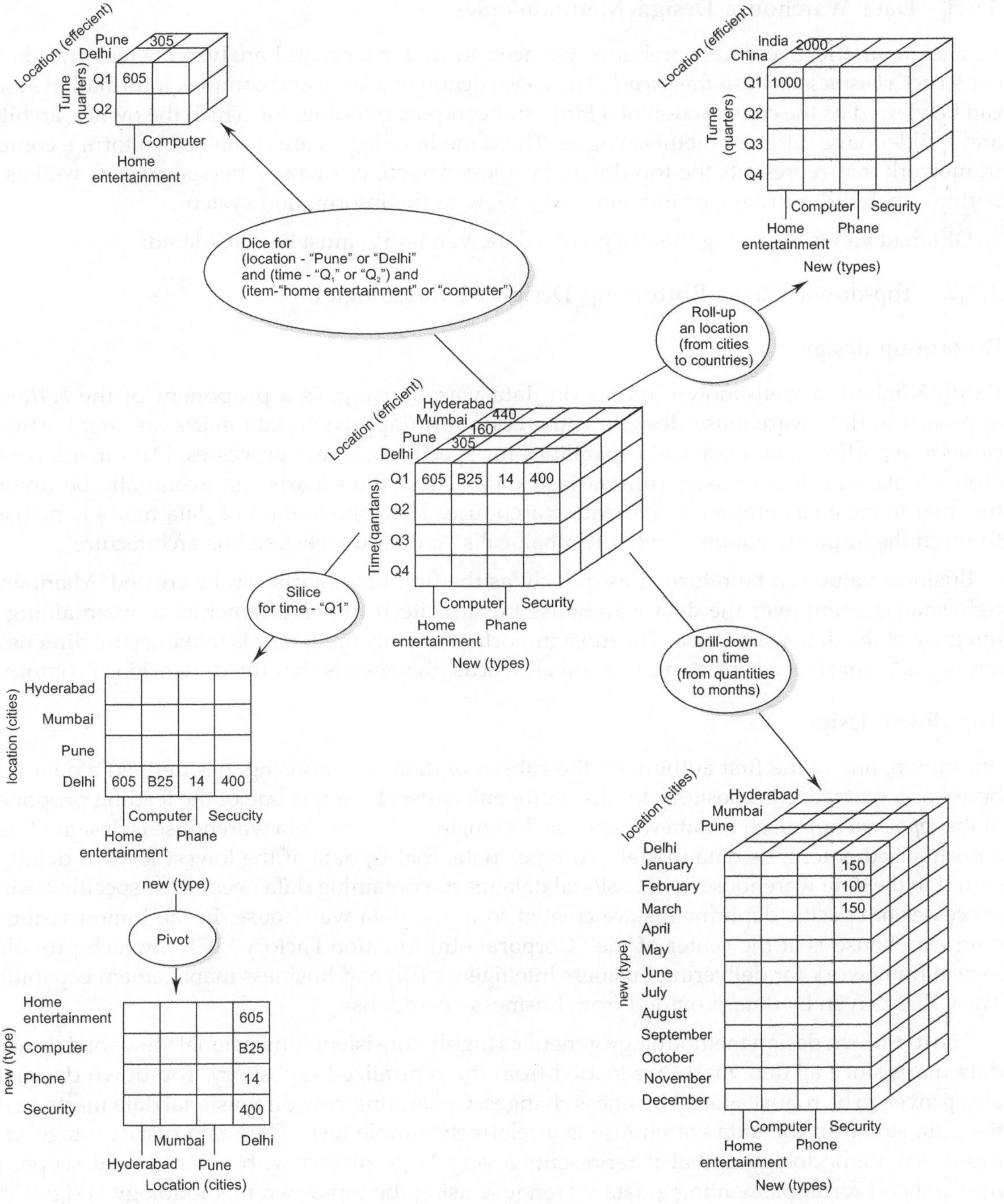

Fig. 3.9 Examples of typical OLAP operations on multidimensional data

3.7 DATA WAREHOUSE DESIGN

In this part outline complete data warehouse architecture, and how to design and construct of data warehouse, data warehouse architecture and metadata.

3.7.1 Data Warehouse Design Methodologies

To design an effective data warehouse we need to understand and analyze business needs and construct a *business analysis framework*. The construction of a large and complex information system can be viewed as the construction of a large and complex building, for which the owner, architect, and builder have different methodologies. These methodologies are combined to form a complex framework that represents the top-down, business-driven, or owner's perspective, as well as the bottom-up, builder-driven, or implementer's view of the information system.

Different views regarding the design of a data warehouse must be considered:

3.7.2 Top-down Versus Bottom-up Design Methodologies

Bottom-up design

Ralph Kimball, a well-known author on data warehousing, is a proponent of the *bottom-up* approach to data warehouse design. In the bottom-up approach data marts are first created to provide reporting and analytical capabilities for specific business processes. Data marts contain atomic data and, if necessary, summarized data. These data marts can eventually be unioned together to create a comprehensive data warehouse. The combination of data marts is managed through the implementation of what Kimball calls "a data warehouse bus architecture".

Business value can be returned as quickly as the first data marts can be created. Maintaining tight management over the data warehouse bus architecture is fundamental to maintaining the integrity of the data warehouse. The most important management task is making sure dimensions among data marts are consistent. In Kimball words, this means that the dimensions "conform".

Top-down design

Bill Inmon, one of the first authors on the subject of data warehousing, has defined a data warehouse as a centralized repository for the entire enterprise. Inmon is one of the leading proponents of the *top-down* approach to data warehouse design, in which the data warehouse is designed using a normalized enterprise data model. "Atomic" data, that is, data at the lowest level of detail, are stored in the data warehouse. Dimensional data marts containing data needed for specific business processes or specific departments are created from the data warehouse. In the Inmon vision the data warehouse is at the center of the "Corporate Information Factory" (CIF), which provides a logical framework for delivering business intelligence (BI) and business management capabilities. The CIF is driven by data provided from business operations

The top-down design methodology generates highly consistent dimensional views of data across data marts since all data marts are loaded from the centralized repository. Top-down design has also proven to be robust against business changes. Generating new dimensional data marts against the data stored in the data warehouse is a relatively simple task. The main disadvantage to the top-down methodology is that it represents a very large project with a very broad scope. The up-front cost for implementing a data warehouse using the top-down methodology is significant, and the duration of time from the start of project to the point that end users experience initial benefits can be substantial. In addition, the top-down methodology can be inflexible and unresponsive to changing departmental needs during the implementation phases.

3.7.3 Hybrid Design

Over time it has become apparent to proponents of bottom-up and top-down data warehouse design that both methodologies have benefits and risks. Hybrid methodologies have evolved to take advantage of the fast turn-around time of bottom-up design and the enterprise-wide data consistency of top-down design.

3.7.4 Data Warehouse Design Process

A data warehouse can be built using a *top-down approach*, a *bottom-up approach*, or a *hybrid*. The top-down approach starts with the overall design and planning. It is useful in cases where the technology is mature and well known, and where the business problems that must be solved are clear and well understood. The bottom-up approach starts with experiments and prototypes. This is useful in the early stage of business modeling and technology development. It allows an organization to move forward at considerably less expense and to evaluate the benefits of the technology before making significant commitments. In the combined approach, an organization can exploit the planned and strategic nature of the top-down approach while retaining the rapid implementation and opportunistic application of the bottom-up approach. From the software engineering point of view, the design and construction of a data warehouse may consist of the following steps: *planning, requirements study, problem analysis, warehouse design, data integration and testing,* and finally *deployment of the data warehouse.*

Large software systems can be developed using two methodologies: the *waterfall method* or the *spiral method.* The waterfall method performs a structured and systematic analysis at each step before proceeding to the next, which is like a waterfall, falling from one step to the next. The spiral method involves the rapid generation of increasingly functional systems, with short intervals between successive releases. This is considered a good choice for data warehouse development, especially for data marts, because the turnaround time is short, modifications can be done quickly, and new designs and technologies can be adapted in a timely manner.

In general, the warehouse design process consists of the following:

3.7.5 Logical Versus Physical Design in Data Warehouses

Your organization has decided to build a data warehouse. You have defined the business requirements and agreed upon the scope of your application, and created a conceptual design. Now you need to translate your requirements into a system deliverable. To do so, you create the logical and physical design for the data warehouse. You then define:

- The specific data content
- Relationships within and between groups of data
- The system environment supporting your data warehouse
- The data transformations required
- The frequency with which data is refreshed

The logical design is more conceptual and abstract than the physical design. In the logical design, you look at the logical relationships among the objects. In the physical design, you look at the most effective way of storing and retrieving the objects as well as handling them from a transportation and backup/recovery perspective.

Orient your design toward the needs of the end users. End users typically want to perform analysis and look at aggregated data, rather than at individual transactions. However, end users might not know what they need until they see it. In addition, a well-planned design allows for growth and changes as the needs of users change and evolves.

By beginning with the logical design, you focus on the information requirements and save the implementation details for later.

3.7.6 Creating a Logical Design

A logical design is conceptual and abstract. You do not deal with the physical implementation details yet. You deal only with defining the types of information that you need.

One technique you can use to model your organization's logical information requirements is entity-relationship modeling. Entity-relationship modeling involves identifying the things of importance (entities), the properties of these things (attributes), and how they are related to one another (relationships).

The process of logical design involves arranging data into a series of logical relationships called entities and attributes. An **entity** represents a chunk of information. In relational databases, an entity often maps to a table. An **attribute** is a component of an entity that helps define the uniqueness of the entity. In relational databases, an attribute maps to a column.

To be sure that your data is consistent, you need to use unique identifiers. A **unique identifier** is something you add to tables so that you can differentiate between the same items when it appears in different places. In a physical design, this is usually a primary key.

While entity-relationship diagramming has traditionally been associated with highly normalized models such as OLTP applications, the technique is still useful for data warehouse design in the form of dimensional modeling. In dimensional modeling, instead of seeking to discover atomic units of information (such as entities and attributes) and all of the relationships between them, you identify which information belongs to a central fact table and which information belongs to its associated dimension tables. You identify business subjects or fields of data, define relationships between business subjects, and name the attributes for each subject.

3.8 DATA WAREHOUSING OBJECTS

Fact tables and dimension tables are the two types of objects commonly used in dimensional data warehouse schemas.

Fact tables are the large tables in your warehouse schema that store business measurements. Fact tables typically contain facts and foreign keys to the dimension tables. Fact tables represent data, usually numeric and additive, that can be analyzed and examined. Examples include sales, cost, and profit.

Dimension tables, also known as lookup or reference tables; contain the relatively static data in the warehouse. Dimension tables store the information you normally use to contain queries. Dimension tables are usually textual and descriptive and you can use them as the row headers of the result set. Examples are customers or products.

3.8.1 Fact Tables

A fact table typically has two types of columns: those that contain numeric facts (often called measurements), and those that are foreign keys to dimension tables. A fact table contains either detail-level facts or facts that have been aggregated. Fact tables that contain aggregated facts are often called summary tables. A fact table usually contains facts with the same level of aggregation. Though most facts are additive, they can also be semi-additive or non-additive. Additive facts can be aggregated by simple arithmetical addition. A common example of this is sales. Non-additive facts cannot be added at all. An example of this is averages. Semi-additive facts can be aggregated along some of the dimensions and not along others. An example of this is inventory levels, where you cannot tell what a level means simply by looking at it.

Creating a new fact table

You must define a fact table for each star schema. From a modeling standpoint, the primary key of the fact table is usually a composite key that is made up of all of its foreign keys.

3.8.2 Dimension Tables

A dimension is a structure, often composed of one or more hierarchies, that categorizes data. Dimensional attributes help to describe the dimensional value. They are normally descriptive, textual values. Several distinct dimensions, combined with facts, enable you to answer business questions. Commonly used dimensions are customers, products, and time.

Dimension data is typically collected at the lowest level of detail and then aggregated into higher level totals that are more useful for analysis. These natural rollups or aggregations within a dimension table are called hierarchies.

3.9 DATA WAREHOUSE ARCHITECTURE

The architecture of a data warehouse is shown in Fig. 3.10. We will describe each of these components in the following sections: The Fig. 3.10 illustrates four things:

- Data Sources (operational systems and flat files)
- Warehouse (metadata, summary data, and raw data)
- Staging Area (where data sources go before the warehouse)
- Users (analysis, reporting, and mining)

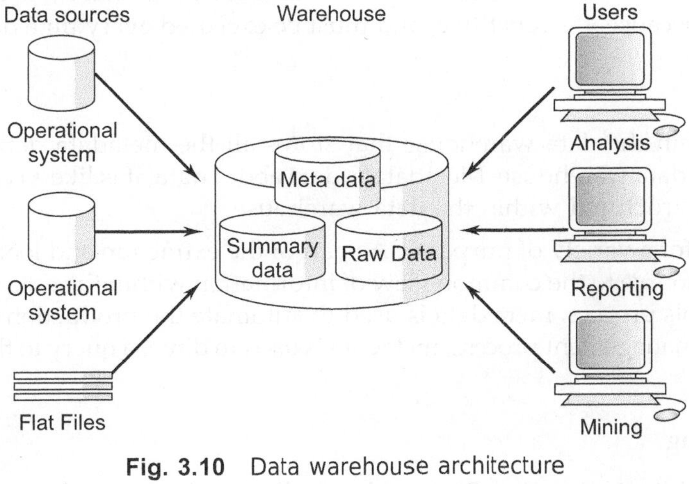

Fig. 3.10 Data warehouse architecture

The architecture of a data warehouse is shown in Fig. 3.10. Data warehouse obtains the data from a number of operational database systems which can be based on RDBMS or ERP packages, etc. These are called data sources. The data from these sources are converted into a form suitable for data warehouse. This process is Extraction, Transformation and Loading (ETL) of data into the target database. In addition to target database, there will be another database to store the metadata, called Metadata repository or simple meta data. This database contains data about data-description of source data, target data and how the source data has been modified into target data. The client software will be used to generate the business intelligence reports. The user interface can be based on a custom-built GUI or it can be a browser interface. An administration console is used to carry out data warehouse administration including the periodic ETL process to update the data into the data warehouse from the data sources.

Data sources

An organization interested in developing a data warehouse has to first study where the existing information is located. There are the data sources. It is likely that most of the data is residing in RDBMS. However, there is no guarantee. Some organizations are using databases developed decades ago, some organizations use advanced systems such as ERP, Customer Relations Management (CRM) and Supply Chain Management (SCM) packages. So, various data sources can be as:

- Flat files, which contain the data with one record per line in a proprietary format.
- Relational databases based on Oracle, MS SQL, Sybase, Informix, IBM DB2, etc., with ODBC connectivity.
- ERP and CRM applications such as Oracle Applications, JDEdwards, PeopleSoft, SAP, etc.
- Mainframe databases such as DB2, VSAM

Warehouse

Generate summaries

Once the source data is loaded and structured for access in the data warehouse, the warehouse tool has to create a set of aggregations to speed up query performance. These aggregations operate on the basis that most queries select a subset of data from a particular dimension.

Summaries are generated automatically by the warehouse tools: that is, no human intervention should be required because it is repetitive, and must be executed every time data is loaded.

Metadata

This is the area within the data warehouse that stores all the metadata definitions used by all processes within the data warehouse. Metadata is data about data: it is like a card index describing how information is structured within the data warehouse.

Metadata is used for a variety of purposes. As part of the extraction and load process, metadata is used to map data source to the common view of information within the data warehouse. As part of the warehouse tools process, meta data is used to automate the production of summary tables. As part of the query management process, metadata is used to direct a query to the most appropriate data source.

3.9.1 Data Staging

Data Warehouse Architecture (with a Staging Area): We need to clean and process our operational data before putting it into the warehouse, as shown in Fig. 3.11 can do this programmatically, although most data warehouses use a staging area*. A staging area simplifies building summaries and general warehouse management. Fig. 3.12 illustrates this typical architecture.

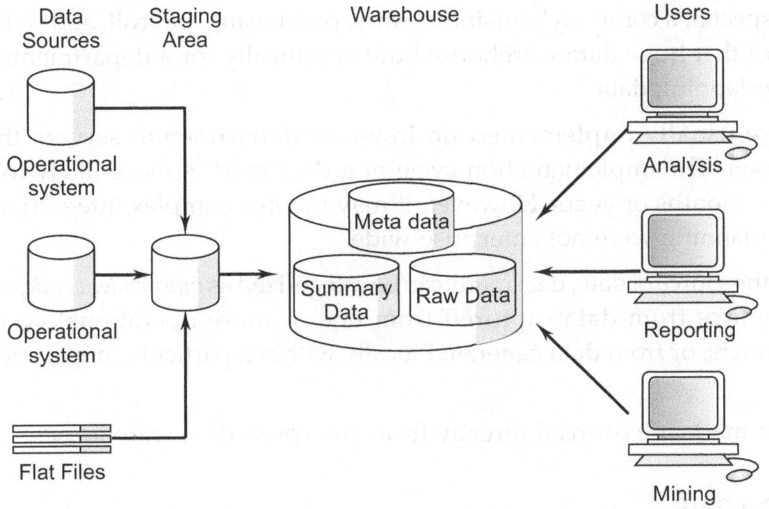

Fig. 3.11 Architecture of a Data Warehouse with a Staging Area

*staging area

Staging area is the place, where data is processed before enter into the warehouse.

Data warehouse architecture (with a staging area and data marts)

Although the architecture in Fig. 3.11 is quite common, we may want to customize our warehouse's architecture for different groups within our organization. We can do this by adding data marts, (data marts will discuss in next sub-section in detail) which are systems designed for a particular line of business. Fig.3.12 illustrates an example where purchasing, sales, and inventories are separated. In this example, a financial analyst might want to analyze historical data for purchases and sales.

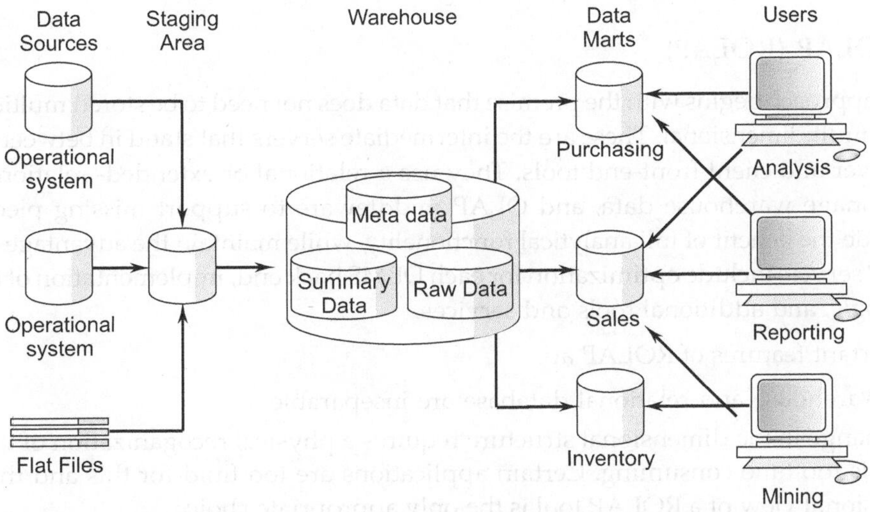

Fig. 3.12 Architecture of a Data Warehouse with a Staging Area and Data Marts

3.9.2 Data Mart

Data marts are partitions of the overall data warehouse. If we visualize the data warehouse as covering every aspect of a company's business (sales, purchasing, payroll, and so forth), then a data mart is a subset of that huge data warehouse built specifically for a department. Data marts may contain some overlapping data.

Data marts are usually implemented on low-cost departmental servers that are UNIX-or Windows/NT-based. The implementation cycle of a data mart is more likely to be measured in weeks rather than months or years. However, it may involve complex integration in the long run if its design and planning were not enterprise-wide.

Depending on the source of data, data marts can be categorized as *independent or dependent. Independent* data marts are source from data captured from one or more operational systems or external information providers, or from data generated locally within a particular department or geographic area.

Dependant data marts are sourced directly from enterprise data warehouses.

3.10 OLAP ENGINE

The main function of the OLAP engine is to present the user a multidimensional view of the data warehouse and to provide tools for OLAP operations. If the warehouse server organizes the data warehouse in the form of multidimensional arrays, then the implementation considerations of the OLAP engine are different from those when the server keeps the warehouse in a relational form. With these considerations in mind, there are three options of the OLAP engine.

3.10.1 Data Warehouse Servers

OLAP servers present business user with multidimensional data from data warehouses or data marts, without concerns regarding how or where the data are stored. However, the physical architecture and implementation of OLAP servers must consider data storage issues. Implementations of a warehouse server for OLAP processing include the following.

Relational OLAP (ROLAP)

The ROLAP approach begins with the premise that data does not need to be stored multidimensional to be viewed multidimensional. These are the intermediate servers that stand in between a relational back-end server and client front-end tools. They use a relational or extended- relational DBMS to store and manage warehouse data, and OLAP middleware to support missing pieces. ROLAP servers provide the benefit of full analytical functionality, while maintain the advantage of relational data. ROLAP servers include optimization for each DBMS back end, implementation of aggregation navigation logic, and additional tools and services.

Two important features of ROLAP are

1. Data Warehouse and relational database are inseparable
2. Any change in the dimensional structure requires a physical recoganization of the database, which is too time consuming. Certain applications are too fluid for this and the on-the-fly dimensional view of a ROLAP tool is the only appropriate choice.

Multidimensional OLAP (MOLAP)

MOLAP servers support multidimensional views of data through array-based multidimensional storage engines. They map multidimensional views directly to data cube array structures. The advantage of using a data cube is that it allows fast indexing to precomputed summarized data.

Almost all MOLAP servers adopt a two-level storage representation to handle sparse and dense data sets: the dense subcubes are identified and stored as array structures, while the sparse subcubes employ compression technology for efficient storage utilization.

Hybrid OLAP (HOLAP)

The hybrid OLAP approach combines ROLAP and MOLAP technology, benefiting from the greater scalability of ROLAP and the faster computation of MOLAP.

3.11 DATA WAREHOUSE IMPLEMENTATION

Data warehouse supports business analysis and decision making by creating an enterprise-wide integrated database of summarized, historical information. Data warehouse contains huge volumes of data. OLAP severs demand that decision support queries be answered in the order of seconds. Therefore, it is crucial for data warehouse systems to support highly efficient cube computation techniques, access methods, and query processing techniques.

3.11.1 Data Warehouse Backend Process

Data Warehouse systems use back-end tools and utilities to populate and refresh their data. These tools and facilities include the following functions:

1. **Data extraction:** Data extraction is the process of extracting data for the warehouse from various sources. The data may come from a variety of sources, like
   - External systems
   - Legacy data
   - Production data
   - Internal office systems
   - Meta data
2. **Data cleaning:** Real-world data to be incomplete, noisy, and inconsistent. Since data warehouse are used for decision making. It is essential that the data in the warehouse be correct. However, since large volumes of data from heterogeneous sources are involved, there is a high probability of errors in the data. Therefore, data cleaning is essential in the construction of quality data warehouses. The data cleaning techniques include
   - Using transformation rules, e.g., translating attribute names like 'age' to 'DOB';
   - Using domain specific knowledge;
   - Performing parsing and fuzzy matching, *e.g.*, for multiple data sources, one can designate a preferred source as a matching standard.
   - Auditing, *i.e.*, discovering facts that flag universal patterns.
3. **Data transformation:** The sources of data warehouse are usually heterogeneous. Data transformation is concerned with transforming heterogeneous data to an uniform structure so that the data can be combined and integrated.

4. **Loading:** Since a data warehouse integrates time-varying data from multiple sources, the volumes of data to be loaded into a data warehouse can be huge. Moreover, there is usually an insufficient time interval when the warehouse can be taken off-line and when loading data, indices and summary tables need to be rebuilt. A loading system should also allow system administrators to monitor the status, cancel, suspend, resume loading or change the loading rate, and restart loading after failures without any loss of data integrity.

   There are different data loading strategies

   - Batch loading
   - Sequential loading
   - Incremental loading

5. **Refresh:** When the source data is updated, we need to update the warehouse. This process is called the refresh function. Determining how frequently to refresh is an important issue. One extreme is to refresh on every update. This is very expensive, however, and is normally only necessary when OLAP queries need the most current data, such as active data warehouse.

Besides cleaning, loading, refreshing, and metadata definition tools, data warehouse systems usually provide a good set of data warehouse management tools.

3.11.2 Metadata Repository

Designing the metadata for the data warehouse is one of the more difficult and least well-defined design tasks. The word *meta* comes from the Greek, and means *among, beside or after.* In the context of metadata it means data about something else. Metadata is, in essence, information that describes something else.

In the data warehouse the term **metadata** is used in a number of different situations. Metadata is data about data. When used in a data warehouse, metadata is the data that define warehouse objects. Metadata are created for the data names and definitions of the given warehouse. Additional metadata are created and captured for timestamping any extracted data, the source of the extracted data, and missing fields that have been added by data cleaning or integration process.

The advantage of storing metadata about the data being transformed is that as source data changes the changes can be captured in the metadata, and transformation programs automatically regenerated.

A metadata repository contain the following

- A description of the structure of the data warehouse. This includes the warehouse schema, view, dimensions, hierarchies and derived data definitions, data marts location and contents etc.
- Operational metadata, such as data linkages, currency of data and monitoring information (warehouse usage statistics, error reports, and its trails)
- The summarization processes which include dimension definition, data on granularity, partitions, summary measure, aggregation, summarization etc.
- Details of the data sources which include source databases and their contents, gateway descriptions, a data partitions, data extractions, cleaning, transformation rules and defaults.
- Data related to system performance, which include indices and profiles that improve data access and retrieval performance, in addition to rules for timing and scheduling of refresh, update, and replication cycles.
- Business metadata, which includes business terms and definitions, data ownership information, and changing policies.

3.11.3 Efficient Processing of OLAP Queries

In the data warehouse query management process is the system process that manages the queries and speeds them up by directing queries to the most effective data source. This process must also ensure that all the system resources are used in the most effective way, usually by scheduling the execution of queries. The query management process may also be required to monitor the actual query profiles.

Unlike the other system processes, query management does not generally operate during the regular load of information into the data warehouse.

There are set of facilities that are constantly in operation.

Directing queries

Date warehouse that contain summary data potentially provide a number of distinct data source to respond to a specific query. These are the detailed information itself, and any number of aggregations that satisfy the query's information need.

Maximizing the system resources

Regardless of the processing power available to run the data warehouse, it is all too possible that a single large query can soak up all the system resources, affecting the performance of the entire system. The query management process must ensure that no single query can effect the overall system performance.

3.11.4 Indexing OLAP Data

For efficient data accessing, most data warehouse systems support index structures and materialized views (using cuboids).

The **bitmap** indexing method is popular in OLAP products because it allows quick searching in data cubes. Bitmap indexing is advantageous compared to hash and tree indices. It is especially useful for low-cardinality domains because comparison, join, and aggregation operations are then reduced to bit arithmetic, which substantially reduces the processing time. Bitmap indexing leads to significant reductions in space and I/O since a string of charters can be represented by a single bit. For higher cardinality domains, the method can be adapted using compression techniques. The join indexing method gained popularity from it use in relational database query processing.

Base table

RID	item	city
R1	H	V
R2	C	V
R3	P	V
R4	S	V
R5	H	T
R6	C	T
R7	P	T
R8	S	T

Item bitmap index table

RID	H	C	P	S
R1	1	0	0	0
R2	0	1	0	0
R3	0	0	1	0
R4	0	0	0	1
R5	1	0	0	0
R6	0	1	0	0
R7	0	0	1	0
R8	0	0	0	1

City bitmap index table

RID	V	T
R1	1	0
R2	1	0
R3	1	0
R4	1	0
R5	0	1
R6	0	1
R7	0	1
R8	0	1

Note: H for "home entertainment," C for "computer," P for "phone," S for "security," V for "Vancouver," T for "Toronto."

Fig. 3.13 Bitmap indexing

For example, if two relations R((RID,A) and S(B,SID) join on the attributes A and B, then the join index record contains the pair (RID,SID), where RID and SID are record identifiers from the R and S relations, respectively. Hence, the join index records can identify joinable tuples without performing costly join operations. Join indexing is especially useful for maintaining the relationship between a foreign key and its matching primary key, from the joinable relation.

3.12 FROM DATA WAREHOUSING TO DATA MINING

In this section we study the usages of data warehousing for information processing, analytical processing, and data mining.

3.12.1 Data Warehousing Usage

Data warehouse and data marts are used in a wide range of applications. Business executives in almost every industry use the data collected, integrated, processed, and stored in data warehouses and data marts to perform data analysis and make strategic decisions. Data Warehouse are used extensively in banking and financial services, consumer goods and retail distribution sectors, and controlled manufacturing such as demand-based production.

Some of the benefits that a data warehouse provides are as follows:

- A data warehouse provides a common data model for all data of interest regardless of the data's source. This makes it easier to report and analyze information than it would be if multiple data models were used to retrieve information such as sales invoices, order receipts, general ledger charges, etc.
- Prior to loading data into the data warehouse, inconsistencies are identified and resolved. This greatly simplifies reporting and analysis.
- Information in the data warehouse is under the control of data warehouse users so that, even if the source system data is purged over time, the information in the warehouse can be stored safely for extended periods of time.
- Because they are separate from operational systems warehouses provide retrieval of data without slowing down operational systems.
- Data warehouses can work in conjunction with and, hence, enhance the value of operational business applications, notably customer relationship management (CRM) systems.
- Data warehouses facilitate decision support system applications such as trend reports (*e.g.*, the items with the most sales in a particular area within the last two years), exception reports, and reports that show actual performance versus goals.

3.12.2 From On-Line Analytical Processing to On-Line Analytical Mining

Data Warehouses are used for information processing (querying and reporting), analytical processing (which allow users to navigate through summarized and detailed data by OLAP operations), and data mining (which supports knowledge discovery). OLAP-based data mining is referred to as OLAP mining or on-line analytical mining (OLAM), which emphasizes the interactive and exploratory nature of OLAP mining.

Among many different patterns and architectures of data mining systems, on-line analytical mining(OLAM) also called OLAP mining, which integrates on-line analytical processing(OLAP) with data mining and mining knowledge in multidimensional databases, is particularly important for the following reasons:

- High quality of data in data warehouses
- Available information processing infrastructure surrounding data warehouses
- OLAP-based exploratory data analysis
- On-line selection of data mining functions

SUMMARY

- A data warehouse is a **subject-oriented, integrated, time-variant, and nonvolatile** collection of data in support of management's decision making process.
- Several factors distinguish data warehouses from operational databases. Because the two systems provide quite different functionalities and require different kinds of data, it is necessary to maintain data warehouses separately from operational databases.
- The most popular data model for a data warehouse is a multidimensional data model. This model is typically used for the design of corporate data warehouses and departmental data marts.
- The multidimensional model can exist in the form of a star schema, and snowflake schema, or fact constellation schema.
- In the multidimensional model, a cube represents all measures with the same shape, that is, the exact same dimensions. In a cube shape, each edge represents a dimension. The dimension members are aligned on the edges and divide the cube shape into cells in which data values are stored.
- Concept hierarchies organize the values of attributes or dimensions into gradual levels of abstraction. They are useful in mining at multiple levels of abstraction.
- Data warehouse in the form of multidimensional model, it is necessary to explore the different analytical tools with which to perform the complex analysis of data.
- The OLAP is mainly used to access the live data online and to analyze it with the operations include roll-up, drill-down, slice and dice, pivot (rotate) as well as statistical operations such as ranking, computing averages and growth rates, and so on.
- To design an effective data warehouse need to understand and analyze business needs and construct a business analysis framework.
- A data warehouse can be built using a *top-down approach*, a *bottom-up approach*, or a *hybrid*. The top-down approach starts with the overall design and planning. The bottom-up approach starts with experiments and prototypes. In hybrid approach, an organization can exploit the planned and strategic nature of the top-down approach while retaining the rapid implementation and opportunistic application of the bottom-up approach.
- Data marts are partitions of the overall data warehouse or subset of data warehouse is also called as data mart.

REVIEW QUESTIONS

1. Define Data Warehouse.
2. What is the difference between the three main types of data warehouse usage information processing, analytical processing, and data mining?
3. Briefly discuss the data warehouse applications.

4. Differentiate OLTP and OLAP.
5. Differentiate operational database systems and data warehousing.
6. Discuss the issues regarding data warehouse architecture.
7. Briefly compare the following concepts. Use an example to explain your points.
   (*a*) Snowflake schema, fact constellation, starnet query model.
   (*b*) Discovery driven cube, multifeature cube, and virtual warehouse.
8. Explain the three-tier data warehousing architecture.

4

DATA PREPROCESSING

4.1 INTRODUCTION

Data Preprocessing is essential part of work to improve the efficiency and ease of the data mining process. Real-world data is dirty. Dirty data can cause confusion for the mining procedure, resulting in unreliable output. *What is dirty data*? The data which is Incomplete, Noisy, and Inconsistent, that data is called as dirty data. The data is dirty due to their typically huge size, often several gigabytes or more and other kind of reasons.

So we should get correct and exact results from data mining system, the data must be clean, then we should preprocess our data with using preprocessing techniques.

There are number of data preprocessing techniques. These preprocessing techniques are listed below are important.

- Data cleaning
- Data integration
- Data transformation
- Data reduction

These preprocessing techniques briefly discuss below, and discuss completely in the subsequent part of this chapter.

Data cleaning can be applied to remove noise and correct inconsistencies in the data.

Data integration merges data from multiple sources into a coherent data store, such as a data warehouse or a data cube.

Data transformation, a data are transformed or consolidated into one forms to another form which is appropriate for mining.

Data reduction can reduce the data size by aggregating, eliminating redundant features, or clustering, for instance.

These data processing techniques, when applied prior to mining, can substantially improve the overall quality of the patterns mined and/or the time required for the actual mining.

4.2 WHY PREPROCESSING?

The data we wish to analyze by data mining techniques are generally incomplete, noisy and inconsistent.

Now let us see the meaning of these words (incomplete, noisy, and inconsistent) in terms of data mining point of view.

Incomplete: lacking attribute values, lacking certain attributes of interest, or containing only aggregate data

Noisy: containing errors or outliers that deviate from the expected

Inconsistent: containing discrepancies in codes or names, there may be inconsistency due to data integration, where a given attribute can have different names in different databases.

Incomplete, noisy, and inconsistent data are common of large real-world databases and data warehouses. Incomplete data can occur for a number of reasons. Attribute of interest may not always be available, such as customer information for sales transaction data. Other data may not be included simple because it was not considered important at the time of entry.

There are many possible reasons for noisy data (having incorrect attribute values). The data collection instruments used may be faulty. There may have been human or computer errors occurring at data entry and errors in data transmission can also occur. There may be technology limitations, like limited buffer size.

Data that were inconsistent with other recorded data may have been deleted. Further more, the recording of the history or modifications to the data may have been overlooked. Missing data, particularly for tuples with missing values for some attributes, may need to be inferred.

So ultimately real-world data tend to be dirty, *i.e.*, data is incomplete, inconsistent and noisy. Data preprocessing techniques can improve the quality of the data, there by helping to improve the accuracy and efficiency of the subsequent mining process. Data preprocessing is an important step in the knowledge discovery process, since quality decision must be based on quality data.

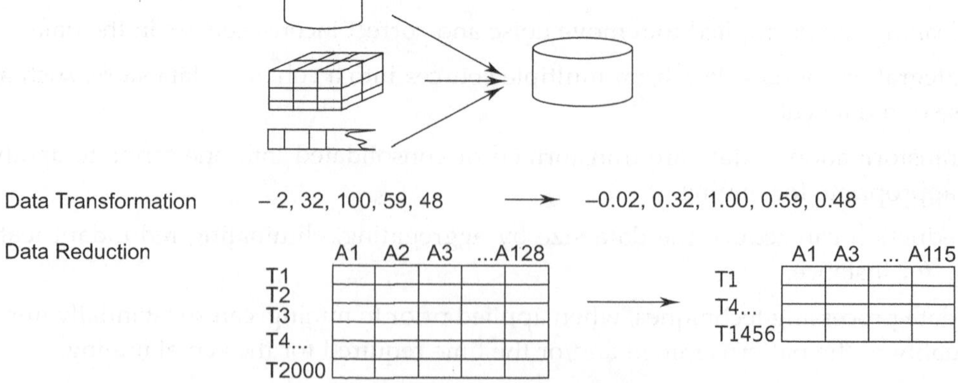

Fig. 4.1 Forms of data preprocessing

4.3 DATA CLEANING

The need for data cleaning is centered around improving the quality of the data to make them "fit for use" by users through reducing errors in the data improving their documentation and presentation.

As we mentioned earlier real-world data tend to be incomplete, noisy, and inconsistent. Data cleaning routines attempt to fill in *missing values, smooth out noise while identifying outliers, and correct inconsistencies* in the data.

4.3.1 Missing Values

In general some database tuples have no recorded values for several attributes. There may be a many reasons the tuples does not contain attributes, but the missing attribute may have important (if it contains) data that may useful for extract knowledge.

How can we go about filling in the missing values for these attributes? Let's look at the following methods:

1. **Eliminate the tuples:** This method is not very effective, unless the tuple contains several attributes with missing values. This is usually done when the class label is missing. It is especially poor when the percentage of missing values per attribute varies considerably.
2. **Fill in the missing value manually:** In general, this approach is time consuming and may not be feasible given a large data set with many missing values.
3. **Substitute a global constant to fill in the missing value:** Replace all missing attribute values by the same constant, such as a label like "Unknown" or - ~. if missing values are replaced by, say, "Unknown", then the missing program may mistakenly think that they form an interesting concept , since they all have a value in common.
4. **Calculate the attribute mean for all samples belonging to the same class as the given tuple:** Replace the missing value with the average value for that of given tuple.

   For example, if a customer customers according to credit_risk, replace the missing value with the average income value for customers in the same credit risk category as that of the given tupel.
5. **Calculate the attribute mean to fill in the missing value:** Replace the missing value with the average value of the attribute. For example, suppose that the average mark of the student is some value. Use this value to replace the missing value for mark.
6. **Use the most probable value to fill in the missing value:** This may be determined with regression, inference-based tools using a Bayesian formalism, or decision tree induction. (Decision trees are discussed in detail in chapter-8)

The methods are discussed for filling missing values may not be correct , but it uses the most information from the present data to predict missing values. By considering the values of the other attributes in its estimation of the missing value for *marks,* there is a great chance that the relationship between *marks* and other attribute are preserved.

4.3.2 Inconsistent Data

Inconsistency in the data may several reasons. There may be inconsistencies in the data recorded for some transactions. Some data inconsistencies may be corrected manually using external references. For example, errors made at data entry may be corrected by performing a paper trace. This may be coupled with routines designed to help correct the inconsistent use of codes.

There may also be inconsistencies due to data integration, where a given attribute can have different names in different databases. For example, in student database *student rank* field have the data A, B, C as rank, in another database *student rank* is 1, 2,3 as rank. When we integrate these two databases there is inconsistency exist.

4.3.3 Noisy Data

Noise is a random error or variance in a measured variable. We can use many techniques to remove noisy. Let us see some of the data smoothing techniques.

1. **Binning:** Binning methods smooth a sorted data values by consulting its "neighborhood", that is , the values around it. The sorted values are distributed into a number of "buckets", or bins. Because binning methods consult the neighborhood of values, they perform *local* smoothing.

   Steps for binning

   Step 1: Partition sorted values into equal size bins.

   Step 2: Smooth by bin means/medians/boundaries.

   Binning method for data smoothing

   Sorted data 4,8,15,21,21,24,25,28,34

   (Partition into (equal depth) bins

   Bin 1: 4, 8, 15

   Bin 2: 21, 21, 24

   Bin 3: 25, 28, 34

   Smoothing by bin mean:

   Bin1: 9, 9, 9;

   Bin 2: 22, 22, 22 ;

   Bin 3: 29, 29, 29;

   Smoothing by bin boundary

   Bin 1: 4, 4, 15;

   Bin 2: 21, 21, 24;

   Bin 3: 25, 25, 34

2. **Clustering:** In clustering the similar values are organized into groups, or "clusters". A cluster is a collection of data objects that are similar to one another within the same cluster and are dissimilar to the objects in other cluster. Outlier may be detected by clustering. (Details of these topics will see incoming chapters).

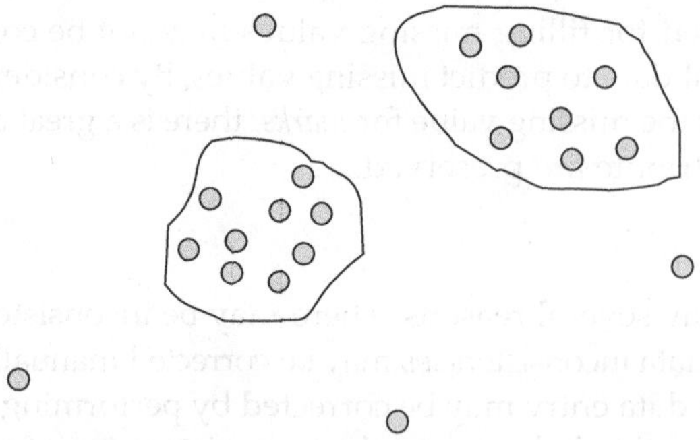

Fig. 4.2 Outlier detected by clustering analysis

3. **Regression:** Regression helps smooth out the noisy data. Using regression to find a mathematical equation to fit the data help smooth out the noise. Through regression data can be smoothed by fitting the data to a function. *Linear regression* involves finding the "best" line to fit two variables, so one variable can be used to predict the other. *Multiple linear regression* is an extension of linear regression, where more than two variables are involved and the data are fit to a multidimensional surface.

Many methods are for data smoothing. And also methods are for data reduction involving discretization. Concept hierarchies are a form of data discretization that can also be used for data smoothing.

4.4 DATA INTEGRATION

Merging multiple databases is called data integration. Data integration often required for data mining. In this section, we will discuss data integration.

Data integration combines data from multiple sources into a coherent data store, as in data warehousing. These sources may include multiple databases, data cubes, or flat files.

There are a number of issues to consider during data integration. Schema integration can be tricky. Here is required to match up the real-world entities from multiple data sources. This is called as the entity identification problem. For example, data analyst or the computer be sure that *student_id* in one database and *stud_number* in another refer to the same entity. Because of database or data warehouse typically have metadata, such metadata can used to help avoid errors in schema integration.

Redundancy is another important issue. An attribute may be redundant if it can be "derived" from another table, such as *annual revenue*. Inconsistencies in attribute or dimension naming can also cause redundancies in the resulting data set.

Some redundancies can be detected by **correlation analysis.** For example, given two attributes, such analysis can measure how strongly one attribute implies the other, based on the available data. The correlation between attributes A and B can be measured by

$$r_{A,B} = \frac{\sum(A-\bar{A})(B-\bar{B})}{(n-1)\sigma A\ \sigma B} \qquad \ldots(4.1)$$

Where n is the number of tuples, $\bar{A}$ and $\bar{B}$ are the respective mean values of A and B, and σA and σB are the respective standard deviations of A and B.

The mean of A is

$$\bar{A} = \frac{\Sigma A}{n}$$

The standard deviation of A is

$$\sigma_A = \sqrt{\frac{\sum(A-\bar{A})^2}{n-1}}$$

If the resulting value of Equation 4.1 is greater than 0, then A and B are positively correlated, meaning that the values of A increase as the values of B increase. The higher the value, the more each attribute implies the other. Hence, a high value may indicate that A (or B) may be removed as a redundancy. If the resulting value is equal to 0, then A and B are independent and there is no correlation between them. The resulting value is less than 0, and then A and B are negatively correlated, where the value of one attribute increases as the value of the other attribute decrease. This means that each attribute discourages the other.

In addition to detecting redundancies between attributes, duplication should also be detected at the tuple level (that means there are two or more identical tuples for a given unique data entry case)

Another important issue in data integration is the *detection and resolution of data value conflicts*. Suppose for example the same real-world entity, attribute values from different sources may different. This may be due to differences in representations scaling, or encoding.

Multiple sources of data integration process may produce redundancies and inconsistencies in the resulting data set. So carefully integrate different sources of data to avoid the redundancies and inconsistencies, that may help improve the accuracy and speed of the subsequent mining process.

4.5 DATA TRANSFORMATION

Data transformation is the mapping and conversion of data from one form to another. The transformed form of data may useful for data mining. Data transformation can involve the following.

- **Smoothing,** This method works to remove the noise from data. This technique include binning, clustering , and regression
- **Aggregation,** Where summary or aggregation operations are applied to the data. For example, the first semester marks data may be aggregated so as to compute all semester marks.
- **Generalization,** of the data, where raw data are replaced by higher-level concepts through the use of concept hierarchies.
- **Normalization** is typically a refinement process after the initial exercise of identifying the data objects that should be in the database, identifying their relationships, and defining the tables required and the columns within each table.
  Scaling attribute values to fall within a specified range.
  - Example: to transform V in [min, max] to V′ in [0,1], apply V′=(V-Min)/(Max-Min)
    Scaling by using mean and standard deviation (useful when min and max are unknown or when there are outliers): V′=(V-Mean)/StDev
- **Attribute construction,** where new attributes are constructed and added from the given set of attributes to help the mining process.

Smoothing and aggregations are already discussed in this chapter briefly. Now it is time to discuss about normalization.

An attribute is normalized by scaling its values so that they fall within a small specified range, such as 0.0 to 1.0. Normalization is particularly useful for classification algorithms, involving neural networks, or distance measurements such as nearest neighbor classification and clustering.

There are many methods for data normalization. We study three of them.

1. Min-max normalization
2. Z-score normalization
3. Normalization by decimal scaling

Min-max normalization performs a linear transformation on the original data. Suppose that min_A and max_A are the minimum and maximum values of an attribute A. Min-max normalization maps a value v of A to v' in the range[new_min_A, new_max_A] by computing

$$v' = \frac{v - min_A}{max_A - min_A}(new\_max_A - new\_min_A) + new\_min_A \quad ...(4.2)$$

Min-max normalization preserves the relationships among the original data values. It will encounter an "out of bounds" error if a future input case for normalization falls outside of the original data range for A.

In z-score normalization (or zero-mean normalization), the values for an attribute A are normalization based on the mean and standard deviation of A. A value v of A is normalized to v' by computing

$$v' = \frac{v - mean_A}{stand\_dev_A}$$

(OR)

$$v' = \frac{v - \bar{A}}{\sigma_A} \quad ...(4.3)$$

Where $\bar{A}$ and σA are the mean and standard deviation, respectively, of attribute A. This method of normalization is useful when the actual minimum and maximum of attribute A are unknown, or when there are outliers that dominate the min-max normalization.

Normalization by decimal scaling normalizes by moving the decimal point of values of attribute A. The number of decimal points moved depends on the maximum absolute value of A. A value v of A is normalized to v' by computing

$$v' = \frac{v}{10^j} \quad ...(4.4)$$

where j is the smallest integer such that $Max(|v'|) < 1$.

4.6 DATA REDUCTION

Data warehouse is for analysis, the data set will be a huge, and the data analysis and mining on huge amounts of data can take a long time, making such an analysis impractical and infeasible.

Data reduction techniques can be applied to obtain a reduced representation of the data set that is much smaller in volume, yet closely maintains the integrity of the original data. That is, mining on the reduced data set should be more efficient yet produce the same (or almost the same) analytical results.

Strategies for data reduction include the following

1. **Data cube aggregation:** Data cube aggregation, where aggregation operations are applied to the data in the construction of a data cube.
2. **Attribute subset selection,** where irrelevant, weakly relevant or redundant attributes or dimensions may be detected and removed.
3. **Dimensionality reduction,** where encoding mechanisms are used to reduce the data set size.

4. **Numerosity reduction,** where the data are replaced or estimated by alternative, small data representations such as parametric models (which need store only the model parameters instead of the actual data) or nonparametric methods such as clustering, sampling, and the use of histograms.
5. **Discretization and concept hierarchy generation,** where raw data values for attributes are replaced by ranges or higher conceptual levels. Data discretization is a form of numerosity reduction that is very useful for the automatic generation of concept hierarchies.

Discretization and concept hierarchy generation are powerful tools for data mining, in that they allow the mining of data at multiple levels of abstraction.

4.6.1 Data Cube Aggregation

Users of decision support systems often see data in the form of data cubes. The cube is used to represent data along some measure of interest. Although called a "cube", it can be 2-dimensional, 3-dimensional, or higher-dimensional. Each dimension represents some attribute in the database and the cells in the data cube represent the measure of interest. For example, they could contain a count for the number of times that attribute combination occurs in the database, or the minimum, maximum, sum or average value of some attribute. Queries are performed on the cube to retrieve decision support information.

Example: We have a database that contains transaction information relating company sales of a part to a customer at a store location. The data cube formed from this database is a 3-dimensional representation, with each cell (*p,c,s*) of the cube representing a combination of values from *part, customer* and *store-location*. A sample data cube for this combination is shown in Fig. 4.3. The contents of each cell are the count of the number of times that specific combination of values occurs together in the database. Cells that appear blank in fact have a value of zero. The cube can then be used to retrieve information within the database about, for example, which store should be given a certain part to sell in order to make the greatest sales.

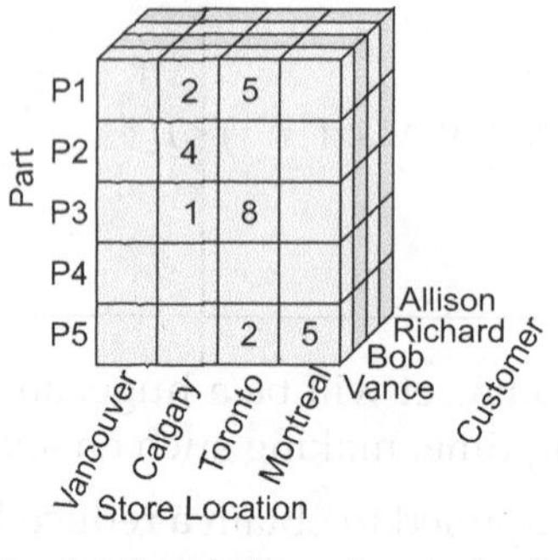

Fig. 4.3 (a) Front view of sample data cube

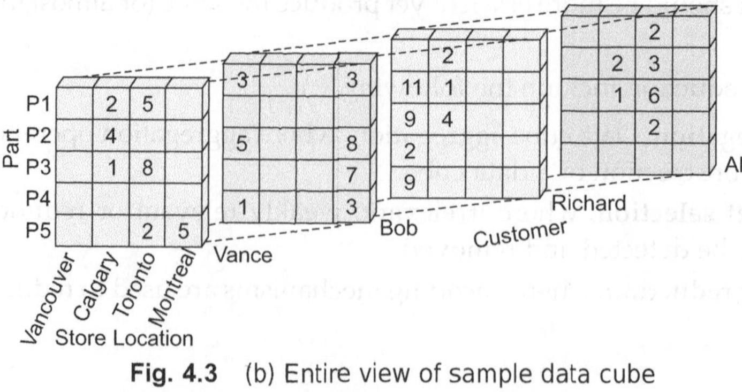

Fig. 4.3 (b) Entire view of sample data cube

Data analysis applications typically aggregate data across many dimensions looking for unusual patterns.

We have collected the data for analysis. This data consists of sales per quarter, for the year 1997 to 1999. We are interested in the annual sales (total per year), rather than the total per quarter. Thus the data can be *aggregated* so that the resulting data summarize the total sales per year instead of per quarter. This aggregation is illustrated in Fig. 4.4. The resulting data set is smaller in volume, without loss of information necessary for the analysis task.

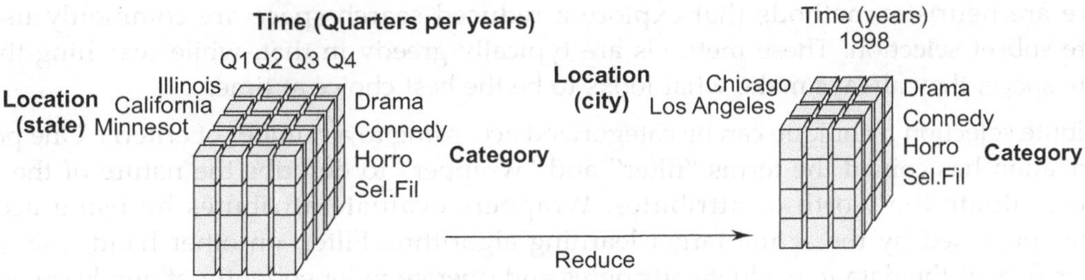

Fig. 4.4 Sales data for the year 1997 to 1999. on the left side, the sales are shown per quarter. On the right, the data are aggregated to the annual sales.

Data cubes store multidimensional aggregated information. Figure 4.4 shows a data cube for multidimensional analysis of sales data with respect to annual sales per item type. The last slice in the Fig. 4.5 each cell holds an aggregate data value, corresponding to the data point in multidimensional space.

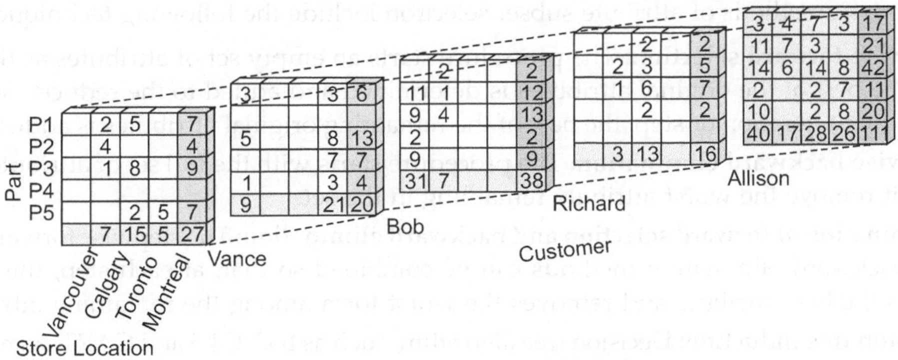

Fig. 4.5 Cube with Aggregation

Concept hierarchies may exist for each attribute, allowing the analysis of data at multiple levels of abstraction. For example, a hierarchy for *branch* could allow branches to be grouped into regions, based on their address. Data cube provide fast access to precomputed, summarized data, there by benefiting on-line analytical processing as well as data mining.

The cube created at the lowest level of abstraction is referred to as the *base cuboid*. The base cuboid should correspond to an individual entry of interest such as sales or customer.

4.6.2 Attribute Subset Selection

Data set for analysis may contain hundreds of attributes, many of which may be irrelevant to the mining task or redundant. It may be possible for a domain expert to pick out some of the useful attributes; this can be a difficult and time-consuming task, especially when the behavior of the data is not well known. Leaving out relevant attributes or keeping irrelevant attributes may be detrimental, causing confusion for the mining algorithms employed.

Attribute subset selection reduces the data set size by removing irrelevant or redundant attributes or dimensions. The goal of attribute subset selection in to find a minimum set of attributes such that the resulting probability distribution of the data classes is as close as possible to the original distribution obtained using all attributes. Mining on a reduced set of attributes has as additional patterns, helping to make the pattern easier to understand.

There are heuristic methods that explore a reduced search space are commonly used for attribute subset selection. These methods are typically greedy in that, while searching through attribute space, they always make what looks to be the best choice at time.

Attribute selection technique can be categorized according to a number of criteria. One popular categorization has coined the terms "filter" and "wrapper" to describe the nature of the metric used to evaluate the worth of attributes. Wrappers evaluate attributes by using accuracy estimates provided by the actual target learning algorithm. Filter, on other hand, use general characteristics of the data to evaluate attributes and operate independently of any learning algorithm. Another useful taxonomy can be drawn by dividing algorithms into those which evaluate (and hence rank) individual attributes and those which evaluate (and hence rank) *subset of attributes*. Some attribute selection techniques can handle regression problems, that is when the class is a numeric rather than a discrete valued variable.

Many other attribute evaluation measures can be used, such as the *information gain* measure used in building decision trees for classification.

Basic heuristic methods of attribute subset selection include the following techniques.

1. **Stepwise forward selection:** The procedure starts an empty set of attributes as the reduced set. The best of the original attributes is determined and added to the reduced set. At each subsequent iteration or step, the best of the remaining original attributes is added to the set.
2. **Stepwise backward elimination:** The procedure starts with the full set of attributes. At each step, it remove the worst attribute remaining in the set.
3. **Combination of forward selection and backward elimination:** The stepwise forward selection and backward elimination methods can be combined so that, at each step, the procedure selects the best attribute and removes the worst form among the remaining attributes.
4. **Decision tree induction:** Decision tree algorithm, such as ID3, C4.5 and CART, were originally intended for classification. Decision tree induction constructs a flowchart like structure where each internal (non leaf) mode denotes a test on an attribute, each branch corresponds to an outcome of the test, and each external (leaf) node denotes a class prediction. At each node, the algorithm chooses the "best" attribute to partition the data into individual classes.

When decision tree induction is used for attribute subset selection, a tree is constructed from the given data. All attributes that do not appear in the tree are assumed to be irrelevant. The set of attributes appearing in the tree form the reduced subset of attributes.

4.6.3 Dimensionality Reduction

Dimension reduction is the process of reducing the number of random variables under consideration, and can be divided into feature selection and feature extraction. Dimensionality reduction reduces the data set size by removing such attributes (or dimensions) from it. Typically, methods of attribute subset selection are applied.

Data Compression

In data compression, data encoding or transformations are applied so as to obtain a reduced or "compressed" representation of the original data. If the original data can be reconstructed from the compressed data without any loss of information, the data compression technique is called lossless.

Here we focus two popular and effective methods of data compression: wavelet transforms and principal components analysis.

Wavelet Transforms

The usefulness of the wavelet transforms is that the data can be truncated. A compressed approximation of the data can be retained by storing only a small fraction of the strongest of the wavelet coefficients. For example, all wavelet coefficients lager than some user-specified threshold can be retained. The remaining coefficients is set to o. The resulting data representation is therefore very sparse, so that operations that can take advantage of data sparsity are computationally very fast if performed in wavelet space. The technique also works to remove noise without smoothing out the main features of the data, making it effective for data cleaning as well. Given a set of coefficients, an approximation of the original data can be constructed by applying the inverse of the DWT (Discrete Wavelet Transforms) used.

Principal Components Analysis

In data mining we often encounter situations where there are a large number of variables in the database. In such situations it is very likely that subsets of variables are highly correlated with each other. The accuracy and reliability of a classification or prediction model will suffer if you include highly correlated variables or variables that are unrelated to the outcome of interest. Superfluous variables can increase the data-collection and data-processing costs of deploying a model on a large database. The dimensionality of a model is the number of independent or input variables used by the model. One of the key steps in data mining is finding ways to reduce dimensionality without sacrificing accuracy.

Principal component analysis (PCA) is a mathematical procedure that transforms a number of (possibly) correlated variables into a (smaller) number of uncorrelated variables called principal components. The objective of principal component analysis is to reduce the dimensionality (number of variables) of the dataset but retain most of the original variability in the data. The first principal component accounts for as much of the variability in the data as possible, and each succeeding component accounts for as much of the remaining variability as possible.

This procedure performs Principal Component Analysis on the selected dataset. A principal component analysis is concerned with explaining the variance covariance structure of a high dimensional random vector through a few linear combinations of the original component variables. Consider a p-dimensional random vector $X = (X_1, X_2, \ldots, X_p)$. k principal components ($k \leq p$) of X are k (univariate) random variables $Y_1, Y_2, \ldots, Y_k$ which are defined by the following formulae.

$$Y_1 = l_1' \underline{X} = l_{11} X_1 + l_{12} X_2 + \ldots + l_{1p} X_p$$

$$Y_2 = l_2' \underline{X} = l_{21} X_1 + l_{22} X_2 + \ldots + l_{2p} X_p$$

$$\vdots$$

$$Y_k = l_k' \underline{X} = l_{k1} X_1 + l_{k2} X_2 + \ldots + l_{pk} X_p$$

Where the coefficient vectors l_1, l_2,..etc are chosen such that they satisfy the following conditions:

First Principal Component = Linear combination $l_1'X$ that maximizes $Var(l_1'X)$ and $\| l_1 \| = 1$

Second Principal Component = Linear combination $l_2'X$ that maximizes $Var(l_2'X)$ and $\| l_2 \| = 1$ and $Cov(l_1'X, l_2'X) = 0$

*j*th Principal Component = Linear combination $l_j'X$ that maximizes $Var(l_j'X)$ and $\| l_j \| = 1$ and $Cov(l_k'X, l_j'X) = 0$ for all $k < j$

This says that the principal components are those linear combinations of the original variables which maximize the variance of the linear combination and which have zero covariance (and hence zero correlation) with the previous principal components.

It can be proved that there are exactly p such linear combinations. However, typically, the first few of them explain most of the variance in the original data. So instead of working with all the original variables $X_1, X_2, ..., X_p$, you would typically first perform PCA and then use only first two or three principal components, say Y_1 and Y_2, in subsequent analysis.

4.6.4 Numerosity Reduction

We can reduce the data volume by choosing 'smaller' forms of data representation with using numerosity reduction techniques. These techniques may be parametric or nonparametric. For parametric methods, a model is used to estimate the data, so that typically only the data parameters need to stored, instead of the actual data. Log-linear models, which estimate discrete multidimensional probability distribution, are an example. Nonparametric methods for storing reduced representations of the data include histograms, clustering, and sampling.

Let's have a look at some of the numerostiy reduction techniques discussed below.

Regression and Log-Linear Models

Regression and log-linear models can be used to approximate the given data. In linear regression, the data are modeled to fit a straight line. For example, a random variable, Y(called a response variable), can be modeled as a linear function of another random variable, X(called a predictor variable), with the equation.

$$Y = \alpha + \beta X \quad ...(4.5)$$

Where the variance of Y is assumed to be constant. The coefficients α and β(called regression coefficients) specify the Y-intercept and slope of the line, respectively. These coefficients can be solved for by the method of least squares, which minimizes the error between the actual line separating the data and the estimate of the line.

Multiple regression is an extension of linear regression allowing a response variable Y to be modeled as a linear function of a multidimensional feature vector.

$$Y = b_0 + b_1 X_1 + b_2 X_2. \quad ...(4.6)$$

Many non-linear functions can be transformed into the above.

Log-linear models approximate discrete multidimensional probability distributions. The method can be used to estimate the probability distributions. The method can be used to estimate the probability of each cell in a base cuboid of a set of discretized attributes, based on the smaller cuboids making up the data cube lattice. This allows higher-order data cubes to be constructed from lower-order ones. Log-linear models are therefore also useful for data compression and data smoothing.

Histograms Histograms are used widely to capture data distribution, to represent the data by small number of step functions.

Histogram or Frequency Histogram is a bar graph. The horizontal axis depicts the range and scale of observations involved and vertical axis shows the number of data points in various intervals *i.e.*, the frequency of observations in the intervals. Histograms are popular among statisticians. Though they do not show the exact values of the data points they give a very good idea about the spread of the data and shape.

Let us try drawing a histogram of percentage scores in a test. The scores are as follows:-

82.5, 78.3, 76.2, 81.2, 72.3, 73.2, 76.3, 77.3, 78.2, 78.5, 75.6, 79.2, 78.3, 80.2, 76.4, 77.9, 75.8, 76.5, 77.3, 78.2

When any data is provided it decides the size and number of intervals amongst which the data should be distributed. Five to Twenty intervals are fixed on the dataset depending on its range.

Let us see the histogram of the same data in Fig. 4.6.

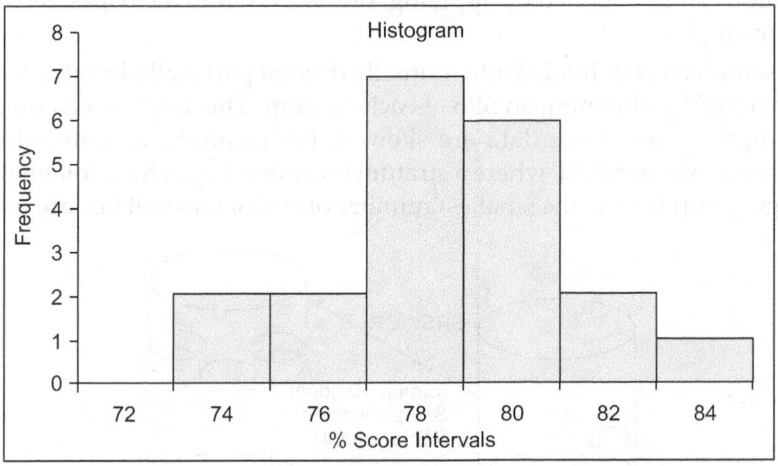

Fig. 4.6 Histogram

The values on the horizontal axis are the upper limits of bins (intervals) of data points, and not the mid-points of the intervals, although they may appear to be so. This is in keeping with the way the Analysis of Excel works. As an example, the bar shown against 78 has a frequency of 7. That means 7 data points lie in the range above 76 and upto (including) 78.

As is evident, the histogram gives a fairly good idea about the shape and spread of data at a glance.

Clustering

Clustering techniques consider data tuples as objects. They partition the objects into groups or clusters, so that objects within a cluster are "similar" to one another and "dissimilar" to objects in other cluster. Similarity is commonly defined in terms of how "close" the objects are in space, based on a distance function. The "quality" of a cluster may be represented by its diameter, the maximum distance between any two objects in the cluster. Centroid distance is an alternative measure of cluster quality and is defined as the average distance of each cluster object from the cluster centroid.

In data reduction, the cluster representations of the data are used to replace the actual data. The effectiveness of this technique depends on the nature of the data. It is much more effective for data that can be organized into distinct clusters than for smeared data.

Sampling

Sampling can be used as a data reduction technique since it allows a large data set to be represented by a much smaller random sample(or subset) of the data. Suppose that a large data set, D, contains N tuples. Let's have a look at some possible samples for D.

- **Simple random sample without replacement(SRSWOR) of size *n*:** This is created by drawing *n* of the N tuples from D(n<N), where the probability of drawing any tuple in D is 1/N, that is all tuples are equally likely.
- **Simple random sample with replacement (SRSWR) of size *n*:** This is similar to above one, except that each time a tuple is drawn from D, it is recorded and then replaced. That is, after a tuple is drawn, it is placed back in D so that it may be drawn again.
- **Cluster sample:** If a tuples in D are grouped into M mutually disjoint "clusters" then an SRS of *m* clusters can be obtained, where m < M. For example, tuples in a database are usually retrieved a page at a time, so that each page can be considered a cluster. A reduced data representation can be obtained by applying, say, SRSWOR to the pages, resulting in a cluster sample of the tuples.
- **Stratified sample:** If D is divided into mutually disjoint parts called strata. A stratified sample of D is generated by obtaining an SRS at each stratum. This helps to ensure a representative sample, especially when the data are skewed. For example, a stratified sample may be obtained from customer data, where a stratum is created for each customer age group. In this way, the age group having the smallest number of customers will be sure to be represented.

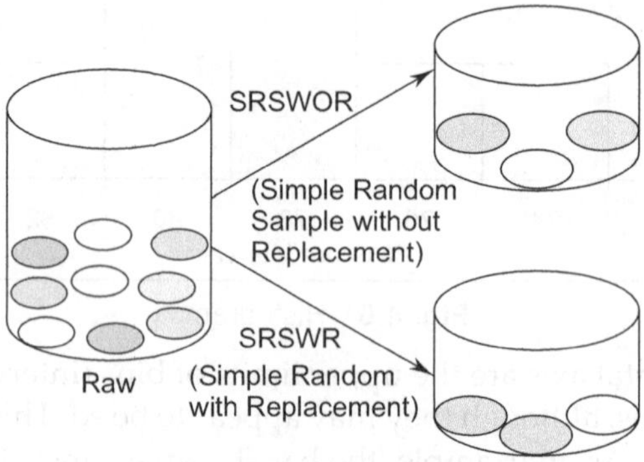

Fig. 4.7 Sampling

4.7 DISCRETIZATION AND CONCEPT HIERARCHY GENERATION

Discretization is a data-processing procedure that transforms quantitative data into qualitative data. Discretization transforms one type of data to another type. Discretization techniques can be used to reduce the number of values for a given continuous attribute, by dividing the range of the attribute into intervals. Interval labels can then be used to replace actual data values. Reducing the number of values for an attribute is especially beneficial if decision-tree-based methods of classification mining are to be applied to the preprocessed data.

Many discretization techniques can be applied recursively in order to provide a hierarchical or multiresolution partitioning of the attribute values, knows as a concept hierarchy.

A concept hierarchy for a given numeric attribute defines a discretization of the attribute. Concept hierarchies can be used to reduce the data by collecting and replacing low-level concepts by higher-level concepts. Although detail is lost by such a data generalization, the generalized data may be more meaningful and easier to interpret, and will require less space than the original data. Mining on a reduced data set will require fewer input/output operations and be more efficient than mining on a large, ungeneralized data set.

Let us look at the generation of concept hierarchies for numeric and categorical data.

4.7.1 Discretization and Concept Hierarchy Generation for Numeric Data

Specify concept hierarchies for numeric attributes is difficult task due to wide diversity of possible data ranges and the frequent updates of data values. Such a manual specification can also be quite arbitrary.

Concept hierarchies for numeric attribute can be constructed automatically based on data distribution analysis. List the five methods for numeric concept hierarchy generation listed below and we examine few of them.

The methods are Binning, Histogram analysis, cluster analysis, entropy-based discretization, and data segmentation by natural partitioning.

Binning

We discussed this method in section 4.3.3 for data smoothing. These methods are also forms of discretization. For example, attribute values can be discretized by distributing the values into bins, and replacing each bin value by the bin mean or median, as in smoothing by bin means or smoothing by bin medians, respectively. These techniques can be applied recursively to the resulting partitions in order to generate concept hierarchies.

Histogram Analysis

Histograms discussed in section 4.6.4. Histograms are also used for discretization. The histogram analysis algorithm can be applied recursively to each partition in order to automatically generate a multilevel concept hierarchy, with the procedure terminating once a prespecified number of concept levels has been reached. A minimum interval size can also be used per level to control the recursive procedure. This specifies the minimum width of a partition, or the minimum number of values for each partition at each level

Cluster Analysis

Clustering techniques can be applied to partition data into clusters or groups. Each cluster forms a node of a concept hierarchy, where all nodes of a concept hierarchy, where all nodes are at the same conceptual level. Each cluster may be further decomposed into several sub clusters, forming a lower level of the hierarchy. Clusters may also be grouped together in order of form a higher conceptual level of the hierarchy. Clustering methods we will study in the chapter 8.

Entropy-Based Discretization

An information-based measure called *entropy* can be used to recursively partition the values of a numeric attribute A, resulting in a hierarchical discretization. Such a discretization forms a numerical concept hierarchy for the attribute. Given a set of data tuples, S, the basic method for entropy-based discretization of A is as follows.

Each value of A can be considered a potential interval boundary or threshold T. For example, a value v of A can partition the samples in S into two subsets satisfying the conditions $A < v$ and $A >= v$, respectively, thereby creating a binary discretization.

Given a set of samples S, if S is partitioned into two intervals S_1 and S_2 using boundary T, the entropy after partitioning is

$$E(S, T) = \frac{|S|}{|S|} \text{Ent}(S) + \frac{|S|}{|S|} \text{Ent}(S) \quad \ldots(4.7)$$

The boundary that minimizes the entropy function over all possible boundaries is selected as a binary discretization. The process is recursively applied to partitions obtained until some stopping criterion is met.

$$\text{Ent}(S) - E(T, S) > \delta \quad \ldots(4.8)$$

4.7.2 Concept Hierarchy Generation for Categorical Data

Categorical data are discrete data. Categorical attributes have a finite (but possibly large) number of distinct values, with no ordering among the values. There are several methods for the generation of concept hierarchies for categorical data.

Specification of a partial ordering of attributes explicitly at the schema level by users or experts

Concept hierarchies for categorical attributes or dimensions typically involve a group of attributes. A user or expert can easily define a concept hierarchy by specifying a partial or total ordering of the attributes at the schema level.

Specification of portion of a hierarchy by explicit data grouping

This is essentially the manual definition of a portion of a concept hierarchy. In a large database, it is unrealistic to define an entire concept hierarchy by explicit value enumeration. However, it is realistic to specify explicit grouping for a small portion of intermediate-level data.

Specification of a set of attributes, but not of their partial ordering

A user may specify a set of attributes forming a concept hierarchy, but omit to explicitly state their partial ordering. The system can then try to automatically generate the attribute ordering so as to construct a meaningful concept hierarchy.

Consider some observations that since higher-level concepts generally cover several subordinate lower-level concepts, an attribute defining a high concept level will usually contain a smaller number of distinct values than an attribute defining a lower concept level. Based on this observation, a concept hierarchy can be automatically generated based on the number of distinct values per attribute in the given attribute set. The attribute with the most distinct values is placed at the lowest level of the hierarchy. The lower number of distinct values an attribute has, the higher it is in the generated concept hierarchy.

Specification of only a partial set of attributes

The user may have included only a small subset of the relevant attributes in a hierarchy specification. For example, instead of including all the hierarchically relevant attributes for *location*, the user may have specified only *street* and *city*. To handle such partially specified hierarchies, it is important to embed data semantic in the database schema so that attributes with tight semantic connections can be pinned together. In this way, the specification of one attribute may trigger a whole group of semantically tightly linked attributes to be "dragged in" to form a complete hierarchy. Users, however, should have the option to override this feature, as necessary.

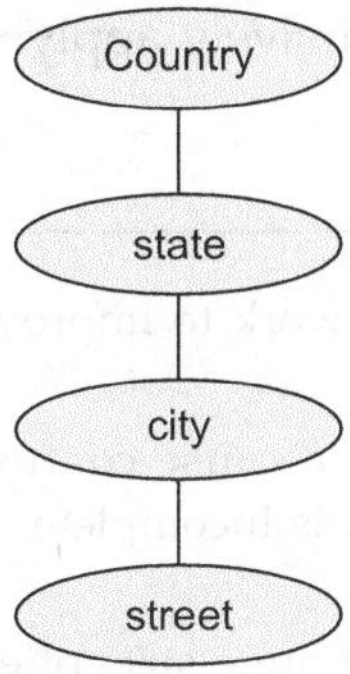

Fig. 4.8 Automatic generation of a schema concept hierarchy based on the number of distinct attribute values

Discretization and generating concept hierarchies

1. Unsupervised discretization - class variable is not used.
   - Equal-interval (equiwidth) binning: split the whole range of numbers in intervals with equal size.
   - Equal-frequency (equidepth) binning: use intervals containing equal number of values.
2. Supervised discretization - uses the values of the class variable.
   - Using class boundaries. Three steps:
     - Sort values.
     - Place breakpoints between values belonging to different classes.
     - If too many intervals, merge intervals with equal or similar class distributions.
   - Entropy (information)-based discretization. Example:
     - Information in a class distribution:
     - Denote a set of five values occurring in tuples belonging to two classes (+ and –) as `[+,+,+,-,-]`
     - That is, the first 3 belong to "+" tuples and the last 2 – to "–" tuples
     - Then, `Info([+,+,+,-,-]) = -(3/5)*log(3/5)-(2/5)*log(2/5)` (logs are base 2)
     - 3/5 and 2/5 are relative frequencies (probabilities)
     - Ignoring the order of the values, we can use the following notation: `[3,2]` meaning 3 values from one class and 2 – from the other.
     - `Then, Info([3,2]) = -(3/5)*log(3/5)-(2/5)*log(2/5)`
   - Information in a split `(2/5 and 3/5 are weight coefficients):`
     - `Info([+,+],[+,-,-]) = (2/5)*Info([+,+]) + (3/5)*Info([+,-,-])`
     - Or, `Info([2,0],[1,2]) = (2/5)*Info([2,0]) + (3/5)*Info([1,2])`
   - Method:
     - Sort the values;
     - Calculate information in all possible splits;
     - Choose the split that minimizes information;

- Do not include breakpoints between values belonging to the same class (this will increase information);
- Apply the same to the resulting intervals until some stopping criterion is satisfied.

3. Generating concept hierarchies: recursively applying partitioning or discretization methods

SUMMARY

- Data Preprocessing is essential part of work to improve the efficiency and ease of the data mining and data warehousing process.
- Real-world data is dirty. Dirty data can cause confusion for the mining procedure, resulting in unreliable output. The dirty data which is Incomplete, Noisy, and Inconsistent, that data is called as dirty data.
- The data is dirty due to their typically huge size, often several gigabytes or more and other kind of reasons.
- Data preprocessing includes data cleaning, data integration, data transformation and data reduction.
- Data cleaning is centered around improving the quality of the data to make them "fit for use" by users through reducing errors in the data improving their documentation and presentation.
- Data cleaning methods can be used to full fill the missing values, smooth noisy data and correct the data inconsistencies.
- Data integration combines data from multiple sources into a coherent data store, as in data warehousing. These sources may include multiple databases, data cubes, or flat files.
- Data transformation is the mapping and conversion of data from one form to another. The transformed form of data may useful for data mining.
- Data reduction techniques can be applied to obtain a reduced representation of the data set that is much smaller in volume, yet closely maintains the integrity of the original data. That is, mining on the reduced data set should be more efficient yet produce the same (or almost the same) analytical results.
- Discretization is a data-processing procedure that transforms quantitative data into qualitative data. Discretization transforms one type of data to another type. Discretization techniques can be used to reduce the number of values for a given continuous attribute, by dividing the range of the attribute into intervals.

REVIEW QUESTIONS

1. Briefly discuss the role of data cube aggregation and dimension reduction in the data reduction process.
2. Briefly discuss the data smoothing techniques.
3. Explain about concept hierarchy generation for categorical data.
4. Explain various data reduction techniques.
5. Explain about the graph displays of basic statistical class description.
6. Discuss data cleaning, data transformation methods
7. Briefly discuss the data smoothing techniques.
8. Discuss about data integration and data transformation.
9. Discuss the role of data compression and numerosity reduction in data reduction process.
10. Explain data discretization and concept hierarchy generation.

5

DATA MINING PRIMITIVES AND DMQL

5.1 INTRODUCTION

Data mining system can dig lot of patterns from the given large databases. Most of the patterns discovered would be irrelevant to the analysis task. Furthermore, many of the patterns found, may related to the analysis task, but difficult to understand or lack validity, novelty, utility, it make them uninteresting. A more realistic scenario is to expect that users can communicate with the data mining system using a set of data *mining primitives* designed in order to facilitate efficient and fruitful knowledge discovery. The primitives of data mining system allow the users to interactively communicate with the data mining system during discovery in order to examine the findings from different angles or depths, and direct the mining process.

In this chapter we will learn about data mining primitives and study the designing of a data mining query language based on data mining primitive principles. A data mining query language can be designed to incorporate data mining primitives, allowing users to flexibly interact with data mining systems. Data mining query language provides a foundation on user-friendly graphical interfaces can be built.

5.2 DATA MINING PRIMITIVES

Data mining primitives include the specification of the portions of the database or the set of data in which the user is interested including the database attributes or data warehouse dimensions of interest, the kinds of knowledge to be mined, background knowledge useful in guiding the discovery process, interestingness measures for pattern evaluation, and how the discovered knowledge should be visualized.

Users will have a data mining task in mind, that is, some form of data analysis that would like to have performed. Data mining primitives are listed below:

- Task-relevant data
- The kind of knowledge to be mined

- Background knowledge
- Pattern interestingness measures
- Visualization of discovered patterns

The data mining primitives are discussed detailed in the subsequent sections.

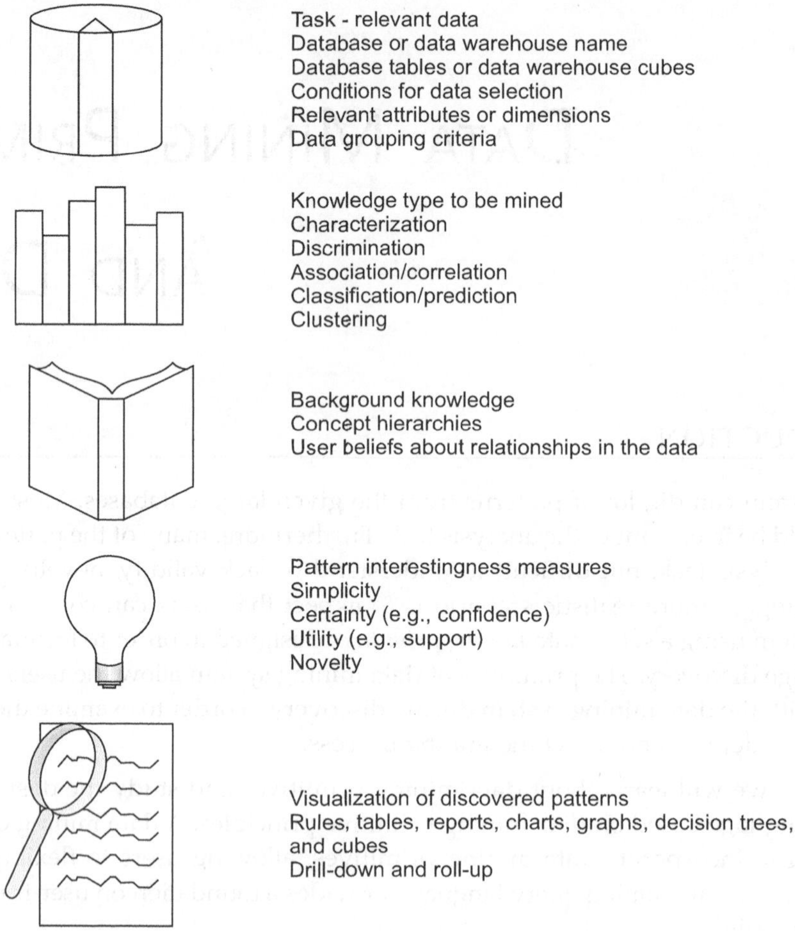

Fig. 5.1 Primitives for specifying a data mining task

5.2.1 Task-Relevant Data

The first data mining primitive is the specification of the data on which mining is to be performed. Typically, a user is interested in only a subset of the database. It is impractical to indiscriminately mine the entire database, particularly since the number of patterns generated could be exponential with respect to the database size. Furthermore, many of the patterns found would be irrelevant to the interests of the user.

For example, suppose that you are a managing director of *supermarket* in charge of sales in India. You would like to study the buying trends of customers in country, rather than mining the entire database, you can specify that only the data relating to customer purchases in India need to be retrieved, along with the related customer profile information. You can also specify attributes of interest to be considered in the mining process. These are referred to as relevant attributes.

In a relational database, the set of task-relevant data can be collected via a relational query involving operations like selection, projection, join, and aggregation. This retrieval of data can be thought of as a "subtask" of the data mining task. The data collection process results in a new data relation, called the initial data relation.

The initial data relation can be ordered or grouped according to the conditions specified in the query. The data may be cleaned or transformed (*e.g.*, aggregated on certain attributes) prior to applying data mining analysis. The initial relation may or may not correspond to a physical relation in the database. Since virtual relations are called views in the field of databases, the set of task-relevant data for data mining is called minable view.

For example, we mentioned *supermarket* example if you are interested only in studying possible relationships between the items purchased and customer annual income and *age*, then the attributes *name* of the relation *item*, and *income* and *age* of the relation *customer*, can be specified as the relevant attributes for mining.

If the data mining task is to study associations between items frequently purchased at *supermarket* by customer in India, the task-relevant data can be specified by providing the following information:

- The name of the *database* or *data warehouse* to be used (*i.e.*, supermarket_db)
- The names of the *tables* or *data cubes* containing the relevant data (*e.g.*, *item, customer, purchases and items_sold*)
- *Conditions* for selecting the relevant data (*e.g.*, retrieve data pertaining to purchases made in India for the current year)
- The *relevant attributes or dimensions* (*e.g.*, *name* and *price* from the *item* table, and *income* and *age* from the customer table)

In additional, the user may specify that the data retrieved be grouped by certain attributes, such as "**group by** date". Given this information, an SQL query can be used to retrieve the task-relevant data.

Specification of the relevant attributes or dimensions can be a difficult task for users. A user may have only a rough idea of what the interesting attributes for exploration might be. Furthermore, when specifying the data to be mined, the user may overlook additional relevant data having strong semantic links to them. For example, the sales of certain items may be closely linked to particular occasions like Diwali, Christmas etc, or to particular groups of customers, yet these factors may not be included in the general data analysis request. For each cases, mechanisms can be used that help give amore precise specification of he task-relevant data. These include functions to evaluate and rank attributes according to their relevance with respect to the operation specified. In addition, techniques that search for attributes with strong semantic ties can be used to enhance the initial data set specified by the user.

5.2.2 The Kind of Knowledge to be Mined

The kind of knowledge is important to specify what kind of knowledge to be mined, as this determines the data mining function to be performed. The kinds of knowledge include concept description, clustering, and evolution analysis.

In addition to specifying the kind of knowledge to be mined for a given data mining task, the user can be more specific and provide pattern templates that all discovered patterns must match. These templates or **metapatterns** (also called **metarules** or **metaqueris**), can be used to guide the discovery process.

For example, A user studying the buying habits of *Supermarket* customers may choose to mine association rules of the form

$$P(X: \text{customer}, W) \wedge Q(X,Y) \rightarrow \text{buys}(X, Z)$$

where X is key of the customer relation: P and Q are predicate variables that can be instantiated to the relevant attributes or dimensions specified as part of the task-relevant data, and W,Y, and Z are object variables that can take on the values of their respective predicates for customer X.

The search for association rules is confined to those matching the given metarule, such as

Age (X,"25...35) ^ income (X,"40K...49K") → buys(X, "camera")

[2.2%,60%] ...(5.1)

and

occupation (X," student") ^age(X, "20...29") → buys(X,"computer")

[1.4%,70%] ...(5.2)

The above rule 5.1 states that customers in their age within 25 to 35 years, with an annual income of between 40K and 49K, are likely (with 60% confidence) to purchase a camera, and such cases represent about 2.2% of the total number of transactions. The second rule 5.2 states that customers who are students and in their age in between 20 to 29 years are likely to purchase a computer, and such cases represent about 1.4% of the total number of transactions.

5.2.3 Background Knowledge: Concept Hierarchies

In this section, we focus on a simple yet powerful form of background knowledge known as *concept hierarchies*. Background knowledge is information about the domain to be mined that can be useful in the discovery process. Concept hierarchy for the dimension *location* is shown in Figure 5.2 mapping low-level concepts to (*i.e.*, cites) to more general concepts (*i.e.*, countries).

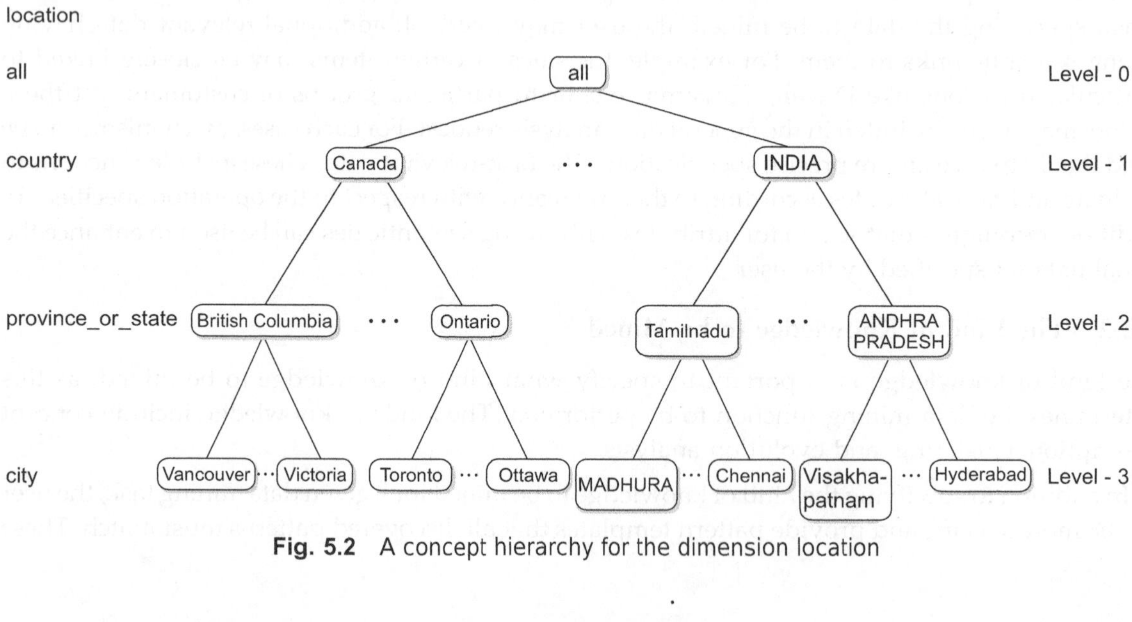

Fig. 5.2 A concept hierarchy for the dimension location

In the Fig. 5.2 showing that concept hierarchy is represented as a set of nodes organized in a tree, where each node, in itself, represents a concept. A special node, **all,** is reserved for the root of the tree. It denotes the most generalized value of the given dimension. If not explicitly shown, it is implied. This concept hierarchy consists of four levels. For our convention, levels within a concept hierarchy are numbered from the top to bottom, starting with level 0 fro the **all** node. In our example figure 5.2 ***level 1*** represents the concept *country,* while levels 2 and 3 represent the concepts *procince_or_state* and *city,* respectively. The leaves of the hierarchy correspond to the dimension's raw data values (primitive level data). These are the most specific values, or concepts, of the given attribute or dimension. Although a concept hierarchy often defines a taxonomy represented in the shape of a tree, it may also be in the form of a general lattice or partial order.

Concept hierarchies are a useful form of background knowledge in that they allow raw data to be handled at higher, generalized levels of abstraction. Generalization of the data, or **rolling up,** is achieved by replacing primitive-level data by higher level concepts. This allows the user to view the data at more meaningful and explicit abstraction, and make the discovered patterns easier to understand. Generalization has an added advantage of compressing the data. Mining on a compressed data set will require fewer input/output operations and be more efficient than mining on a larger, uncompressed data set.

If the resulting data appear over generalized, concept hierarchies also allow specialization, or **drilling down,** whereby concept values are replaced by lower-level concepts. By rolling up and drilling down, users can view the data from different perspectives, gaining further insight into hidden data relationships.

Concept hierarchies can be provided by system users, domain experts, or knowledge engineers. The mappings are typically data-or application-specific. Concept hierarchies can often be automatically discovered or dynamically refined based on statistical analysis of the data distribution.

There are more than one concept hierarchy for a given attribute or dimension, based on different user viewpoint. There are four major types of concept hierarchies.

- Schema hierarchies
- Set-grouping hierarchies
- Operation-driven hierarchies
- Rule-based hierarchies

We will discuss below these four concept hierarchies

Schema hierarchies

A schema hierarchy (also called schema-defined hierarchy) is total or partial order among attributes in the database schema. Schema hierarchies may formally express existing semantic relationships between attributes. Typically, a schema hierarchy specifies a data warehouse dimension.

For example, the schema of a relation for *address* containing the attributes street, city province_or_state, and *country,* we can define a *location* schema hierarchy by the following total order

```
street<city <province_or_state<country
```

This means that *street* is at a conceptually lower level than *city*, which is lower than province_or_state, which is conceptually lower than *country*. A schema hierarchy provides metadata information, that is , data about the data. Its specification in terms of a total or partial order among attributes is more concise than an equivalent definition that lists all instances of streets, provinces or states, and countries.

Set-grouping hierarchies

A set-grouping hierarchy organizes values for a given attribute or dimension into groups of constants or range values. A total or partial order can be defined among groups. Set-grouping hierarchies, when the two types of hierarchies are combined. They are typically used for defining small sets of object relationships.

For example, a set-group hierarchy for the attribute *age* can be specified in term of ranges, as in the following;

{*young, middle-aged, senior*} ⊂ all(age)

{20…39} ⊂ *young*

{40…59} ⊂ *middle_aged*

{60…89} ⊂ *senior*

Operation-derived hierarchies

An *operation-derived hierarchy* is based on operations specified by users, experts, or the data mining system. Operations can include the decoding of information-encoded strings, information extraction from complex data objects, and data clustering.

For example, the e-mail address or URL of the WWW may contain hierarchy information relating departments, universities or (companies), and countries. Decoding operations can be defined to extract such information in order to form concept hierarchies.

Alternatively, mathematical and statistical operations, such as data clustering and data distribution analysis algorithms, can be used to form concept hierarchies.

Ruled-based hierarchies: *A rule-based hierarchy* occurs when either a whole concept hierarchy or a portion of it is defined by a set of rules and is evaluated dynamically based on the current database data and the rule definition.

5.2.4 Interestingness Measures

Data mining processes still generate a large number of patterns. Typically, only a small fraction of these patterns will actually be of interest to the given user. Thus users need to further confine the number of uninteresting pattern returned by the process. This can be achieved by specifying interestingness measures that estimate the simplicity, certainty, utility, and novelty of patterns.

Objective measures are based on the structure of patterns and the statistics underlying them. In general, each measure is associated with a *threshold* that can be controlled by the user. Rules do not meet the threshold are considered uninteresting, and hence are not presented in the user knowledge.

Simplicity: Objective measures of pattern's overall simplicity for human comprehension. Objective measures of pattern simplicity can be viewed as functions of the pattern structure, defined in terms of the pattern size in bits, or the number of attributes or operators appearing in the patterns. For example, the more complex the structure of a rule is, the more difficult it is to interpret, and, hence, the less interesting it is likely to be.

Rule length, for instance, is a simplicity measure. For rules expressed in conjunctive normal form, rule length is typically defined as the number of conjuncts in the rule. Association, discrimination, or classification rules whose lengths exceed a user-defined threshold can be considered uninteresting. For patterns expressed as decision trees, simplicity may be a function of the number of tree leaves or tree nodes.

Certainty: Each discovered pattern should have a measure of certainty associated with it that assesses the validity or "trustworthiness" of the pattern. A certainty measure for association rules of the form "A=> B" is defined as

$$\text{Confidence (A=>B)} = \frac{\#\_\text{tuples\_containing\_both\_A\_and\_B}}{\#\_\text{tuples\_containing\_A}} \qquad \text{...(5.3)}$$

Suppose that the set of task-relevant data consists of transactions of items purchased from the food department of *supermarket.* A confidence of 85% for the association rule.

Utility: The potential usefulness of a patterns is a factor defining its interestingness. It can be estimate by a utility function, such as support. The **support** of an association pattern refers to the percentage to task-relevant data tuples (or transactions) for which the pattern is true. For association rules of the form "A=>B" where A and B are sets of items, it is defined as

$$\text{Support (A=>B)} = \frac{\#\_\text{tuples\_containing\_both\_A\_and\_B}}{\text{total\_\#\_of\_tuples}} \qquad \text{...(5.4)}$$

Association rules that satisfy both a user-specified *minimum confidence threshold* and user-specified minimum support threshold are referred to as ***strong association rules*** and are considered interesting. Rules with low support likely represent noise, or rare or exceptional cases.

The numerator of the support equation is also known as the rule **count.** Quite often, this number is displayed instead of support. Support can easily be derived from it.

Characteristic and discriminate descriptions are, in essence, generalized tuples. Any generalized tuple representing less than Y% of the total number of task-relevant tuples can be considered noise. Such tuple are not displayed to the user. The value of Y is referred to as the *noise threshold.*

Novelty: Novelty patterns are those that contribute new information or increased performance to the given pattern set. For example, a data exception may be considered novel in that it differs from that expected based on a statistical model or user beliefs.

Another strategy for detecting novelty is to remove redundant patterns. If a discovered rule can be implied by another rule that is already in the knowledge base or in the derived rule set, then either rule should be reexamined in order to remove the potential redundancy.

Mining with concept hierarchies can result in a large number of redundant rules. Data mining system should allow user to flexible and interactively specify, test, and modify interestingness measures and their respective thresholds. There are many other objective measures, apart from the basic ones studied above. Subjective measures exist as well, which consider user beliefs regarding relationship in the data, in addition to objective statistical measures.

5.2.5 Presentation and Visualization of Discovered Patterns

For data mining to be effective, data mining systems should be able to display the discovered patterns in multiple forms, such as rules, tables, crosstabs (cross-tabulations), pie or bar charts, decision trees, cubes, or other visual representations. Allowing the visualization of discovered patterns in various forms can help users with different backgrounds to identify patterns in interest and to interact or guide the system in further discovery. A user should be able to specify the forms of presentation to be used for displaying the discovered patterns.

The use of concept hierarchies plays an important role in aiding the user to visualize the discovered patterns. Mining with concept hierarchies allows the representation of discovered knowledge in high-level concepts, which may be more understandable to users than rules expressed in terms of primitive data, such a functional or multivalued dependency rules, or integrity constraints. Furthermore, data mining system should employ concept hierarchies to implement drill-down and roll-up operations, so that users may inspect discovered patters at multiple levels of abstraction. In addition, pivoting (or rotating), slicing, and dicing operations aid the user in viewing generalized data and knowledge from different perspectives.

Some representation forms may be better suited than others for particular kinds of knowledge. For example, generalized relations and their corresponding crosstabs or pie/bar charts are good for presenting characteristic descriptions, whereas decision trees are a common choice for classification.

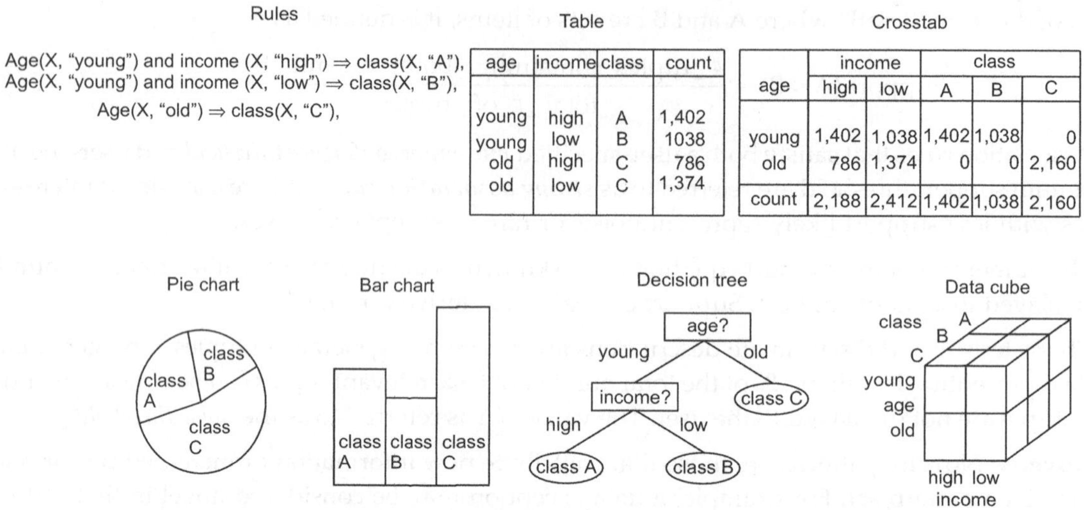

Fig. 5.3 Various form of presenting and visualizing the discovered patterns

5.3 A DATA MINING QUERY LANGUAGE (DMQL)

The desired feature of data mining systems is the ability to support adhoc and interactive data mining in order to facilitate flexible and effective knowledge discovery. Data mining query languages are designed to support such features.

The importance of the design of a good data mining query language can also be seen from observing history of relational database systems. Each commercial relational database system has its own graphical user interface; the underlying core of each interface is a standardized relational query language. The standardization of relational query languages provided a foundation on which relational systems were developed and evolved. The recent standardization activities in database systems, such as SQL-3 and so on further illustrate the importance of having a standard database language for commercialization of database systems. So, having a query language for data mining may help standardize the development of platforms for database systems.

Designing a comprehensive data mining language is challenging because data mining covers a wide spectrum of tasks. Each task has different requirements. The design of an effective data mining query language requires a deep understanding of power, limitation and underlying mechanisms of the various kinds of data mining tasks. We design a data mining query language based on the five data mining task primitives. The primitives specify again following.

- The set of task-relevant data to be mined
- The kind of knowledge to be mined
- The background knowledge to be used in the discovery process
- The interestingness measures and thresholds for pattern evaluation
- The expected representation for visualizing the discovered patterns

Query language for data mining called DMQL(Data Mining Query Language) allows adhoc mining of several kinds of knowledge from relational databases and data warehouses at multiple levels of abstraction. The language adopts SQL syntax, so that it can easily be integrated with SQL. The syntax of DMQL is defined in extended BNF grammar where "[ ]" represents 0 or 1 occurrence,"{ }" represents 0 or more occurrences and words in sans serif font represents keywords.

Specify background knowledge	→	**use database** <database_name> {**use hierarchy** <hierarchy_name> for <attribute>}
Specify rules to be discovered	→	<rule_spec>
Relevant attributes or aggregations	→	**related to** <attr_or_agg_list> **from** <relation(s)> [**where** <conditions>] [**order by** <order list>]
Specify threshold parameters	→	{with [<kinds of>] threshold =<threshold_value> [for <attribute(s)>]} <rule_spec> find **classification** rules [as <rule_name>] [according to <attributes>] find **association** rules [as <rule_name>] **generalize** data [into <relation_name>] others

5.3.1 Syntax for Task-Relevant Data

A data mining task is the specification of the task-relevant data, that is, the data on which mining is to be performed.

Task relevant data kind of primitive will perform on the following points.

- Database or data warehouse name
- Database tables or data warehouse cubes
- Condition for data selection
- Relevant attributes or dimensions
- Data grouping criteria

Syntax for the task-relevant data

use databasedatabase_name, or **use data warehouse**data_warehouse_name

from relation(s)/cube(s)[**where**condition]

in relevance toatt_or_dim_list

order byorder_list

group bygrouping_list

havingcondition

5.3.2 Syntax for Kind of Knowledge to be Mined

This primitive can perform the data mining functionalities. Knowledge to be mined indicates and performs the following important mining functionalities.

- Characterization
- Discrimination
- Association
- Classification / prediction
- Clustering
- Outlier Analysis
- Other data mining tasks

Characterization:

Mine_Knowledge_Specification::=

mine characteristics[aspattern_name]

analyzemeasure(s)

(*e.g.*, sum, count etc.)

The characterization specifies that characteristic descriptions are to be mined. The **analyze** clause specifies aggregate measures, example sum, count, average etc.

Discrimination:

Mine_Knowledge_Specification::=

mine comparison[aspattern_name]

for target_classwheretarget_condition

{versus contrast_class_iwherecontrast_condition_i}

analyzemeasure(s)

These descriptions compare a given target class of objects with one or more other contrasting classes. The kind of knowledge is indexed to as a comparison.

Association:

Mine_Knowledge_Specification::=

mine associations[aspattern_name]

[**matching** <metapattern>]

When it specifies the user has the option of providing templates with the matching clause. This matching clause find the metapatterns be used to focus the discovery towards the pattern that match given meta pattern.

Classification:

Mine_Knowledge_Specification::=

mine classification[aspattern_name]

analyzeclassifying_attribute_or_dimension

Classification specifies that patterns for data classification are to be mined. The analyze class specifies that the classification is performed according to the values.

5.3.3 Syntax for Concept Hierarchy

Concept hierarchies allow the discovery of knowledge at multiple levels of abstraction. It map from a set of low-level concepts to higher-level concepts. Definition of concept hierarchies with DMQL is shown below.

To specify what concept hierarchies to use

use hierarchy <hierarchy>**for** <attribute_or_dimension>

We use different syntax to define different type of hierarchies

Schema hierarchies:

define hierarchy time_hierarchy **on** dateas [date,month quarter,year]

Set-grouping hierarchies

define hierarchy age_hierarchyfor age **on** customeras

level1: {young, middle_aged, senior} < level0: all

level2: {20, ..., 39} < level1:young

level2: {40, ..., 59} < level1: middle_aged

level2: {60, ..., 89} < level1: senior

Operation-driven hierarchies

Define hierarchy age_hierarchy forage oncustomer as

{age_category(1), ..., age_category(5)} := cluster(default, age, 5) < all(age)

Rule-based hierarchies

define hierarchy profit_margin_hierarchy onitem as

level_1: low_profit_margin < level_0: all

if (price -cost)< $50

level_1: medium-profit_margin < level_0: all

if ((price -cost) > $50) and ((price -cost) <= $250))

level_1: high_profit_margin < level_0: all

if (price -cost) > $250

5.3.4 Specification of Interestingness Measure Syntax

Interestingness measures and thresholds can be specified by a user with the statement:

with <interest_measure_name>**threshold** = threshold_value

Example:

with support **threshold**= 0.05

with confidence **threshold** = 0.7

The interestingness measures and threshold values can be set and modified interactively.

5.3.5 Specification of Pattern Presentation and Visualization Syntax

The data mining query language for pattern presentation syntax that allows users to specify the display of discovered patterns in one or more forms mentioned below.

- Rules
- Tables
- Crosstabs
- Pie or bar charts
- Decision trees
- Cubes
- Curves or surfaces.

The syntax for this task is as follows

display as <result_form>

where the <result_form> could be any of the knowledge presentation or visualization forms listed above.

To facilitate interactive viewing at different concept level, the following syntax is defined:

Multilevel_Manipulation::= **roll up on** attribute_or_dimension

| **drill down on** <attribute_or_dimension >

| **add**<attribute_or_dimension >

| **drop**<attribute_or_dimension >

5.4 OTHER DATA MINING LANGUAGES AND STANDARDIZATION EFFORTS

Association rule language specifications

MSQL (Imielinski& Virmani'99)

MineRule(MeoPsailaand Ceri'96)

Query flocks based on Datalogsyntax (Tsuret al'98)

OLEDB for DM (Microsoft'2000)

Based on OLE, OLE DB, OLE DB for OLAP

Integrating DBMS, data warehouse and data mining

CRISP-DM (CRoss-Industry Standard Process for Data Mining)

Providing a platform and process structure for effective data mining

Emphasizing on deploying data mining technology to solve business problems

SUMMARY

- The primitives of data mining system allow the users to interactively communicate with the data mining system during discovery in order to examine the findings from different angles or depths, and direct the mining process.
- Data mining primitives are task-relevant data, the kind of knowledge to be mined, background knowledge, pattern interestingness measures and visualization of discovered patterns.
- First data mining primitive is task-relevant data that specification of the data on which mining is to be performed. The data might be a database file, data warehouse and in particularly attributes and dimensions.
- The second data mining primitive is kind of knowledge to be mined. It is important to specify what kind of knowledge to be mined, as this determines the data mining function to be performed. The kinds of knowledge include concept description, clustering, and evolution analysis.
- Background knowledge is information about the domain to be mined that can be useful in the discovery process.
- Data mining processes still generate a large number of patterns. Typically, only a small fraction of these patterns will actually be of interest to the given user. Thus users need to further confine the number of uninteresting pattern returned by the process.
- Data mining systems should be able to display the discovered patterns in multiple forms, such as rules, tables, cross-tabs (cross-tabulations), pie or bar charts, decision trees, cubes, or other visual representations.
- Query language for data mining called DMQL (Data Mining Query Language) allows adhoc mining of several kinds of knowledge from relational databases and data warehouses at multiple levels of abstraction.

REVIEW QUESTIONS

1. Write the syntax for the following data mining primitives:
   (*a*) Task-relevant data.
   (*b*) Concept hierarchies.

2. List and describe the five data mining primitives.
3. Describe why concept hierarchies are useful in data mining.
4. Write the syntax for the following data mining primitives:
   (*a*) The kind of knowledge to be mined.
   (*b*) Measures of pattern interestingness.
5. Briefly discuss the various forms of Presenting and visualizing the discovered patterns.
6. Describe why is it important to have a data mining query language.
7. How can we specify a data mining query for characterization with DMQL?
8. Describe the transformation of a data mining query to a relational query.

6

ASSOCIATION RULES MINING

6.1 INTRODUCTION

Among the areas of data mining, the problem of deriving associations from data has received a great deal of attention. A huge amount of data stored electronically in most enterprises. In particular, in all retail outlets the amount of data stored has grown enormously. In this, we are given a set of items and a large collection of transactions, which are subsets of these items. The task is to find relationships between the presences of various items within these baskets.

There are numerous applications of data mining which fit into this framework. The classic example from which the problem gets its name is the supermarket. In this context, the problem is to analyze customer's buying habits by finding association between the different items that customers place in their shopping baskets. The discovery of such association rules can help the retailer develop marketing strategies, by gaining insight into matters like "which items are most frequently purchased by customers". It also helps in inventory managements, sale promotion strategies, etc.

6.2 FUNDAMENTAL CONCEPTS

Let us first Discuss the association rules mining task, and also define some of the terminology by using an example of a super market. To keep the example simple, we assume that the super market sells only a small variety of products:

Bread	Cheese	Coffee	Chocolate
Juice	Milk	Tea	Oil
Biscuits	Newspaper	Sugar	Butter

We assume that the shopkeeper keeps records of what each customer purchases. Such records of ten customers are given in Table 6.1. Each row in the table gives the set of items that customer bought.

Table 6.1: Transactions of Supermarket

Transaction ID	*Items*
10	Bread, Cheese, Newspaper, Butter
20	Bread, Cheese, Juice, Oil
30	Bread, Milk, Chocolate
40	Cheese, Juice, Milk, Coffee, Tea, Butter
50	Sugar, Tea, Coffee, Biscuits, Newspaper
60	Sugar, Tea, Coffee, Biscuits, Milk, Juice, Newspaper
70	Bread, Cheese, Butter
80	Bread, Cheese, Juice, Coffee, Chocolate, Oil
90	Bread, Milk, Tea, Sugar, Chocolate
100	Sugar, Tea, Coffee, Bread, Milk, Juice, Newspaper

The shopkeeper wants to find which products (call them items) are sold together frequently. If for example, sugar and tea are the two items that are sold together frequently then the shopkeeper might consider having a sale on one of them in the hope that it will not only increase the sale of that item but also increase the sale of the other.

We will not find a solution to this example just now. Similar examples are used later in the chapter where we illustrate a number of methods for solving them.

6.2.1 Terminology

We now define some terminology. We assume that the number of items the shop stocks is n (for example, $n = 12$ for this shop) and these items are represented by I$\{i_1, i_2, i_3, \ldots, i_n\}$. We assume that there are N transactions (N = 10 for the shop data Table 6.1). We denote them by T $\{t_1, t_2, \ldots, t_N\}$ each with a unique identifier (TID) and each specifying a subset of items (possibly a small subset) from the item set I purchased by one customer. Let each transaction of m items be $\{i_1, i_2, \ldots, i_m\}$ with $m <= n$. Typically, transactions differ in the number of items. We now wish to find association relationships, given a large number of transactions, such that items that tend to occur together are identified. It should be noted that association rules mining does not take into account the quantities of items bought.

Association rules are often written as X → Y meaning that whenever X appears Y also tends to appear. X and Y may be single items or sets of items (in which the same item does not appear in both sets). X is often referred to as the rule's *antecedent* and Y as the *consequent*.

X → Y is a probabilistic relationship found empirically. It indicates only that X and Y have been found together frequently in the given data and does not show a causal relationship implying that buying of X by a customer causes him/her to buy Y.

As noted above, we assume that we have a set of transactions, each transactions being a list of items. Suppose items (or itemsets) X and Y appear together in only 10% of the transactions but whenever X appears there is an 80% chance that Y also appears. The 10% presence of X and Y together is called the support (or *prevalence*) of the rule and the 80% chance is called the *confidence* (or *predictability*) of the rule. Essentially, the support and confidence are measures of the interestingness of the rule. A high level of support indicates that the rule is frequent enough for the business to be interested in it. A high level of confidence shows that the rule is true often enough to justify a decision based on it.

Let us define support and confidence more formally. As noted earlier, the total number of transactions is N. Support of X is the number of times it appears in the database divided by N and support for X and Y together is the number of times they appear together divided by N. Therefore using P(X) to mean probability of X in the database, we have:

$$\text{Support}(X) = (\text{Number of times X appears})/N = P(X)$$

$$\text{Support}(X/Y) = (\text{Number of times X and Y appear together})/N = P(X \wedge Y)$$

Confidence for $X \rightarrow Y$ is defined as ratio of the support for X and Y together to the support for X. Therefore if X appears much more frequently then X and Y appear together, the confidence will be low. It does not depend on how frequently Y appears.

$$\text{Confidence of } (X \rightarrow Y) = \text{Support}(X/Y)/\text{Support}(X) = P(X \wedge Y)/P(X) = P(YX)$$

P(Y/X) is the probability of Y once X has taken place, also called the conditional probability of Y.

Some time the term lift is used to measure the power of association between items that are purchased together. Lift essentially indicates how much more likely an item Y is to be purchased if the customer has bought the item X that has been identified as having an association with the first item Y, compared to the likelihood of Y being purchased. Obviously, lift must be above 1.0 for association to be of interest. Lift may be defined as P(Y/X)/P(Y).

It should be noted that considerable care is needed in interpreting association rules. For example, if the consequent is very popular, like Coca Cola which is a very frequently bought item in most Australian supermarkets, then the confidence of the rule is likely to be high irrespective of whether the two items are associated. We will discuss such issues later in the chapter.

6.3 THE APRIORI ALGORITHM

The basic algorithm for finding the association rules was first proposed in 1993. In 1994, an improved algorithm was proposed. Our discussion is based on the 1994 algorithm called the Apriori algorithm. This algorithm may be considered to consist of two parts. In the first part, those itemsets that exceed the minimum support requirement are found. As noted earlier, such itemsets are called frequent itemsets. In the second part, the association rules that meet the minimum confidence requirement are found from the frequent itemsets. The second part is relatively straight forward, so much of the focus of the research in this field has been to improve the first part.

First Part – Frequent Itemsets

The first part of the algorithm itself many be divided into two steps (Steps 2 and 3 below). The first step essentially finds itemsets that are likely to be frequent or candidates for frequent itemsets. The second step finds a subset of these candidate itemsets that are actually frequent.

The algorithm works as follows for a given set of transactions(it is assumed that we require minimum support of $p\%$):

Step 1: Scan all transactions and found all frequent items that have support above $p\%$. Let these frequent items be L_1. ($p\%$ is minimum support count)

Step 2: Build potential sets of k items from L_{k-1} by using pairs of itemsets in L_{k-1} such that each pair has the first $k-2$ items in common. Now the $k-2$ common items and the one remaining item from each of the two itemsets are combined to forma k-itemset. The set of such potentially frequent k itemsets is the candidate set C_k. (For $k = 2$, build the potential frequent pairs by using the frequent item set L_1 so that every item in L_1 appears with every other item in L_1. The ser so generated is the candidate set C_2.) This step is called Apriori-gen.

Step 3: Scan all transactions and find all *k*-itemsets in C_k that are frequent. The frequent set so obtained is L_k. (For $k = 2$, C_2 is the set of candidate pairs. The frequent pairs are L_2.)

Terminate when no further frequent itemsets are found, otherwise continue with step 2.

The main notation for association rule mining that is used in the Apriori algorithm is the following.

- A *k*-itemset is a set of *k* items.
- The set C_k is a set of candidate *k*-itemsets that are potentially frequent.
- The set L_k is a subset of C_k and is the set of *k*-itemsets that are frequent.

It is now worthwhile to discuss the algorithmic aspects of the Apriori algorithm. Some of the issues that need to be considered are:

1. **Computing L_1:** We scan the disk-resident database only once to obtain L_1. An item vector of length *n* with count for each item stored in the main memory may be used. Once the scan of the database is finished and the count for each item found, the items that meet the support criterion can be identified and L_1 determined.
2. **Apriori-gen Function:** This is step 2 of the Apriori algorithm. It takes an argument L_{k-1} and returns a set of all candidates *k*-items. In computing C_3 from L_2, we organize L_2 so that the itemsets are stored in their lexicographic order. Observe that if an item set in C_3 is (a, b, c) then L_2 must have items (a, b) and (a, c) since all subsets of C_3 must be frequent. Therefore to find C_3 we only need to look at pairs in L_2 that have the same first item. Once we find two such matching pairs in L_2, they are combined to form a candidate itemset in C_3. Similarly when forming C_i from L_{i-1}, we sort the itemsets in L_{i-1} and look for a pair of item sets in L_{i-1} that have same first $i-2$ items. If we such a pair, we can combine them to form a candidate itemset for C_i.
3. **Pruning:** Once a candidate set C_1 has been reduced. We can prune some of the candidate itemsets by checking that all subsets of every itemset in the set are frequent. For example, if we have derived $\{a, b, c\}$ from $\{a, b\}$ and $\{a, c\}$ we check that $\{b, c\}$ is also in L_2. If it is not, $\{a, b, c\}$ may be removed from C_3. The task of such pruning becomes harder as the number of items in the itemsets grows, but the number of the large itemsets tends to be small.
4. **Apriori Subset Function:** To improve the efficiency of searching, the candidate itemsets C_k are stored in a hash tree. The leaves of the hash tree store itemsets while the internal nodes provide a root map to reach the leaves. Each leaf node is reached by traversing the tree whose root is at he depth 1. Each internal node of depth *d* points to all the related nodes at depth +1 and the branch to be taken is determined by applying a hash function on the *d*th item. All the nodes are initially created as leaf nodes and when the number of itemsets in a leaf node exceeds a specified threshold, the leaf node is converted to an internal node. We do not discuss the data structure any further.
5. **Transactions Storage:** We assume the data is too large to be stored in the main memory. Should it be stored as a set of transactions, each transaction being a sequence of item numbers? Alternatively, should each transaction be stored as a Boolean vector of the length *n*(*n* being the number of items in the store) with 1s showing for the items purchased? We discuss this issue later in this section.
6. **Computing L_2 (and more generally L_k):** Assuming that C_2 is available in the main memory, each candidate pair needs to be tested to finds if the pair is frequent. Given that C_2 is likely to

be large, this testing must be done efficiently. In one scan, each transaction can be checked for the candidate pairs.

Second Part—Finding the Rules

To find the association rules from the frequent itemsets, we take a large itemset, say p, and find each nonempty subset a. the rule $a \to (p - a)$ is possible if it satisfies the confidence. Confidence of this rule is given by support (p)/support(a).

It should be noted that when considering rules like $a \to (p - a)$, it is possible to make the rule generation process more efficient as follows. We only want rules that have the minimum confidence required. Since confidence is given by support (p)/support(a), it is clear that for some a, the rule $a \to (p - a)$ does not have the minimum confidence then all rules like $b \to (p - b)$, where b is a subset of a, will also not have the confidence since support(b) cannot be smaller than support(a). It therefore makes sense to generate all subsets a in a recursive fashion and once we find a subset a for which the rule $a \to (p - a)$ does not have minimum confidence then no smaller subsets need to be checked. As an example, if ABC $\to$ D does not have the minimum confidence then AB $\to$ CD or A $\to$ BCD also will not have the confidence.

Another way to improve rule generation is to consider rules like $(p - a) \to a$. If this rule has the minimum confidence then all rules $(p - b) \to b$ will also have minimum confidence if b is a subset of a since $(p - b)$ has more items than $(p - a)$, given that b is smaller than a and so cannot have support higher than that of $(p - a)$. As an example, if A $\to$ BCD has the minimum confidence then all rules like AB $\to$ CD, AC $\to$ BD and ABC $\to$ D will also have the minimum confidence. Once again this can be used in improving the efficiency of rule generation.

In both the improvements noted above, the total number of items, and therefore the support of (p), stays the same.

Implementation Issue—Transaction Storage

Let us now deal with the representation of the transactions as an example. To illustrate the different options, let the number of items be six. Let them be {A, B, C, D, E, F}, Let there be only eight transactions with transaction IDs { 10, 20, 30, 40, 50, 60, 70, 80 }. This set of eight transactions with six items can be represented in at least three different ways as follows.

The first representation (Table 6.2) is the most obvious horizontal one. Each row in the table provides the transaction ID and the items that were purchased.

Table 6.2: A Simple Representation of Transactions as an Item List

Transaction ID	*Items*
10	A, B, D
20	D, E, F
30	A, F
40	B, C, D
50	E, F
60	D, E, F
70	C, D, F
80	A, C, D, F

In the second horizontal representation (Table 6.3), rather than listing the items that were purchased we may list all the items and indicate purchases by putting a 1 against the item that occurs in a transaction and 0 against the rest. Each row is still a transaction, but the items purchased are represented by a binary string.

Table 6.3: Representing Transactions as a Binary Item List

TID	*A*	*B*	*C*	*D*	*E*	*F*
10	1	1	0	1	0	0
20	0	0	0	1	1	1
30	1	0	0	0	0	1
40	0	1	1	1	0	0
50	0	0	0	0	1	1
60	0	0	0	1	1	1
70	0	0	1	1	0	1
80	1	0	1	1	0	1

In the third representation (Table 6.4), call it the vertical representation, the transaction list is turned around. Rather than using each row to represent a transaction of the items purchased, each row now represents an item and indicates transactions in which the item appears. The columns now represent the transactions. This representation is also called a *TID-list* since for each item it provides a list of TIDs.

Table 6.4: Representing Transactions as Binary Columns

Items	*TID*							
	10	20	30	40	50	60	70	80
A	1	0	1	0	0	0	0	1
B	1	0	0	1	0	0	0	0
C	0	0	0	1	0	0	1	1
D	1	1	0	1	0	1	1	1
E	0	1	0	0	1	1	0	0
F	0	1	1	0	1	1	1	1

How the data is represented can have an impact on the efficiency of the algorithm. A vertical representation can facilitate counting of items by counting the number of 1s in each row and for example, the number of 2-itemsets can be counted by finding the intersection of the two TID lists, but the representation is not storage efficient if there is very large number of transactions involved. Also if an algorithm needs data in the vertical representation then there would be a cost in transforming data from the horizontal representation to the vertical one.

We now present two examples of using the Apriori algorithm, one very simple and another more complex.

Example 6.1 —A Simple Apriori Example

Let us first consider an example of only five transactions and six items. We still want to find association rules with 50% support and 75% confidence. The transactions are given in Table 6.5.

Table 6.5: Transactions

Transaction ID	*Items*
100	Bread, Cheese, Eggs, Juice
200	Bread, Cheese, Juice
300	Bread, Milk, Yogurt
400	Bread, Juice, Milk
500	Cheese, Juice, Milk

We first find L_1. Since we have only a small number of items, we can see that Bread appears 4 times, Cheese 3 times, Juice 4 times, Milk 3 times, and Eggs and Yogurt only once. We require 50% support and therefore each frequent item must appear in at least three transactions. Therefore L_1 is given by items in Table 6.6

Table 6.6: Frequent Items

Items	*Frequency*
Bread	4
Cheese	3
Juice	4
Milk	3

The candidate 2-itemsets or C_2 therefore has six pairs. These pairs and their frequencies are given in Table 6.7:

Table 6.7: Candidate Item Pairs C_2

Item pairs	*Frequency*
(Bread, Cheese)	2
(Bread, Juice)	3
(Bread, Milk)	2
(Cheese, Juice)	3
(Cheese, Milk)	1
(Juice, Milk)	2

We therefore have only two frequent items pairs which are {Bread, Juice} and {Cheese, Juice}. This is L_2. From these two frequent 2-item sets. We do not obtain a candidate 3-itemset since we do not have two 2-itemsets that have the same first item.

The two frequent 2-itemsets above lead to the following possible rules:

$$\text{Bread} \rightarrow \text{Juice}$$
$$\text{Juice} \rightarrow \text{Bread}$$
$$\text{Cheese} \rightarrow \text{Juice}$$
$$\text{Juice} \rightarrow \text{Cheese}$$

The confidence of these rules is obtained by dividing the support for both items in the rule by the support for the item on the left-hand side of the rule. The confidence of the four rules therefore are 3/4 = 75%, 3/4 = 75%, 3/3 = 100% and 3/4 = 75% respectively. Since all of them have a minimum 75% confidence, they all qualify.

Example 6.2—A Larger Apriori Example

Consider a store having 16 items for sale as listed in Table 6.8. Now consider the 25 transactions given in Table 6.9. As usual, each row in the table represents one transaction, *i.e.*, the items bought by one customer.

In this example, we want to find association rules that satisfy the requirement of 25% support and 70% confidence.

Table 6.8: The List of Grocery Items

Item number	*Item name*
1	Biscuits
2	Bread
3	Cereal
4	Cheese
5	Chocolate
6	Coffee
7	Donuts
8	Eggs
9	Juice
10	Milk
11	Newspaper
12	Pastry
13	Rolls
14	Sugar
15	Tea
16	yogurt

Transaction Storage

In Table 6.9 showing 25 transactions, we list the names of items for interest but it would be more storage efficient to use item numbers.

Table 6.9: Transaction Data

TID	*Items*
1	Biscuits, Bread, Cheese, Coffee, Yogurt
2	Bread, Cereal, Cheese, Coffee
3	Cheese, Chocolate, Donuts, Juice, Milk
4	Bread, Cheese, Coffee, Cereal, Juice
5	Bread, Cereal, Chocolate, Donuts, Juice
6	Milk, Tea
7	Biscuits, Bread, Cheese, Coffee, Milk
8	Eggs, Milk, Tea
9	Bread, Cereal, Cheese, Chocolate, Coffee,
10	Bread, Cereal, Chocolate, Donuts, Juice

Contd....

11	Bread, Cheese, Juice
12	Bread, Cheese, Coffee, Donuts, Juice
13	Biscuits, Bread, Cereal
14	Cereal, Cheese, Chocolate, Donuts, Juice
15	Chocolate, Coffee
16	Donuts
17	Donuts, Eggs, Juice
18	Biscuits, Bread, Cheese, Coffee
19	Bread, Cereal, Chocolate, Donuts, Juice
20	Cheese, Chocolate, Donuts, Juice
21	Milk, Tea, Yogurt
22	Bread, Cereal, Cheese, Coffee
23	Chocolate, Donuts, Juice, Milk, Newspaper
24	Newspaper, Pastry, Rolls
25	Rolls, Sugar, Tea

Computing L_1

To find the frequent set L_1 we count the number of times each of the 16 items has been sold. Since we wish to scan the transaction database only once, we first set up the list of items and we locate one transaction at a time and update the count of every item that appears in that transaction. We obtain the list given in Table 6.10:

Table 6.10: Frequency Count for all Items

Item no.	*Items name*	*Frequency*
1	Biscuits	4
2	Bread	13
3	Cereal	10
4	Cheese	11
5	Chocolate	9
6	Coffee	9
7	Donuts	10
8	Eggs	2
9	Juice	11
10	Milk	6
11	Newspaper	2
12	Pastry	1
13	Rolls	2
14	Sugar	1
15	Tea	4
16	Yogurt	2

The items that have the necessary support (25% support in 25 transactions) must occur in at least 7 transactions. The frequent 1-itemset or L_1 is now given in Table 6.11.

Table 6.11: The Frequent 1-itemset or L_1

Item	*Frequency*
Bread	13
Cereal	10
Cheese	11
Chocolate	9
Coffee	9
Donuts	10
Juice	11

Computing C_2

Given L_1, we now form candidate pairs or C_2. The 7 items in Table 6.11 form 21 pairs, or $(d)(d-1)/2$ pairs for d frequent items, shown in Table 6.12. The number of pairs in this list is a quadratic function of the number of frequent items and grows rapidly with the number of frequent items. It may also be written as $L_1 \times L_1$ where X is a special concatenation operation. These 21 pairs are the only ones worth investigating since they are the only ones that could be frequent.

Table 6.12: The 21 Candidate 2-itemsets of c_2

{Bread, Cereal}
{Bread, Cheese}
{Bread, Chocolate}
{Bread, Coffee}
{Bread, Donuts}
{Bread, Juice}
{Cereal, Cheese}
{Cereal, Chocolate}
{Cereal, Coffee}
{Cereal, Donuts}
{Cereal, Juice}
{Cheese, Chocolate}
{Cheese, Coffee}
{Cheese, Donuts}
{Cheese, Juice}
{Chocolate, Coffee}
{Chocolate, Donuts}
{Chocolate, Juice}
{Coffee, Donuts}
{Coffee, Juice}
{Donuts, Juice}

Computing L_2

This step is the most resource intensive step. We scan the transaction database once and look at each transaction and find out which of the candidate pairs occurs in that transaction. This then requires scanning the list C_2 for every pair of items that appears in the transaction that is being scanned. Table 6.13 presents the number of items each candidate 2-itemset appears in the example transaction database in Table 6.9.

Table 6.13: Frequency Count of Candidate 2-itemsets

Candidate 2-itemset	*Frequency*
{Bread, Cereal}	9
{Bread, Cheese}	8
{Bread, Chocolate}	4
{Bread, Coffee}	8
{Bread, Donuts}	4
{Bread, Juice}	6
{Cereal, Cheese}	5
{Cereal, Chocolate}	4
{Cereal, Coffee}	5
{Cereal, Donuts}	4
{Cereal, Juice}	6
{Cheese, Chocolate}	4
{Cheese, Coffee}	9
{Cheese, Donuts}	3
{Cheese, Juice}	4
{Chocolate, Coffee}	1
{Chocolate, Donuts}	7
{Chocolate, Juice}	7
{Coffee, Donuts}	1
{Coffee, Juice}	2
{Donuts, Juice}	9

From this list we can find the frequent 2-itemsets or the set L_2. It is given in Table 6.14. Usually L_2 is smaller than L_1 but in this example they both have seven itemsets and each member of L_1 appears as a subset of some member of L_2. This is unlikely to be true when the number of items is large.

Table 6.14: The Frequent 2-itemsets or L_2

Frequent 2-itemset	*Frequency*
{Bread, Cereal}	9
{Bread, Cheese}	8
{Bread, Coffee}	8
{Cheese, Coffee}	9
{Chocolate, Donuts}	7
{Chocolate, Juice}	7
{Donuts, Juice}	9

Computing C_3

To find the candidate 3-itemsets or C_3, we combine the appropriate frequent 2-itemsets from L_2 (these must have the same first item) and obtain four such itemsets. Now we again scan the transaction database to find frequencies. These are given in Table 6.15.

Table 6.15: Candidate 3-itemsets or C_3 and their Frequencies

Candidate 3-itemset	*Frequency*
{Bread, Cereal, Cheese}	4
{Bread, Cereal, Coffee}	4
{Bread, Cheese, Coffee}	8
{Chocolate, Donuts, Juice}	7

Computing L_3

Table 6.16 now presents the frequent 3-itemsets or L_3. Note that only one member of L_2 is not a subset of any itemset in L_3. That 2-itemset is {Bread, Cereal}.

Table 6.16: The Frequent 3-itemsets or L_3

Frequent 3-itemset	*Frequency*
{Bread, Cheese, Coffee}	8
{Chocolate, Donuts, Juice}	7

This is the end of frequent itemset generation since there cannot be candidate 4-itemsets.

Finding the Rules

To derive association rules, we find the rules and their confidence and proceed as follows. We know that:

$$\text{Confidence}(A \to B) = P(B \mid A) = P(A \cap B)/P(A)$$

The rules obtained from frequent 3-itemsets would always include some rules that we could obtain from L_2 embedded in them, but some additional rules will be obtainable from itemsets in L_2 which are not subsets of itemsets in L_3, for example, {Bread, Cereal}. We now use a single letter for each item for brevity. Thus we write {Bread, Cheese, Coffee} as {B, C, D} and obtain a rule $B \to CD$ which may be written as $B \to C$ and $B \to D$.

A 3-itemset, for example BCD, will always result in six possible rules—three possible association rules with one item on the left side and three rules with one item on the right side. The three rules with one item on left side are:

$$B \to CD$$
$$C \to BD$$
$$D \to BC$$

The three rules with one item on right side are:

$$C \to DB$$
$$B \to DC$$
$$B \to CD$$

The support for all these rules is 8. We need to compute (Table 6.17) the frequencies of the left hand side itemsets to compute confidence.

Table 6.17: Confidence of Association Rules from {Bread, Cheese, Coffee}

Rule	*Support of BCD*	*Frequency of LHS*	*Confidence*
B → CD	8	13	0.61
C → BD	8	11	0.72
D → BC	8	9	0.89
CD → B	8	9	0.89
BD → C	8	8	1.0
BC → D	8	8	1.0

The confidence of all these rules, except the first one, is higher than 70% and so five association rules qualify. Similarly, looking at the other 3-itemset {Chocolate, Donuts, Juice} and writing it as {N, M, P} we find values as given in Table 6.18.

Table 6.18: Confidence of Association Rules from {Chocolate, Donuts, Juice}

Rule	*Support*	*Frequency of LHS*	*Confidence*
N → MP	7	9	0.78
M → NP	7	10	0.70
P → NM	7	11	0.64
MP → N	7	9	0.78
NP →M	7	7	1.0
NM → P	7	7	1.0

Again, the confidence of all these rules, except the third, is higher than 70%, and so five of them also qualify.

As noted earlier, the rules obtained from L_3 do not always include all the rules that could be derived from L_2 if there are frequent 2-itemsets that are not subsets of frequent–itemsets. For each member of L_3 there should be three 2-itemsets in L_2 although these might overlap. We therefore need to check L_2.

The only rules that may be derived from L_2 that have not been derived already are Bread → Cereal and Cereal → Bread and they both have the confidence required.

The full list of all the rules is now given below in Table 6.19

Table 6.19: All Association Rules for Example 6.2

Cheese → Bread
Cheese → Coffee
Coffee → Bread
Coffee → Cheese
Cheese, Coffee → Bread
Bread, Coffee → Cheese
Bread, Cheese → Coffee
Chocolate → Donuts
Chocolate → Juice
Donuts → Chocolate

Donuts → Juice
Donuts, Juice → Chocolate
Chocolate, Juice → Donuts
Chocolate, Donuts → Juice
Bread → Cereal
Cereal → Bread

Note that we have replaced rules like Cheese → (Bread, Coffee) by two rules Cheese → Coffee in Table 2.24. That concludes this example.

Comments about the Apriori Algorithm and Further Terminology

1. In the three examples that we have used so far in this chapter, we have required support of 25% and 50%. These support values are high if the number of items and/or number of transactions is large. For example, 25% support in a supermarket transaction database of a day would mean searching for items that have been purchased by one in four customers! Not many items would probably qualify. Practical applications therefore deal with much smaller support, sometimes even down to 1% or lower.
2. A and B are related events, they are not independent so we cannot use probability theory for independent events. The interestingness of a rule A → B can in fact be related to $P(A \cap B) - P(A)P(B)$.
3. **Closed and maximal itemsets:** A frequent *closed* itemset is a frequent itemset X such that there exists no superset of X with the same support count as X. A frequent itemset Y is *maximal* if it is not a proper subset of any other frequent itemset. Therefore a maximal itemset is a closed itemset, but a closed itemset is not necessarily a maximal itemset. In Example 6.2, we found that {B,D} and {B,C,D} and the same support of 8 while {C,D} had a support of 9. {C, D} is therefore a closed itemset but not maximal. On the other hand, {Bread, Cereal} was frequent but no superset of the two items is frequent. These pair therefore is maximal as well as closed.
4. **Frequent maximal itemsets:** The frequent maximal itemsets uniquely determine all frequent itemsets. Therefore the aim of any association rule algorithm is to find all maximal frequent itemsets.

Example 6.3—Closed and Maximal Itemsets

We consider an example to further demonstrate the concepts of closed frequent itemsets and maximal frequent itemsets.

Consider the transaction database in Table 6.20 with minimum support required to be 40%.

Table 6.20: A Transaction Database to Illustrate Closed and Maximal Itemsets

100	Bread, Cheese, Juice
200	Bread, Cheese, Juice, Milk
300	Cheese, Juice, Egg
400	Bread, Juice, Milk, Egg
500	Milk, Egg

All the frequent itemsets from the transaction database in Table 6.20 are given in Table 6.21.

Table 6.21: Frequent Itemsets for the Database in Table 6.20

Itemset	*Support*	*Closed?*	*Maximal?*	*Both?*
{Bread}	3	No	No	No
{Cheese}	3	No	No	No
{Juice}	4	Yes	No	No
{Milk}	3	Yes	No	No
{Egg}	3	Yes	No	No
{Bread, Cheese}	2	No	No	No
{Bread, Juice}	3	Yes	No	No
{Bread, Milk}	2	No	No	No
{Cheese, Juice }	3	Yes	No	No
{Juice, Milk}	2	No	No	No
{Juice, Egg}	2	Yes	Yes	Yes
{Milk, Egg}	2	Yes	Yes	Yes
{Bread, Cheese, Juice}	2	Yes	Yes	Yes
{Bread, Juice, Milk}	2	Yes	Yes	Yes

There are 14 frequent itemsets and the closed and maximal itemsets among the have been identified in the table. The number of closed frequent itemsets is 9 and the number of maximal frequent itemsets is 4.

It should be noted that closed and maximal frequent itemsets are often orders of magnitude fewer than all frequent itemsets and yet all frequent itemsets and the association rules can be generated from them. Therefore, an algorithm mining only the maximal frequent itemsets is likely to be efficient. The reader is encouraged to look at the maximal frequent itemsets and check whether all possible rules from this database can be derived from them.

The relationship between frequent itemsets, closed frequent itemsets and maximal frequent itemsets may be shown as in Fig. 6.1.

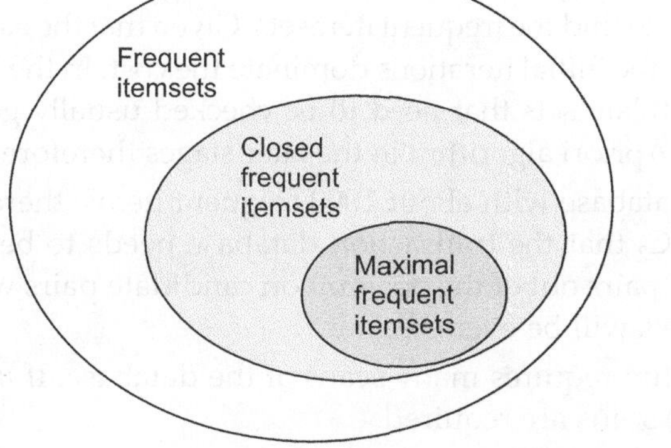

Fig. 6.1 Frequent, closed and maximal itemsets

We consider the Apriori algorithm again since it finds potentially frequent itemsets and then scans the database to find the frequent itemsets. It is useful to look at the following lattice structure (Figure 6.2).

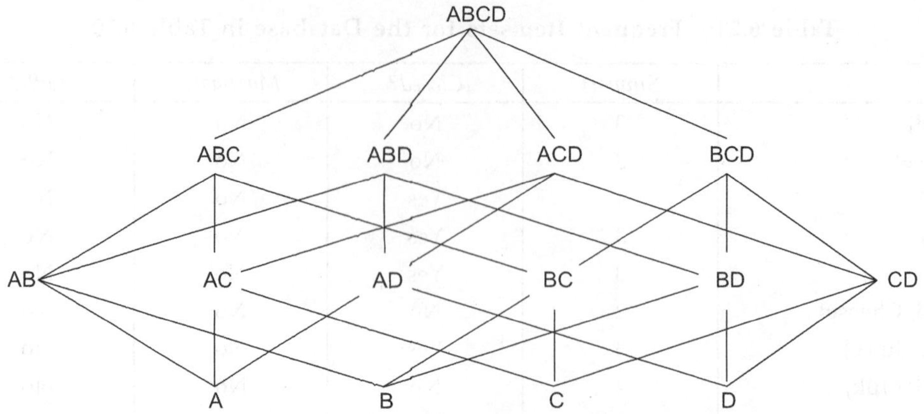

Fig. 6.2 Lattice showing subsets of itemset ABCD

The lattice structure shows the basic concept in association rule mining that an itemset can be frequent only if all the subsets of the itemset are frequent. For the four-itemset ABCD to be frequent itemsets ABC, ABD, ACD and BCD must be frequent which in turn require that AB, AC, AD, BC, BD and CD be frequent which finally require A, B, C and D to be frequent.

Looking at the lattice we can say that the Apriori algorithm works bottom up one level at a time. It first computes the frequent 1-itemsets, then the frequent 2-itemsets, etc. The number of scans of the transactions database is thus equal to the maximum number of items in a candidate itemset. Thus if ABCD is the final candidate itemset, then that would require a final scan of the transaction database whether ABCD is found to be frequent or not.

6.4 IMPROVING THE EFFICIENCY OF THE APRIORI ALGORITHM

The Apriori algorithm is resource intensive for large sets of transactions that have a large set of frequent items. The major reasons for the may be summarized as follows:

1. The number of candidate itemsets grows quickly and can result in huge candidate sets. For example, the size of the candidate set, in particular C_2 is crucial to the performance of the Apriori algorithm. The larger the candidate set, the higher the processing cost for scanning the transaction database to find the frequent itemsets. Given that the early sets of candidate itemsets are often very large, the initial iterations dominate the cost. In the later stages of the algorithm, the number of candidate sets that need to be checked usually goes down dramatically. The performance of the Apriori algorithm in the later stages therefore is not so much of a concern.

   In a supermarket database with about 1000 frequent items, there will be almost one million candidate pairs in C_2 that the transaction database needs to be scanned for. Generally the number of frequent pairs out of the one million candidate pairs will be much smaller and the number of 3-itemsets will be even smaller.
2. The Apriori algorithm requires many scans of the database. If n is the length of the longest itemset, then $(n + 1)$ scans are required.
3. Many trivial rules (*e.g.*, buying milk with Tic Tacs) are derived and it can often be difficult to extract the most interesting rules from all the rules derived. For example, one may wish to remove all the rules involving very frequently sold items. Progress is being made in developing techniques in which constraints may be specified so that, for example, the rules with the most frequent items may be pruned.

4. Some rules can be inexplicable and very fine grained, for example, toothbrush was the most frequently sold item on Thursday mornings.
5. Redundant rules are generated. For example, if A → B is a rule then any rule AC → B is redundant. A number of approaches have been suggested to avoid generating redundant rules.
6. The Apriori algorithm assumes sparsity since the number of items in each transaction is small compared with the total number of items. The algorithm works better with sparsity. Some applications produce dense data (*i.e.*, many items in each transaction) which may also have many frequently occurring items. Apriori is likely to inefficient for such applications.

A number of techniques for improving the performance of the Apriori algorithm have been suggested. They can be classified into four categories:

- Reduce the number of candidate itemsets. For example, use pruning to reduce the number of candidate 3-itemsets and, if necessary, larger itemsets.
- Reduce the number of transactions. This may involve scanning the transaction data after L_1 has been computed and deleting all the transactions that do not have at least two frequent items. More transaction reduction may be done if the frequent 2-itemset L_2 is small.
- Reduce the number of comparisons. There may be no need to compare every candidate against every transaction if we use an appropriate data structure.
- Generate candidate sets efficiently. For example, it may be possible to compute C_k and from it compute C_{k+1} rather than wait for L_k to be available. One could then search for both k-itemsets and $(k + 1)$-itemsets in one pass.

We now discuss a number of algorithms that use one or more of the above approaches to improve the Apriori algorithm. The last method, the Frequent Pattern Growth, does not generate candidate itemsets and is not based on the Apriori algorithm.

1. Apriori-TID
2. Direct Hashing and Pruning (DHP)
3. Dynamic Itemset Counting (DIC)
4. Frequent Pattern Growth

Next section we will discuss only the Apriori-TID method only

6.5 APRIORI-TID

Apriori-TID uses the Apriori's candidate generating function to determine candidate itemsets before the beginning of a pass but it does not use the database for counting support after the first pass. Rather it builds another, hopefully smaller, database by encoding of the candidate itemsets used in the previous pass denoted by T_k, in the first pass, T_1 corresponds to the database. In the following steps, each member of T_k corresponding to a transaction t such that it contains at least one candidate k-itemset, that is T_k, is given by $\{t.TID, c \subset C_k \mid c \text{ contained in } t\}$. If a transaction does not contain any candidate k-itemset, then T_k will not have any entry for that transaction. The size of T_k is therefore expected to be smaller, in particular k grows, then the number of transactions in the original transaction database. Also, for large k values, each entry in T_k is likely to be smaller than the corresponding transaction, as few candidates would be expected to be contained in each transaction. However, f or small values of k, each entry may be larger than the corresponding transaction as we show in the example below.

The Apriori-TID algorithm is outlined below:

1. The entire transaction database is scanned to obtain T_1 in terms of itemsets (*i.e.*, each entry of T_1 contains all items in the transaction along with the corresponding TID).
2. Frequent 1-itemset L_1 calculate with the help of T_1.
3. C_2 is obtained by applying the Apriori-gen function discussed under the Apriori algorithm.
4. The support for the candidates in C_2 is then calculated is then calculated by using T_1.
5. Entries in T_2 are then calculated.
6. L_2 is then generated from C_2 by the usual means and then C_3 can be generated from L_2.
7. T_3 is then generated with the help of T_2 and C_3. This process is repeated until the set of candidate *k*-itemsets is an empty set.

Example 6.4—Apriori-TID

We consider the transactions in Example 6.2 again. As a first step, T_1 is generated by scanning the database. It is assumed throughout the algorithm that the itemsets in each transaction are sorted in each of the itemsets in a transaction is represented as a set of one item.

As is Example 6.2, we will use minimum support of 50% and minimum confidence of 75%.

Step 1

We first scan the entire database and obtain T_1 by treating each item as a 1-itemset. This is given in Table 6.23.

Table 6.22: The Transaction Database T_1

Transaction ID	*Items*
100	{Bread} {Cheese} {Eggs} {Juice}
200	{Bread} {Cheese} {Juice}
300	{Bread} {Milk} {Yogurt}
400	{Bread} {Juice} {Milk}
500	{Cheese} {Juice} {Milk}

Step 2 and 3

The next step is to generate L_1. This is generated with the help of T_1. C_2 is calculated as previously in the Apriori algorithm. See Table 6.23.

Table 6.23: The Sets L_1 and C_2

L_1

Itemset	*Support*
{Bread}	4
{Cheese}	3
{Juice}	4
{Milk}	3

C_2

Itemset
{B, C}
{B, J}
{B, M}
{C, J}
{C, M}
{J, M}

In Table 6.23, we have used single letters B(Bread), C(Cheese), J(Juice) and M(Milk) for C_2.

Step 4

The support for itemsets in C_2 is now calculated with the help of T_1, instead of scanning the actual database as in the Apriori algorithm and the result is shown in Table 6.24.

Table 6.24: Frequency of Itemsets in C_2

Itemset	*Frequency*
{B, C}	2
{B, J}	3
{B, M}	2
{C, J}	3
{C, M}	1
{J, M}	2

Step 5

We now find T_2 by using C_2 and T_1 as shown in Table 6.25.

Table 6.25: Transaction Database T_2

TID	*Set-of-Itemsets*
100	{{B, C}, {B, J}, {C, J}}
200	{{B, C}, {B, J}, {C, J}}
300	{{B, M}}
400	{{B, J}, {B, M}, {J, M}}
500	{{C, J}, {C, M}, {J, M}}

{B, J} and {C, J} are the frequent pairs and they make up L_2. C_3 may now be generated but we find that C_3 is empty. If it was not empty we would have used it to find T_3 with the help of the transaction set T_2. That would result in a smaller T_3 and it might have resulted in the removal of a transaction or two (*e.g.*, TID 300) from T_2. This is the end of this simple example.

The generation of association rules from the derived frequent set can be done in the usual way. The main advantage of the Apriori-TID algorithm is that the size of T_k is usually smaller than the transaction database. Furthermore, each entry in T_k may be smaller, in some cases significantly smaller, than the entry in the corresponding transaction for larger *k* values. Since the support for each candidate *k*-itemset is counted with the help of the corresponding T_k, the algorithm is often faster than the basic Apriori algorithm.

It should be noted that both Apriori and Apriori-TID use the same candidate generation algorithm, and therefore they count the same itemsets. Experiments have shown that the Apriori algorithm runs more efficiently during the earlier phases of the algorithm because for small values of *k*, each entry in T_k may be larger than the corresponding entry in the transaction database. However, in the later phases, Apriori-TID becomes more efficient than the Apriori algorithm because the number of candidate itemsets reduces in the later stages of the algorithm while Apriori still examines every transaction in the database. When T_k can fit in memory, then the process becomes even more efficient, because the cost of writing data to the disk is not incurred.

6.5.1 Iceberg Queries

The Apriori algorithm can be used to improve the efficiency of answering ice-berg queries. Iceberg queries are commonly used in data mining, particularly for market basket analysis. An **iceberg query** computers an aggregate function over an attribute or set of attributes in order to find aggregate values above some specified threshold: Given a relation R with attributes a_1, a_2....a_N and b, and an aggregate function, agg_*f*, an iceberg query is of the form

Select R.a_1, R.a_2,.....R.a_N, agg_*f*(R.*b*) **from** relation R **group by** R.a_1,R.a_2.....R.a_N **having** agg_*f*(R.*b*)>=threshold

Given the large quantity of input data tuples, the number of tuples that will satisfy the threshold in the **having** clause is relatively small. The output result is seen as the "tip of the iceberg," where the "iceberg" is the set of input data.

6.6 MULTILEVEL ASSOCIATION RULES

In many applications, interesting associations among data items often occur at a relatively high concept level. For example, the purchase patterns in a transaction database may not show any substantial regularities at the primitive data level, such as at the bar-code level, but may show some interesting regularities at some high concept level(s), such as milk and bread. Therefore, it is important to study mining association rules at a generalized abstraction level or at multiple levels.

It is difficult to find strong associations among data items at low or primitive levels of abstraction due to the sparsity of data in multidimensional space. Strong associations discovered at high concept levels may represent common sense knowledge. The data mining systems should provide capabilities to mine association rules at multiple levels of abstraction and traverse easily among different abstraction spaces.

Approach to Mining Multilevel Association Rules

We mine multilevel association rules efficiently using concept hierarchies. Generally in concept hierarchy, a top-down strategy is employed , where counts are accumulated for the calculation of frequent itemsets at each concept level, starting at the concept level 1 and working towards the lower, more specific concept levels, until no more frequent item sets can be found. That is, once all frequent itemsets at concept level 1 are found, then the frequent itemsets at level 2 are found, and so on. For each level, any algorithm for discovering frequent itemsets may be used, such as Apriori or its variations.

Concept hierarchies are useful in data mining since they permit the discovery of knowledge at different levels of abstraction, such as multilevel association rules. However, when multilevel association rules are mined, some of the rules found will be redundant due to "ancestor" relationships between items.

6.7 ASSOCIATION MINING TO CORRELATION ANALYSIS

When we discovering association rules are there all association rules are likely to be interesting? Most association rule mining algorithms employ a support-confident framework. In spite of using minimum support and confidence thresholds to help weed out or exclude the exploration of uninteresting rules, many rules that are not interesting to the user may still be produces.

Whether the rule is interesting or not can be judged either subjectively or objectively. Ultimately, only the user cab judge if a given rule is interesting or not, and this decision may be different from one user to another. The support-confidence framework can be misleading in that it may identify a rule A=> B as interesting when, in fact the occurrence of A does not imply the occurrence of B. Now we finding interesting relationships between data itemsets based on correlation.

The occurrence of itemset A is independent of the occurrence of itemset B if P(AUB) = P(A)P(B). Otherwise itemsets A and B are dependent and correlated as events. This definition cab easily be extended to more than two itemsets. The correlation between the occurrence of A and B can be measured by computing

$$\text{Corr} \qquad A, B = P(AUB)/P(A)P(B) \qquad \ldots(6.1)$$

If the resulting value of Equation 6.1 is less than 1 then the occurrence of A is negatively correlated with the occurrence of B. If the resulting value is greater than 1, then A and B are positively correlated, meaning the occurrence of one implies the occurrence of the other. If the resulting value is equal to 1, then A and B are independent and there is no correlation between them.

Equation 6.1 is equivalent to P(B/A)/P(B), which is also called the lift of the association rule A=> B.

6.8 CONSTRAINT-BASED ASSOCIATION MINING

The data mining process may uncover thousands of rules, many of which are uninteresting to the user. In constraint-based mining is performed under the guidance of various kinds of constraints provided by the user. The following are constraints

- **Knowledge type constraints:** These specify the type of knowledge to be mined, such as association
- **Data constraint:** These specify the set of task-relevant data
- **Dimension/level constraints:** These specify the dimension of the data, or levels of the concept hierarchies , to be used.
- **Interestingness constraints:** These specify thresholds on statistical measures of rule interestingness, such as support and confidence.
- **Rule constraints:** These specify the form of rules to be mined. Such constraints may be expressed as metarules, as the maximum or minimum number of predicates that can occur in the rule antecedent or consequent, or as relationship among attributes, attribute values and / or aggregates.

This form of constraint-based mining allows users to specify the rules to be mined according to their intention, thereby making the data mining process more effective. In addition, a sophisticated mining query optimizer can be used to exploit the constraints specified by the user, thereby making the mining process more effective.

6.8.1 Metarule-Guided Mining of Association Rules

A meta-rule-guided data mining approach is proposed and studied which meta-rules as guidance at finding multiple-level association rules in large relational databases. A meta-rule is a rule template in the form of "$P_1 \wedge P_2 \wedge \ldots\ldots \wedge P_m \rightarrow Q_1 \wedge Q_2 \wedge \ldots\ldots \wedge Q_1$ where P and Q are prodicate variables in which some of the predicates (and/or their variables) in the antecedent and/or consequent of the meta-rule could be instantJared. The rule template is used to describe what forms of rules are expected to be found from the database, and such a rule template is used as a guidance or constraint in the data mining process. Note that the predicate variables in a meta-rule can be instantJared against a database schema, whereas the variables or some high-level constants inside a predicate can be bound to multiple (but more specific) levels of concepts in the corresponding conceptual hierarchies.

Metarules allow users to specify the syntactic form of rules that they are interested in mining. The rule forms can be used as constraints to help improve the efficiency of the mining process. Meta rules normally based on the analyst's expectations, or intuition regarding the data, or automatically generated based on the database schema.

Metarules can guide the mining process with the following explanation.

Suppose that we wish to mine interdimension association rules below

$$P_1(A, B) \cap P_2(A, C) \rightarrow \text{buys}(A, \text{"Financial software"}) \quad \ldots(6.2)$$

Where P_1 and P_2 are **predicate variables** that are instantiated to attributes from the given database during the mining process. A is a variable representing a customer, and B and C take on values of the attributes assigned to P_1 and P_2 respectively. User will specify a list of attributes to be considered for instantiation with P_1 and P_2. Otherwise, a default set may be used.

6.9 INCREASING THE EFFICIENCY OF ASSOCIATION RULE MINING

Since the amount of the processed data in mining association rules tends to be huge; it is important to device efficient algorithms to conduct mining on such data. In this section, some techniques to improve the efficiency of mining association rules are presented.

The computational cost of association rule mining can be reduced in four ways:

- By reducing the number of passes over the database
- By sampling the database
- By adding extra constraints on the structure of patterns
- Through parallelization.

In recent years much progress has been made in all these directions.

6.9.1 Reducing the Number of Passes Over the Database

FP-Tree, frequent pattern mining, is another milestone in the development of association rule mining, which breaks the main bottlenecks of the Apriori. The frequent itemsets are generated with only two passes over the database and without any candidate generation process. FP-tree is an extended prefix-tree structure storing crucial, quantitative information about frequent patterns. Only frequent length-1 items will have nodes in the tree, and the tree nodes are arranged in such a way that more frequently occurring nodes will have better chances of sharing nodes than less frequently occurring ones.

FP-Tree also called as FP-Growth algorithm. This algorithm uses an approach that is different from that used by methods based on the Apriori algorithm. The major difference between frequent pattern-growth (FP-Growth) and the other algorithm generates the candidate itemsets and then tests.

The motivation for the FP-tree method is a follows:

- Only the frequent items are needed to find the association rules, so it is best to find the frequent items and ignore the others.

- If the frequent items can be stored in a compact structure, then the original transaction database does not need to be used repeatedly.
- If multiple transactions share a set of frequent items, it may be possible to merge the shared sets with the number of occurrences registered as count.

Generating FP-Trees

The algorithm works as follows:

1. Scan the transaction database once, as in the Apriori algorithm, to find all the frequent items and their support.
2. Sort the frequent items in descending order of their support.
3. Initially, start creating FP-tree with a root "null".
4. Get the first transaction from the database. Remove all non-frequent items and list the remaining items according to the order in the sorted frequent items.
5. Use the transaction to construct the first branch of the tree with each node corresponding to a frequent item and showing that item's frequency, which is 1 for the first transaction.
6. Get the next transaction from the transaction database. Remove all non-frequent items and list the remaining items according to the order in the sorted frequent items.
7. Insert the transaction in the tree using any common prefix that may appear. Increase the item counts.
8. Continue with step 6 until all transactions in the database are processed.

FP-Tree scales much better than Apriori because as the support threshold goes down, the number as well as the length of frequent itemsets increase dramatically. The candidate sets that Apriori must handle become extremely large, and the pattern matching with a lot of candidates by searching through the transactions becomes very expensive. The frequent patterns generation process includes two sub processes: constructing the FT-Tree, and generating frequent patterns from the FP-Tree. The mining result is the same with Apriori series algorithms.

To sum up, the efficiency of FP-Tree algorithm account for three reasons. First the FP-Tree is a compressed representation of the original database because only those frequent items are used to construct the tree, other irrelevant information are pruned.

Secondly this algorithm only scans the database twice. Thirdly, FP-Tree uses a divide and conquer method that considerably reduced the size of the subsequent conditional FP Tree.

Every algorithm has his limitations, for FP-Tree it is difficult to be used in an interactive mining system. During the interactive mining process, users may change he threshold of support according to the rules. However for FP-Tree the changing of support may lead to repetition of the whole mining process. Another limitation is that FP-Tree is that it is not suitable for incremental mining. Since as time goes on databases keep changing, new datasets may be inserted into the database, those insertions may also lead to a repetition of the whole process if we employ FP-Tree algorithm.

Tree Projection is another efficient algorithm recently proposed. The general idea of Tree Projection is that it constructs a lexicographical tree and projects a large database into a set of reduced, item-based sub databases based on the frequent patterns mined so far. The number of nodes in its lexicographic tree is exactly that of the frequent itemsets.

The efficiency of TreeProjection can be explained by two main factors:

1. The transaction projection limits the support counting in a relatively small space;
2. The lexicographical tree facilitates the management and counting of candidates and provides the flexibility of picking efficient strategy during the tree generation and transaction projection phrases.

Wang and Tjortjis presented PRICES, an efficient algorithm for mining association rules. Their approach reduces large itemset generation time, known to be the most time consuming step, by scanning the database only once and using logical operations in the process. Another algorithm for efficient generating large frequent candidate sets is proposed by, which is called Matrix Algorithm. The algorithm generates a matrix which entries 1 or 0 by passing over the cruel database only once, and then the frequent candidate sets are obtained from the resulting matrix.

Finally association rules are mined from the frequent candidate sets. Experiments results confirm that the proposed algorithm is more effective than Apriori Algorithm.

6.9.2 Sampling

Toivonen presented an association rule mining algorithm using sampling. The approach can be divided into two phases. During phase 1 a sample of the database is obtained and all associations in the sample are found. These results are then validated against the entire database. To maximize the effectiveness of the overall approach, the author makes use of lowered minimum support on the sample. Since the approach is probabilistic (*i.e.*, dependent on the sample containing all the relevant associations) not all the rules may be found in this first pass. Those associations that were deemed not frequent in the sample but were actually frequent in the entire dataset are used to construct the complete set of associations in phase 2.

Another progressive sampling algorithm, called Sampling Error Estimation (SEE), which aims to identify an appropriate sample size for mining association rules. SEE has two advantages. First, SEE is highly efficient because an appropriate sample size can be determined without the need of executing association rules. Second, the identified sample size of SEE is very accurate, meaning that association rules can be highly efficiently executed on a sample of this size to obtain a sufficiently accurate result. Especially, if data comes as a stream flowing at a faster rate than can be processed, sampling seems to be the only choice.

Especially, if data comes as a stream flowing at a faster rate than can be processed, sampling seems to be the only choice.

6.9.3 Parallelization

Association rule discovery techniques have gradually been adapted to parallel systems in order to take advantage of the higher speed and greater storage capacity that they offer. The transition to a distributed memory system requires the partitioning of the database among the processors, a procedure that is generally carried out indiscriminately.

Cheung presented an algorithm called FDM. FDM is a parallelization of Apriori to (shared nothing machines, each with its own partition of the database. At every level and on each machine, the database scan is performed independently on the local partition. Then a distributed pruning technique is employed. Schuster and Wolff described another Apriori based D-ARM algorithm - DDM. As in FDM, candidates in DDM are generated levelwise and are then counted by each node in its local database. The nodes then perform a distributed decision protocol in order to find out which of the candidates are frequent and which are not.

Another efficient parallel algorithm FPM (Fast Parallel Mining) for mining association rules on a shared-nothing parallel system has been proposed by. It adopts the count distribution approach and has incorporated two powerful candidate pruning techniques, *i.e.*, distributed pruning and global pruning. It has a simple communication scheme which performs only one round of message exchange each iteration. A new algorithm, Data Allocation Algorithm (DAA), is presented in that uses Principal Component Analysis to improve the data distribution prior to FPM.

SUMMARY

- Mining association rules in transactional or relational databases has recently attracted a lot of attention in database communities. Association rule mining is an interesting problem with many applications.
- Association rules are frequently used in retail stores and also they are used to predict faults in telecommunication networks.
- Apriori constructs a candidate set of large itemsets, counts the number of occurrences of each candidate itemset, and then determines large itemsets based on a pre-determined minimum support.
- The data mining systems should provide capabilities to mine association rules at multiple levels of abstraction and traverse easily among different abstraction spaces.
- Data mining association rules tends to be huge, it is important to device efficient algorithms to conduct mining on such a kind of data.
- The computational cost of association rules mining can be reduced in four ways:
    - By reducing the number of passes over the database
    - By sampling the database
    - By adding extra constraints on the structure of patterns
    - Through parallelization.
- Frequent pattern growth(FP-growth) is a method of mining frequent itemsets without candidate generation. It constructs a highly compact data structure to compress the original transaction database.

REVIEW QUESTIONS

1. What is association rule mining? What purpose it is being used explain with example?
2. Define support and confidence for an association rule.
3. Explain apriori algorithm with example.
4. Write the FP-growth algorithm. Explain.
5. Which algorithm is an influential algorithm for mining frequent item sets for Boolean association rules? Explain.
6. What are additional rule constraints to guide mining? Explain.
7. What are the approaches for mining multilevel Association rules? Explain.
8. How can we mine multilevel Association rules efficiently using concept hierarchies? Explain.
9. Can we design a method that mines the complete set of frequent item sets without candidate generation? If yes, explain with example.
10. Consider an example with the following set of transactions

TID	Item bought
100	B,M,T,Y
101	B,M
102	A,T,S,P
103	A,B,C,D
104	A,B
105	T,Y,E,M
106	A,B,M
107	B,C,D,T,P
108	D,T,S
109	A,B,M

Find the frequent itemsets and association rules with at least 30% support and 60% confidence.

7

CLASSIFICATION

7.1 INTRODUCTION

If we think for a minute about how we classify common everyday objects such as people and cars, it's pretty clear that we are using *features* of those objects to do the job. People have legs, which are a feature that cars don't have. Cars have wheels that are a feature that people don't have. By selecting the ***appropriate set of features***, we can do a good job of classification.

To make this kind of feature-based classification work, we need to have some knowledge of what features make good predictors of class membership for the classes we are trying to distinguish. For example, having wheels or not distinguishes people from cars, but doesn't distinguish cars from trains. These are two different classification tasks. Depending on the classification task we are facing, different features or sets of features may be important, and knowing how we arrive at our knowledge of which features are useful to which task is essential.

7.2 LEARNING

The general process by which we gain knowledge of certain features matter in a given discrimination task is called *learning*. For those of us who are parents, one example of this type of learning (feature selection) involves teaching our children about types of animals. We (endlessly) point to animals and say words like *dog* or *cat* or *horse*. We don't generally give our children a feature list that a biologist might use to define *Canis familiaris* or *Felis catus*. Instead, we present examples and expect our children to figure out for themselves what the important features are. And when they make a correct guess about an animal (a correct classification or prediction), we give copious amounts of positive feedback.

This procedure is called ***supervised learning***. We present our children or our computer programs with examples and tell them what category each example belongs to, so they learn under our *supervision*. This is in contrast to ***unsupervised learning***. In unsupervised learning objects are grouped together based on perceptions of similarity (or more properly, relative lack of difference) without anything more to go on. While unsupervised learning is indispensable, supervised learning has a substantial advantage over unsupervised learning.

In particular, supervised learning allows us to take advantage of our own knowledge about the classification problem we are trying to solve. Instead of just letting the algorithm work out for itself what the classes should be, we can tell it what we know about the classes: how many there are and what examples of each one look like. The supervised learning algorithm's job is then to find the features in the examples that are most useful in predicting the classes.

Table 7.1: There are Several Types of Classification

Type of Classification	*Description*	*Example*
Categorical (Nominal)	Classification of entities into particular categories.	That thing is a dog. That thing is a car.
Ordinal	Classification of entities in some kind of ordered relationship.	You are stronger than him. It is hotter today than yesterday.
Adjectival or Predicative	Classification based on some quality of an entity.	That car is fast. She is smart.
Cardinal	Classification based on a numerical value.	He is six feet tall. It is 25.3 degrees today.

Categorical classification is also called nominal classification because it classifies an entity in terms of the name of the class it belongs to. This is the type of classification we focus on in this document.

The clustering algorithms are examples for *unsupervised* learning algorithms. The classification algorithms are examples for *supervised* learning algorithms. Classification algorithms are more complex than clustering, and sometimes more frustrating due to their additional complexity, but they have considerable advantages.

The classification process with supervised learning always involves two steps:

1. **Training** (with assessment) – This is where we discover what features are useful for classification by looking at many pre classified examples.
2. **Classification** (with assessment) – This is where we look at new examples and assign them to classes based on the features we have learned about during training.

This process isn't perfect, particularly if the number of examples used in training is small. A difficult problem is how to handle objects that don't fall into any of the classes we know about. There is a tendency to categorize them as belonging to one of the classes we do know about, even if the fit is rather poor. For example, upon seeing a horse for the first time, my son announced, 'Look! Big dog! Classification algorithms are capable of making this kind of error.

Definition of classification: Classification is the task of learning a target function that maps each attribute set x to one of the predefined class labels y

The target function is also known informally as a Classification model.

A classification model is useful for the following two purposes.

1. Descriptive modeling
2. Predictive modeling

Earlier in the chapter 2 already mention these issues but here these two things belongs for the classification we will discuss again

Descriptive modeling: A classification model can serve as an explanatory tool to distinguish between objects of different classes.

Predictive modeling: A classification model can also be used to predict the class label of unknown records.

We use the different kind of data for the classification but the following way different data is useful for different purposes.

Classification techniques are most suited for predicting or describing data sets with binary or nominal categories. They are less effective for ordinal categories(*e.g.*, to classify a person as a member of high, medium, or low-income group) because they do not consider the implicit order among the categories. Other forms of relationships, such as the subclass-superclass relationships among categories (*e.g.*, humans and apes are primates, which in turn is a subclass of mammals) are also ignored.

Classification is perhaps the most familiar and most popular data mining technique. Classification applications include image and pattern recognition, medical diagnosis, loan approval, detecting faults in industry applications, and classifying financial market trends.

The classification problem can be simply stated as follows.

1. How do we find a set of features that is a good predictor of what class a sample belongs to?
2. Having found a good set of features, how do we use it to predict what classes new samples belong to?

The first part of the classification problem, which is by far the hardest, is proprietary data mining algorithms. The second is solved by artificial neural networks (ANNs) or support vector machines (SVMs).

7.3 DIFFERENCE BETWEEN CLASSIFICATION AND PREDICTION

Classification is a two-step process. In the first step, a model is constructing for a predetermined set of data classes or concepts. In the second step the model is used for classification.

The term Prediction is usually applied to identify data mining projects with the goal to identify a statistical or neural network model or set of models that can be used to predict some response of interest. For example, a credit card company may want to engage in predictive data mining, to derive a (trained) model or set of models (*e.g.*, neural networks) that can quickly identify transactions which have a high probability of being fraudulent.

Classification and prediction both has many applications, for example prediction of customer behavior and identifying fraud. In many applications, for example in assessing credit card applications, a credit card company may already have a sample data based on past applications and knowledge about the applicants that were good credit risks and those that were not.

7.3.1 When Classification and Prediction Are Not the Same?

It is a matter of definition. If you are trying to classify existing data, *e.g.*, group patients based on their known medical data and treatment outcome, I would call it a classification. If you use a classification model to predict the treatment outcome for a new patient, it would be a prediction.

In the book "Data Mining Concepts and Techniques", by Han and Kamber's view is that predicting class labels is **classification**, and predicting values (*e.g.*, using regression techniques) is **prediction**.

Other people prefer to use "**estimation**" for predicting continuous values.

Classification and prediction are two forms of data analysis that can be used to extract models describing important data classes or to predict future data trends. Classification is the task of examining the features of a newly presented objects and assigning it to one of a predefined set of classes. Prediction is the constructions and use of a model to assess the class of an unlabelled object or to assess the value or value range of a given object is likely to have the most popular classification and prediction methods are listed below.

1. Decision trees.
2. Neural Networks.
3. Genetic algorithms.
4. K-Nearest Neighbor.
5. Naïve-Bayes.

7.4 CLASSIFICATION BY DECISION TREE

A decision tree is a predictive modeling technique used to classify, and predict tasks. It uses "divide-and-conquer" technique to split the problem search space into subsets.

Decision tree is a classifier in the form of a tree structure, where root node and each internal node are labeled with question.

If one does a decision tree analysis, what is the result? Is it classification or a prediction?

The decision tree is a classification model, applied to existing data. If you apply it to new data, for which the class is unknown, you also get a prediction of the class.

The assumption is that the new data comes from the similar distribution as the data you used to build your decision tree. In many cases this is a correct assumption and that is why you can use the decision tree for building a predictive model.

Decision tree is a flow chart like tree structure, where each internal node denotes a test on an attribute, each branch represents an outcome of the test, and Leaf nodes represent class labels or class distribution. The top most node in a tree is the root node. The typical decision tree is shown in the Fig. 7.1

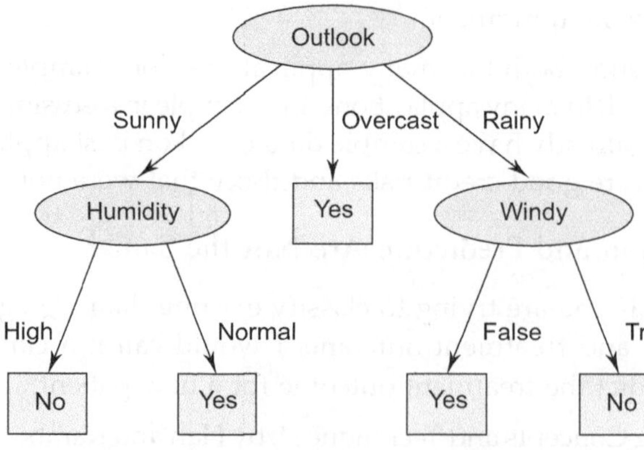

Fig. 7.1 Decision tree for weather data

Table 7.2: Weather Data Example for Construction of Decision Tree

ID code	*Outlook*	*Temperature*	*Humidity*	*Windy*	*Play*
100	Sunny	Hot	High	False	No
101	Sunny	Hot	High	True	No
102	Overcast	Hot	High	False	Yes
103	Rainy	Mild	High	False	Yes
104	Rainy	Cool	Normal	False	Yes
105	Rainy	Cool	Normal	True	No
106	Overcast	Cool	Normal	True	Yes
107	Sunny	Mild	High	False	No
108	Sunny	Cool	Normal	False	Yes
109	Rainy	Mild	Normal	False	Yes
110	Sunny	Mild	Normal	True	Yes
111	Overcast	Mild	High	True	Yes
112	Overcast	Hot	Normal	False	Yes
113	Rainy	Mild	High	True	No

7.4.1 Decision Tree Construction

Decision tree induction is a typical inductive approach to learn knowledge on classification. Constructs decision tree in a top-down recursive divide-and conquer manner. The tree construction procedure is as follows.

Step 1: Tree starts as a single node representing the training samples

Step 2: If all the samples are same class then the node becomes a leaf node and it labeled with that class.

Step 3: Otherwise, (it means samples are not belongs to same class) uses attribute selection measures like entropy-based known as information gain for selecting the attribute that will best separate the samples into individual classes.

Step 4: Selected attribute becomes the "decision" or "test" attribute at the node.

Step 5: A branch of tree is created for each known value of the test or decision attribute, and the samples are partitioned accordingly.

Step 6: Repeat the above process recursively until all samples belong to the same class or there is no remaining attributes on which the samples may be further partitioned.

Attribute selection measure in the decision tree algorithm is the selection of an attribute to test at each decision node in the tree. The goal is to select the attribute that is most useful for classifying samples. A good quantitative measure of an attribute is a statistical property called *information gain* that measure how well a given attribute separates the training examples according to their target classification. This measure is used to select among the candidate attributes at each step while growing the tree.

Let S be a set consisting of s data samples. Suppose the class label attribute has m distinct values defining m distinct classes, c_i (for $i = 1,....m$). Let s_i be the number of samples of S in class C_i. The expected information needed to classify a given sample is given by

$$I(s_1, s_2, \ldots, s_m) = -\sum_{i=1}^{m} p_i \log_2 (p_i),$$

where p_i is the probability that an random sample belongs to class C_i and is estimated by s_i/s. Note that a long function to the base 2 is used since the information is encoded in bits.

Let attribute A have n distinct values, $\{a_1, a_2, \ldots a_n\}$. Attribute A can be used to partition S into v subsets, $\{S_1, S_2, \ldots, S_n\}$, where S_j contains those samples in S that have value a_j of A. If A were selected as the test attribute(that attribute is best for splitting), then these subsets would correspond to the branch grown from the node containing the set S. Let s_{ij} be the number of samples of class C_i in a subset S_j. The entropy, or expected information based on the partitioning into subsets by A is given by

$$E(A) = \sum_{j=1}^{v} \frac{s_{1j} + \ldots + s_{mj}}{s} I(s_{1j}, \ldots, s_{mj}).$$

The term $s_{1j} + .s_{mj}/s$ acts as the weight of the jth subset and is the number of samples in the subset divided by the total number of samples in S. The smaller the entropy value,the greater the purity of the subset partitions. Note that for a given subset Sj,

$$I(s_{1j}, s_{2j}, \ldots, s_{mj}) = -\sum_{i=1}^{m} p_{ij} \log_2 (p_{ij})$$

Where $P_{ij} = S_{ij}/|s_j|$ and is the probability that a sample in S_j belongs to class C_i.

The encoding information that would be gained by branching on A is

$$\text{Gain}(A) = I(S_1, S_2, \ldots\ldots, S_m) - E(A).$$

That is Gain(A) is the expected reduction in entropy caused by knowing the value of attribute A.

Example In the weather data there are 9 instances of which the decision to play is "yes" and there are 5 instances of which the decision to play is "no". Then, the information gained by knowing the result of the decision is

$$I(S_1, S_2) = I(9, 5) = \frac{9}{14} \times \left(-\log \frac{9}{14}\right) + \left(\frac{5}{14}\right) \times \left(-\log \frac{5}{14}\right) = 0.940 \text{ bits.}$$

Next, we need to compute the entropy of each attribute.

$$\text{Entropy of a decision} = -P_1 \times \log P_1 - P_2 \times \log P_2 - \cdots - P_n \times \log P_n$$

Here $P_1, P_2 \ldots\ldots\ldots, P_n$ are the probilities of the n possible outcomes Informaiton further required if *outlook* is placed at the root

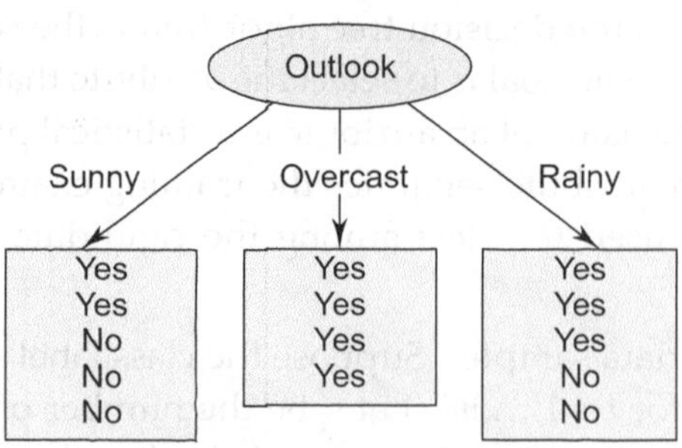

Fig. 7.2 Decision rules for weatherforecasting data

$$\text{Information further required} = \left(\frac{5}{14}\right)\times 0.971 + \left(\frac{4}{14}\right)\times 0 + \left(\frac{5}{14}\right)\times 0.971 = 0.693 \text{ bits.}$$

Information gained by placing each of the four attributes

Gain (Outlook) = 0.940 – 0.692 = 0.247

Gain (temperature) = 0.029

Gain(humidity) = 0.152

Gain(windy) = 0.048

Select the attribute that gives us the largest information gain. In the above example "outlook" is the attribute have the highest information gain and therefore becomes a test attribute at the root node of the decision tree.

When a decision tree is built, many of the branches will reflect anomalies in the training data due to noise or outlier. So tree pruning methods address this problem of overfitting the data.

7.4.2 Tree Pruning

The decision tree building algorithm discussed earlier is having the problem of overfitting due to noise and outlier data set. When the objects being classified have a large number of attributes and a tree of maximum possible depth is built, the tree quality may not be high since the tree is built to deal correctly with the training data set. In fact it may becomes quite complex, with long and very uneven paths.

Such decision tree are a result of overfitting the training data and may result in poor accuracy for unseen samples.

Pruning is a technique to make an overfitted decision tree simpler and more general. There are number of techniques for pruning a decision tree by removing some splits and subtrees created.

One approach involves removing branches from a "fully grown" tee to obtain a sequence of progressively pruned trees. The accuracy of these trees is then computed and a pruned tree that is accurate enough and simple enough is selected. It is advisable to use a set of data different from the training data to decide which is the "best pruned trees".

Another approach is called pre-pruning in which tree construction is halted early. Essentially a node is not split if this would result in the goodness measure of the tree falling below a threshold. It is, however, quite difficult to choose an appropriate threshold.

Detailed pruning concepts of decision tree is discussed in this chapter in the subtopic of comparisions of classification problems in the subsection number 7.7.1

7.4.3 Strengths and Weaknesses of Decision Tree Classifications

Strengths:

- Decision trees are able to understand to generate understandable rules.
- Decision trees are able to handle both numerical and the categorical attributes.
- Decision trees are providing a clear indication of which fields are most important for prediction or classification.

Weaknesses:

- Some decision trees can only deal with binary-valued target classes. Others are able to assign records to an arbitrary number of classes, but error-prone when the number of training examples per class gets small. This can happen rather quickly in a tree with many levels and/or many branches per node.

The process of growing a decision tree is computationally expensive.

7.5 BAYESIAN CLASSIFICATION

Classification is an important task in data mining because it helps to address a verity of problems, statistical techniques can provide the means to solve these problems in a simple way. Statistical decision theory deals with situations where decisions have to be made under a state of uncertainty, and its goal is to provide a rational framework for dealing with such situations. The Bayesian approach is a particular way of formulating and dealing with statistical decision problems. More specifically, it offers a method of formalizing a priori beliefs and of combining them with the available observations, with the goal of allowing a rational (formal) derivation of optimal (in some sense) decision criteria. The Bayesian approach provides a natural and flexible way to approach classification problems and other probability-related questions.

The Bays methodology has a wide range of application in many different fields such as medicine, genetics and business.

7.5.1 Bayesian Methodology

The Bayes approach defines the classification problem in terms of probabilities. More specifically, the three main concepts required are conditional probability, Bayes theorm, and the Bayes decision rule.

The conditional probability P(A/B), which is used to define independent event is defined by

$$P(A/B) = \frac{P(A \cup B)}{P(B)}.$$

Where P(A/B) is the probability that event A happen, given that B is observed

Similarly

$$P(B/A) = \frac{P(A \cup B)}{P(A)}$$

Where P(B/A) is the probability that event B happens, given that A is observed. It follows that

$$P(A \cap B) = P(A)\,P(B/A)$$

The premise of Bayes theorm starts with an initial degree of belief that an event will occur, and then with new information this degree of belief can be "updated". These two degrees are represented, respectively by the prior probability P(A/B) and the posterior probability P(B/A) which are

$$P(A/B) = \frac{P(A)\,P(B/A)}{P(B)}$$

The Bayes decision rule states that based on the posterior probabilities, it is possible to assign an element x to a class with the largest probability.

In particular, for the classification problem the conditional probabilities described above can be defined as follows:

Generally speaking the Bayesian methodology for classification follows the below five steps

1. Collect data, and estimate parameters such as mean and covariance for each class
2. Choose a set of features.

3. Choose a model and derive a decision rule with these parameters.
4. Train the classifier and apply the decision rule by using a discriminant function, and apply it to a test data set to classify each sample.
5. Evaluate the decision rule in order to impove the choice of features and the overall design of the classifier.

7.6 CLASSIFICATION BY NEURAL NETWORKS CONCEPTS

Neural networks fundamentals discussed in separate Chapter 11. For better understanding please go through the chapter and comeback and follow this topic

Neural networks can also be used to classify data. Unlike regression problems, where the goal is to produce a particular output value for a given input, classification problems require us to label each data point as belonging to one of n classes. Neural networks can do this by learning a **discriminant** function which **separates** the classes. For example, a network with a single linear output can solve a two-class problem by learning a discriminant function which is greater than zero for one class, and less than zero for the other. Figure 7.3 shows two such two-class problems, with filled dots belonging to one class, and unfilled dots to the other. In each case, a line is drawn where a discriminant function that separates the two classes is zero.

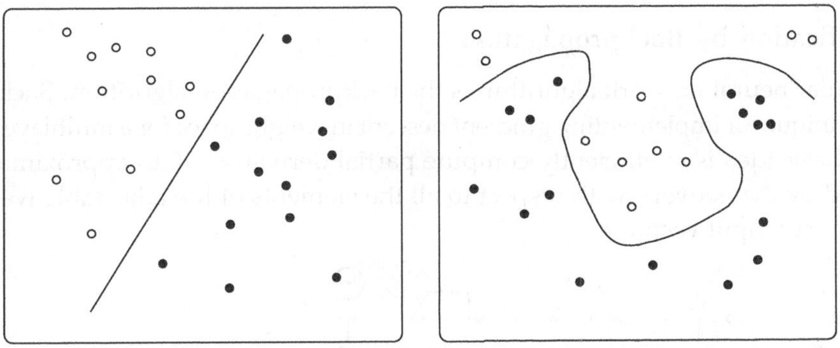

Fig. 7.3 Two-class problem classifiers

On the left side, a straight line can serve as a discriminant: we can place the line such that all filled dots lie on one side, and all unfilled ones lie on the other. The classes are said to be **linearly separable**. Such problems can be learned by neural networks without any hidden units. On the right side, a highly non-linear function is required to ensure class separation. This problem can be solved only by a neural network with hidden units.

To use a neural network for classification, we need to construct an equivalent function approximation problem by assigning a target value for each class. For a **binomial** (two-class) problem we can use a network with a single output y, and binary target values: 1 for one class, and 0 for the other. We can thus interpret the network's output as an estimate of the probability that a given pattern belongs to the '1' class. To classify a new pattern after training, we then employ the **maximum likelihood** discriminant, $y > 0.5$.

A network with linear output used in this fashion, however, will expend a lot of its effort on getting the target values *exactly* right for its training points - when all we actually care about is the correct positioning of the discriminant. The solution is to use an activation function at the output that saturates at the two target values: such a function will be close to the target value for any net input that is sufficiently large and has the correct sign. Specifically, we use the logistic sigmoid function

$$f(u) = \frac{1}{1+e^{-u}} \quad f'(u) = f(u)\,(1 - f(u))$$

Given the probabilistic interpretation, a network output of, say, 0.01 for a pattern that is actually in the '1' class is a *much* more serious error than, say, 0.1. Unfortunately the sum-squared loss function makes almost no distinction between these two cases. A loss function that is appropriate for dealing with probabilities is the **cross-entropy** error. For the two-class case, it is given by

$$E = -t \ln y - (1-t) \ln (1-y)$$

When logistic output units and cross-entropy error are used together in backpropagation learning, the error signal for the output unit becomes just the difference between target and output:

$$\frac{\partial E}{\partial net} = \ldots = y - t$$

In other words, implementing cross-entropy error for this case amounts to nothing more than omitting the f′(net) factor that the error signal would otherwise get multiplied by. This is not an accident, but indicative of a deeper mathematical connection: cross-entropy error and logistic outputs are the "correct" combination to use for binomial probabilities, just like linear outputs and sum-squared error are for scalar values.

7.6.1 Classification by Backpropagation

The most popular neural network algorithm is the backpropagation algorithm. Back-propagation is a specific technique for implementing gradient descent in weight space for a multilayer feedforward network. The basic idea is to efficiently compute partial derivative of an approximating function F(*w*, *x*) realized by the network with respect to all the elements of the adjustable weight vector *w* for a given value of input vector *x*.

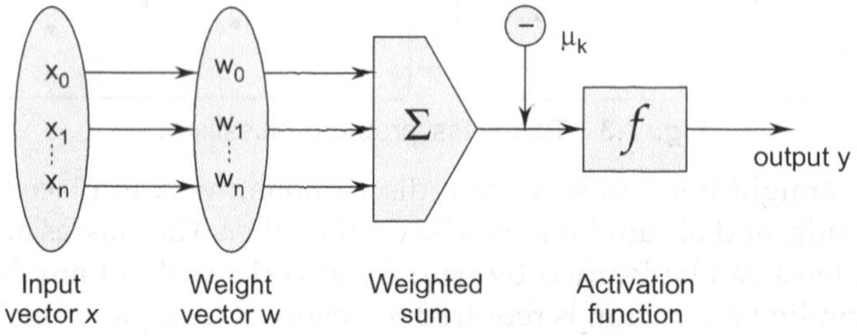

Fig. 7.4 A hidden or output layer unit *j*

The inputs to unit *j* are outputs from the previous layer. These are multiplied by their corresponding weights in order to form a weighted sum, which is added to the bias associated with unit *j*. A nonlinear activation function is applied to the net input.

Steps of the Backpropagation

1. Present a training sample to the neural network.
2. Compare the network's output to the desired output from that sample. Calculate the error in each output neuron.

3. For each neuron, calculate what the output should have been, and a *scaling factor*, how much lower or higher the output must be adjusted to match the desired output. This is the local error.
4. Adjust the weights of each neuron to lower the local error.
5. Assign "blame" for the local error to neurons at the previous level, giving greater responsibility to neurons connected by stronger weights.
6. Repeat from step 3 on the neurons at the previous level, using each one's "blame" as its error.

The backpropogation procedure discussed detailed in the following steps

1. First apply the inputs to the network and work out the output – remember this initial output could be anything, as the initial weights were random numbers.
2. Next work out the error for neuron B. The error is *What you want – What you actually get*, in other words:

   $$Error_B = Output_B\,(1\text{-}Output_B)(Target_B - Output_B)$$

   The *"Output(1-Output)"* term is necessary in the equation because of the Sigmoid Function – if we were only using a threshold neuron it would just be *(Target – Output)*.
3. Change the weight. Let $W_{+\,AB}$ be the new (trained) weight and W_{AB} be the initial weight. $W_{+\,AB} = W_{AB} + (Error_B \times Output_A)$

   Notice that it is the output of the connecting neuron (neuron A) we use (not B). We update all the weights in the output layer in this way.
4. Calculate the Errors for the hidden layer neurons. Unlike the output layer we can't calculate these directly (because we don't have a Target), so we *Back Propagate* them from the output layer (hence the name of the algorithm). This is done by taking the Errors from the output neurons and running them back through the weights to get the hidden layer errors. For example if neuron A is connected as shown to B and C then we take the errors from B and C to generate an error for A.

   $$Error_A = Output_A\,(1 - Output_A)(Error_B\, W_{AB} + Error_C\, W_{AC})$$

   Again, the factor *"Output (1 - Output)"* is present because of the sigmoid squashing function.
5. Having obtained the Error for the hidden layer neurons now proceed as in stage 3 to change the hidden layer weights. By repeating this method we can train a network of any number of layers.

This may well have left some doubt in your mind about the operation, so let's clear that up by explicitly showing *all* the calculations for a full sized network with 2 inputs, 3 hidden layer neurons and 2 output neurons as shown in Fig. 7.4. W_+ represents the new, recalculated, weight.

7.6.2 Problems with Backpropagation

Backpropagtion has some problems associated with it. Perhaps the best known is called "Local Minima". This occurs because the algorithm always changes the weights in such a way as to cause the error to fall. But the error might briefly have to rise as part of a more general falls as shown in figure 7.5. If this is the case, the algorithms will "gets stuck" (because it can't go uphill) and the error will not decrease further.

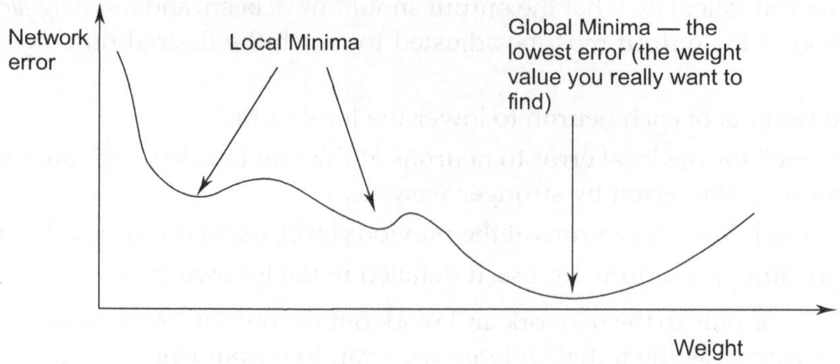

Fig. 7.5 Local minima

There are several solutions to this problem. One is very simple and that is to reset the weights to different random numbers and try training again (this can also solve several other problems). Another solution is to add "momentum" to the weight change. This means that the weight change this iteration depends not just on the current error, but also on previous changes.

7.7 COMPARISON OF CLASSIFICATION METHODS

Here it again each of the classification methods used in the analysis is summarized, followed by a conceptual comparison of the methods and their relative advantages and disadvantages.

7.7.1 Decision Tree Methods

Most decision tree methods learn the decision trees by considering them top-down, beginning with the question "which attribute should be used to define a partition?" To answer this question, each attribute is evaluated using the information gain to determine how well it alone classifies the training examples. The entire process is then repeated using the training examples associated with each descendant node to select the best attribute to test at that point in the tree. This forms a greedy search for a decision tree, in which the algorithm never backtracks to reconsider earlier choices. The decision tree method is a discrete-value function method that is robust to noisy data and capable of learning "or" expressions. The most common decision tree algorithms are ID3. These methods are biased towards small trees over larger trees.

Some advantages are:

1. Human understandable representation : The decision tree can be transferred into a set of "if-then" rules to improve human readability.
2. Decision tree learning methods are robust to errors in classification of the training set. The testing set and pruning algorithms are used to minimize the tree size and the mis classification.
3. Some decision tree methods can be used even when some training examples have unknown values. ID3 does not provide a mechanism to handle the missing attribute values, however, C4.5 does provide such a mechanism.

After the decision tree is generated, an attempt is made to prune the decision tree by eliminating some of the smaller branches. The basic algorithm of reduced error pruning is as follows:

Step 1. Prepare a separate set of examples distinct from the training examples called a validating set to evaluate the effect of pruning.

Step 2. Build the decision tree from the training set. Growing the tree until the training data is fit as well as possible and allow overfitting to occur.

Step 3. Nodes are pruned iteratively from the leaf (bottom) based on the validating set.

Step 4. Pruning of nodes continues until further pruning is not required.

The major difference between a decision tree and a multiple partition decision tree is in terms of the number of variables used for partitioning the data set. In multiple partitioning, the number of subsets for a variable can range from two upto the number of unique values of the predictor variable.

The predictor variable used to form a partition is chosen to be the variable that is most significantly associated with the dependent variable. A chi-squared test of independence for a contingency table is used as the measure of association. The main stopping criteria is the p-value for the chi-square test. If a predictor has more than two categories there may be a large number of ways to partition the data. A combinatorial search algorithm is used to find a partition that has a small p-value for the chi-square test.

This algorithm does not specifically support continuous explanatory variables. Continuous variables are treated as ordinal. Only values of a variable that are adjacent to each other can be combined. With a large number of continuous variables and a large number of objects, this can have a large impact on execution time. The limitations of the decision tree method are

1. The limitation is to ordinal or nominal data and there are execution speed issues that occur when continuous variables are used.
2. This method splits the data by single variables at a time. This can cause high error rates if classes are shaped. This problem can be reduced by adding linear combinations of variables to the list of explanatory variables or by using principal components for the classification. Of course, if linear combinations must be determined from the data, the execution time might greatly increase.
3. One of the major dangers with continuous data is over-fitting. When we are dealing with measured data with random variation it is not uncommon for the measurement variability to be large. This creates a large number of unique values to split the test set on, which may not match-up well with the testing data set. What fits well for a training set may have much higher error rates for the test set.
4. One other issue with this method is the size of the decision tree. A traditional advantage of decision trees is the ease of interpretation and visualization. However, it was not uncommon for the number of nodes generated to exceed 150 using this method. This number of nodes greatly decreases the interpretability of the decision tree.

7.7.2 Discriminant Analysis Methods

The basic concept of discriminant analysis is to estimate the distance from the object to the center of the class and then assign the object to the nearest group. Thus, the primary question becomes one of determining the appropriate distance measure. Usually the Mahalanobis distance, based on the covariance matrix of the observations, is used to estimate these distances. Depending on the assumption of an equal covariance matrix for all classes, either linear (equal variance matrix) or quadratic (non-equal variance matrix) discriminant analysis is used. When the covariance matrices are not equal the Euclidean distance from the class centroids to the discrimination boundary is different for different classes.

Suppose a data set has [*n*.sub.*p*] predictors and *g* classes. The following notation is used: x is the column vector of length [*n*.sub.*p*] containing the values of the predictors for this observation; [*m*.sub.*i*] is a column vector of length [*n*.sub.*p*] containing the means of the predictors calculated from the data in class *i*; [S.sub.*i*] is the covariance matrix calculated from the data in class *i*; \[S.sub.*i*]\ the determinant of [S.sub.*i*]; S is the pooled covariance matrix; [*p*.sub.*i*] is the a prior probability that an observation is in group *i*.

For the equal covariance case, the squared distance (Mahalanobis distance) of observation *x* to the center (mean) of group *i* is given by

[*d*.sup.2.sub.*i*](*x*) = (*x* – [*m*.sub.*i*]) × [S.sup.– 1] (*x* – [*m*.sub.*i*]) ...(7.1)

An observation *x* is classified into group *i*, if the squared distance for *x* to group *i* is the smallest. The equation for the squared distance can be expanded into

[*d*.sup.2.sub.*i*](*x*) = – 2[[*m*′.sub.*i*][S.sup.–1]*x* – 0.5 [*m*′.sub.*i*][S.sup.–1][*m*.sub.*i*]] + *x*′[S.sup.–1]*x*. ...(7.2)

The term in square brackets is a linear function of *x*, and it is called the linear discriminant function for group *i*. For a given *x*, the largest linear discriminant function value occurs for the group with the smallest squared distance.

In quadratic discriminant analysis, the groups are not assumed to have equal covariance matrices. Again, an observation is classified into the group from which it has the smallest squared distance. The squared distance is given by

[*d*.sup.2.sub.*i*](*x*) = (*x* – [*m*.sub.*i*])′ [S.sup.–1.sub.*i*] (*x* – [*m*.sub.*i*]) – ln \[S.sub.*i*]\ . ...(7.3)

This does not simplify into a linear function. In quadratic discriminant analysis, the multivariate distribution of the explanatory variables is assumed to be different in each group.

One expects linear discriminant analysis to perform well when the classes can be approximately described by multivariate normal distributions with identical covariance matrices. This assumption of multivariate normal distribution may seem reasonable for continuous data, but clearly not for categorical explanatory variables. The assumption of equal covariance matrices also seems to be fairly drastic, but this can always be resolved by using quadratic discriminant analysis. Limitations of the method are:

1. Although categorical variables can be converted to indicator variables similar to what is done in regression, discriminant analysis is primarily effective for continuous explanatory variables. Furthermore, these indicator variables are not multivariate normally distribute. Consequently, linear discriminant analysis is not expected to excel in this case
2. The use of the Mahalanobis distance to the centroid of a class can result in problems if unusual shaped classes were encountered.
3. Discriminant analysis is dependent on the estimate of the covariance matrix. Classes with a small membership will result in poorly estimated covariance matrices. The error rates for testing data will tend to be much worse than for the training data, because the covariance matrix estimates may change significantly due to the random sampling of only a few members from that class.
4. There is always the problem of potential overfitting the training set. Information on preventing overfitting is summarized by McLachlan (1992).

7.7.3 Neural Network Methods

The alternative of neural computing emerges from the attempts to emulate the capabilities of biological neural systems in respect to how they store and manipulate information, leading this effort to a class of artificial neural networks or simply neural networks. As it is expected neural networks tend to integrate research in diverse fields such as psychology, neuroscience, cognitive science, and systems theory. Neural networks are relatively new computational paradigms. On one hand good understanding has been gained over the years on some of the paradigms, on the other hand truly brain-like artificial neural systems are still under development, not to mention that there is still much to advance in neurophysiology.

Artificial neural networks are sometimes referred to as "black-box" models. This usually implies the notion of neural networks as nonlinear mapping tools. Artificial neural networks are represented by a set of identical processing units, or simply processing nodes, and connections between the processing units. A neural network renders itself as a parallel processing device. When the processing units are arranged in a layered fashion and the connections are only made from the previous layer to the next layer, the network so obtained is referred to as a feed-forward network. It has been shown that (Haykin, 1999, Section 4.13), a feed-forward network with an input, a middle (or hidden) layer, and an output layer, can approximate any continuous function given that the number of units in the hidden layer is large. By this notion, even without physical insights or a physical model for the problem at hand, one can build a neural network to approximate a nonlinear system as long as the system function under consideration is continuous. This has much to do with neural networks being named a "black-box" method.

In most application problems, the number of nodes in the layers needs to be determined through the evaluation of testing and training error rates for different numbers of nodes. This requires the dividing of the data set into training and testing sets and training the network with a range of nodes in the hidden layer (Haykin, 1999, Section 4.14). The number of hidden nodes is based on having a low error rate for the training set and a minimum difference between the training and testing set error...

SUMMARY

- This chapter has given basic idea of the classification techniques in data mining. The classification problem tends to occur in a wide variety of areas. This widespread need to classify has led to the development of many different classification techniques.
- Some of the techniques are linear and quadratic discriminate analysis decision tree, neural networks, mixed-inter preprocessing and expert rule- based systems. Decision tree induction algorithm uses an information-theoretic measure to select the attribute tested for each nonleaf node in the tree.
- Backpropagation is a neural network algorithm for classification that employs a method of gradient descent. It searches for a set of weights that can model the data so as to minimize the mean squared distance between the network's class predication and the actual class label of data samples.
- Rules may be extracted from trained neural networks in order to help improve the interpretability of the learned network.
- There have been numerous comparisons on the different classification methods, and the matter remains a research topic. No single method has been found to be superior over all others for all data sets.
- Issues such as accuracy, training time, robustness, interpretability, and scalability must be considered and can improve trade-offs, further complicating the quest for an overall superior method.

REVIEW QUESTIONS

1. What is classification? What is prediction?
2. What is Bayes theorem? Explain about Naive Bayesian classification.
3. Discuss about k-Nearest neighbor classifiers and case-based reasoning.
4. An e-mail database is a database that stores a large number of electronic mail messages. It can be viewed as a semistructured database consisting mainly of text data.

   Discuss the following.

   (*a*) How can such an e-mail database be structured so as to facilitate mult- dimensional search, such as by sender, by receiver, by subject, by time, an so on?

   (*b*) What can be mined from such an e-mail database?

   (*c*) Suppose you have roughly classified a set of your previous e-mail messages as junk, unimportant, normal, or important.

   Describe how a data mining system may take this as the training set to automatically classify new e-mail messages or unclassified ones.
5. Discuss about Backpropagation classification.
6. Explain decision tree induction classification.
7. Can any ideas from association rule mining be applied to classification? Explain
8. Explain training Bayesian belief networks.
9. How does tree pruning work? What are some enhancements to basic decision tree induction?
10. Describe the data classification process with a neat diagram.
11. Explain classifier accuracy.
12. Explain about basic decision tree induction algorithm.
13. Discuss about Bayesian classification.

8

CLUSTER ANALYSIS

8.1 INTRODUCTION

Clustering is a division of data into groups of similar objects. Each group, called cluster, consists of objects that are similar between themselves and dissimilar to objects of other groups. Representing data by fewer clusters necessarily loses certain fine details (akin to lossy data compression), but achieves simplification. It represents many data objects by few clusters, and hence, it models data by its clusters. Data modeling puts clustering in a historical perspective rooted in mathematics, statistics, and numerical analysis. From a machine learning perspective clusters correspond to hidden patterns, the search for clusters is unsupervised learning, and the resulting system represents a data concept.

Therefore, clustering is unsupervised learning of a hidden data concept.

Cluster analysis is an important human activity. Early in childhood, once learns how to distinguish between cat and dogs, or between animals and plants, by continuously improving subconscious clustering schemes. Cluster analysis has been widely used in numerous applications, including pattern recognition, data analysis, image processing, and market research. By clustering, one can identify dense and sparse regions and, therefore, discover overall distribution patterns and interesting correlations among data attributes.

Data clustering is under vigorous development. Contributing areas of research include data mining , statistics, machine learning, spatial database technology, biology, and marketing. Owing to the huge amounts of data collected in databases, clustering has recently become a highly active topic in data mining research.

Data mining deals with large databases that impose on clustering analysis additional severe computational requirements. These challenges led to the emergence of powerful broadly applicable data mining clustering methods surveyed below.

8.2 NOTATIONS

To fix the context and to clarify prolific terminology, we consider a dataset X consisting of data points (or synonymously, objects, instances, cases, patterns, tuples, transactions) $x_1 = (x_{i1} \ldots, x_{id}) \in$

A in attribute space A, where i = 1: N, and each component is a numerical or nominal categorical attribute (or synonymously, feature, variable, dimension, component, field). For a discussion of attributes data types, Such point-by-attribute data format conceptually corresponds to a matrix and is used by the majority of algorithms reviewed below. However, data of other formats, such as variable length sequences and heterogeneous data, is becoming more and more popular. The simplest attribute space subset is a direct Cartesian product of sub ranges called a segment (also cube, cell, region).

A unit is an elementary segment whose sub-ranges consist of a single category value, or of a small numerical bin. Describing the numbers of data points per every unit represents an extreme case of clustering, a histogram, where no actual clustering takes place. This is a very expensive representation, and not a very revealing one. User driven segmentation is another commonly used practice in data exploration that utilizes expert knowledge regarding the importance of certain sub-domains. We distinguish clustering from segmentation to emphasize the importance of the automatic learning process.

The ultimate goal of clustering is to assign points to a finite system of k subsets, clusters. Usually subsets do not intersect (this assumption is sometimes violated), and their union is equal to a full dataset with possible exception of outliers.

8.3 CATEGORIES OF CLUSTERING ALGORITHMS

Categorization of clustering algorithms is neither straightforward, nor canonical. In reality, groups below overlap. For reader's convenience we provide a classification closely followed by this survey. Corresponding terms are explained below.

Clustering Algorithms

- Hierarchical Methods
  - Agglomerative Algorithms
  - Divisive Algorithms
- Partitioning Methods
  - Relocation Algorithms
  - Probabilistic Clustering
  - K-medoids Methods
  - K-means Methods
  - Density-Based Algorithms
    - Density-Based Connectivity Clustering
    - Density Functions Clustering
- Grid-Based Methods
- Methods Based on Co-Occurrence of Categorical Data
- Constraint-Based Clustering
- Clustering Algorithms Used in Machine Learning
  - Gradient Descent and Artificial Neural Networks
  - Evolutionary Methods
- Scalable Clustering Algorithms
- Algorithms For High Dimensional Data

- Subspace Clustering
- Projection Techniques
- Co-Clustering Techniques

8.4 IMPORTANT ISSUES

The following properties of clustering algorithms we are concerned with in data mining

These properties include:

Type of attributes algorithm can handle

Scalability to large datasets

Ability to work with high dimensional data

Ability to find clusters of irregular shape

Handling outliers

Time complexity

Data order dependency

Labeling or assignment (hard or strict vs. soft of fuzzy)

Reliance on a priori knowledge and user defined parameters

Interpretability of results

While we try to keep these issues in mind, realistically, we mention only few with every algorithm we discuss. The above list is in no way exhaustive. For example, we also discuss such properties as ability to work in pre-defined memory buffer, ability to restart and ability to provide an intermediate solution.

Clustering is a challenging field of research in which its potential applications pose their own special requirements. The following are typical requirements of clustering in data mining:

Scalability: Many clustering algorithms work well on small data sets containing fewer than several hundred data objects; however, a large database may contain millions of objects. Clustering on a sample of a given large data set may lead to biased results highly scalable clustering algorithms are needed.

Ability to deal with different types of attributes: Many algorithms are designed to cluster interval-based (numerical) data. However, applications may require clustering other types of data, such as binary, categorical (nominal), and ordinal data, or mixtures of these data types.

Discovery of clusters with arbitrary shape: Many clustering algorithms determine clusters based on Euclidean distance measures. Algorithms based on such distance measures tend to find spherical clusters with similar size and density. However, a cluster could be of any shape. It is important to develop algorithms that can detect clusters of arbitrary shape.

Minimal requirements for domain knowledge to determine input parameters: Many clustering algorithms require users to input certain parameters in cluster analysis (such as the number of desired clusters). The clustering results can be quite sensitive to input parameters. Parameters are often difficult to determine, especially for data sets containing high-dimensional objects. This not only burdens users, but it also makes the quality of clustering difficult to control.

Ability to deal with noisy data: Most real-world databases contain outliers or missing, unknown, or erroneous data. Some clustering algorithms are sensitive to such data and may lead to clusters of poor quality.

Incremental clustering and insensitivity to the order of input records: Some clustering algorithms cannot incorporate newly inserted data (*i.e.*, database updates) into existing clustering structures and, instead, must determine a new clustering from scratch. Some clustering algorithms are sensitive to the order of input data. That is, given a set of data objects, such an algorithm may return dramatically different clustering depending on the order of presentation of the input objects. It is important to develop incremental clustering algorithms and algorithms that are insensitive to the order of input.

High dimensionality: A database or a data warehouse can contain several dimensions or attributes. Many clustering algorithms are good at handling low-dimensional data, involving only two to three dimensions. Human eyes are good at judging the quality of clustering for up to three dimensions. Finding clusters of data objects in high dimensional space is challenging, especially considering that such data can be sparse and highly skewed.

Constraint-based clustering: Real-world applications may need to perform clustering under various kinds of constraints. Suppose that your job is to choose the locations for a given number of new automatic banking machines (ATMs) in a city. To decide upon this, you may cluster households while considering constraints such as the city's rivers and highway networks, and the type and number of customers per cluster. A challenging task is to find groups of data with good clustering behavior that satisfy specified constraints.

Interpretability and usability: Users expect clustering results to be interpretable, comprehensible, and usable. That is, clustering may need to be tied to specific semantic interpretations and applications. It is important to study how an application goal may influence the selection of clustering features and methods.

8.5 HIERARCHICAL METHODS

Hierarchical clustering builds a cluster hierarchy or, in other words, a tree of clusters, also known as a *dendrogram*. Every cluster node contains child clusters; sibling clusters partition the points covered by their common parent. Such an approach allows exploring data on different levels of granularity.

Hierarchical clustering methods are categorized into agglomerative (bottom-up) and divisive (top-down) [Jain & Dubes 1988; Kaufman & Rousseeuw 1990]. An agglomerative clustering starts with one-point (singleton) clusters and recursively merges two or more most appropriate clusters. A divisive clustering starts with one cluster of all data points and recursively splits the most appropriate cluster. The process continues until a stopping criterion (frequently, the requested number k of clusters) is achieved. Advantages of hierarchical clustering include:

- Embedded flexibility regarding the level of granularity
- Ease of handling of any forms of similarity or distance
- Consequently, applicability to any attribute types

Disadvantages of hierarchical clustering are related to:

- Vagueness of termination criteria
- The fact that most hierarchical algorithms do not revisit once constructed (intermediate) clusters with the purpose of their improvement.

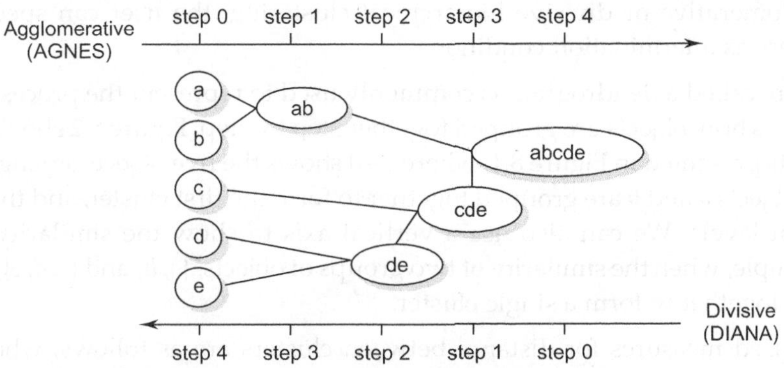

Fig. 8.1 Agglomerative and divisive hierarchical clustering on data objects {*a*, *b*, *c*, *d*, *e*}

8.5.1 Agglomerative and Divisive Hierarchical Clustering

In general there are two types of hierarchical clustering methods

Agglomerative hierarchical clustering: This bottom-up strategy starts by placing each object in its own cluster and then merges these atomic clusters into larger and larger clusters, until all of the objects are in a single cluster or until certain termination conditions are satisfied. Most hierarchical clustering methods belong to this category. They differ only in their definition of intercluster similarity.

Divisive hierarchical clustering: This top-down strategy does the reverse of agglomerative hierarchical clustering by starting with all objects in one cluster. It subdivides the cluster into smaller and smaller pieces, until each object forms a cluster on its own or until it satisfies certain termination conditions, such as a desired number of clusters is obtained or the diameter of each cluster is within a certain threshold.

Figure 8.1 shows the application of AGNES (AGglomerative NESting), an agglomerative hierarchical clustering method, and DIANA (DIvisive ANAlysis), a divisive hierarchical clustering method, to a data set of five objects, {*a*, *b*, *c*, *d*, *e*}. Initially, AGNES places each object into a cluster of its own. The clusters are then merged step-by-step according to some criterion. For example, clusters C_1 and C_2 may be merged if an object in C_1 and an object in C_2 form the minimum Euclidean distance between any two objects from different clusters. This is a single linkage approach in that each cluster is represented by all of the objects in the cluster, and the similarity between two clusters is measured by the similarity of the closest pair of data points belonging to different clusters. The cluster merging process repeats until all of the objects are eventually merged to form one cluster.

In DIANA, all of the objects are used to form one initial cluster. The cluster is split according to some principle, such as the maximum Euclidean distance between the closest neighboring objects in the cluster. The cluster splitting process repeats until, eventually, each new cluster contains only a single object.

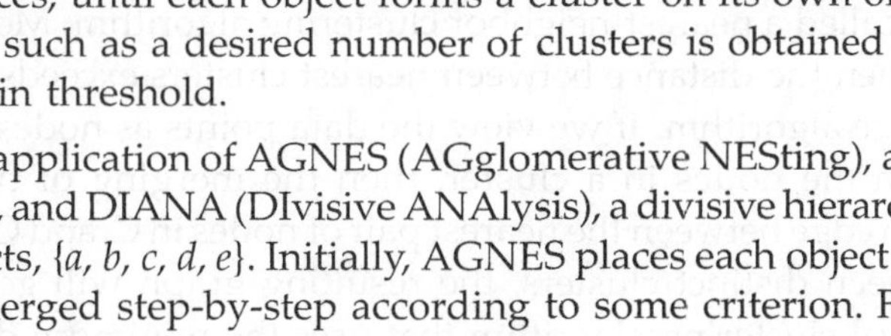

Fig. 8.2 Dendrogram representation for hierarchical clustering of objects {*a*, *b*, c, *d*, *e*}

In either agglomerative or divisive hierarchical clustering, the user can specify the desired number of clusters as a termination condition.

A tree structure called a dendrogram is commonly used to represent the process of hierarchical clustering. It shows how objects are grouped together step by step. Figure 8.2 shows a dendrogram for the five objects presented in Figure 8.1, where l = 0 shows the five objects as singleton clusters at level 0. At l = 1, objects *a* and *b* are grouped together to form the first cluster, and they stay together at all subsequent levels. We can also use a vertical axis to show the similarity scale between clusters. For example, when the similarity of two groups of objects, $\{a, b\}$ and $\{c, d, e\}$, is roughly 0.16, they are merged together to form a single cluster.

Four widely used measures for distance between clusters are as follows, where $|p-p'|$ is the distance between two objects or points, p and p'; m_i is the mean for cluster, C_i; and n_i is the number of objects in C_i.

$$\text{Minimum distance: } d_{\min}(C_i, C_j) = \min_{p \in C_i, p' \in C_j} |p - p'|$$

$$\text{Maximum distance: } d_{\max}(C_i, C_j) = \max_{p \in C_i, p' \in C_j} |p - p'|$$

$$\text{Mean distance: } d_{mean}(C_i, C_j) = |m_i - m_j|$$

$$\text{Average distance: } d_{avg}(C_i, C_j) = \frac{1}{n_i n_j} \sum_{p \in C_i} \sum_{p' \in C_j} |p - p'|$$

When an algorithm uses the minimum distance, dmin (C_i, C_j), to measure the distance between clusters, it is sometimes called a nearest-neighbor clustering algorithm. Moreover, if the clustering process is terminated when the distance between nearest clusters exceeds an arbitrary threshold, it is called a single-linkage algorithm. If we view the data points as nodes of a graph, with edges forming a path between the nodes in a cluster, then the merging of two clusters, C_i and C_j, corresponds to adding an edge between the nearest pair of nodes in C_i and C_j. Because edges linking clusters always go between distinct clusters, the resulting graph will generate a tree. Thus, an agglomerative hierarchical clustering algorithm that uses the minimum distance measure is also called a minimal spanning tree algorithm.

8.5.2 Johnson Algorithm

This algorithm was defined by S.C. Johnson in 1967

Given a set of N items to be clustered, and an N*N distance (or similarity) matrix, the basic process of hierarchical clustering is this:

1. Start by assigning each item to a cluster, so that if you have N items, you now have N clusters, each containing just one item. Let the distances (similarities) between the clusters the same as the distances (similarities) between the items they contain.
2. Find the closest (most similar) pair of clusters and merge them into a single cluster, so that now you have one cluster less.
3. Compute distances (similarities) between the new cluster and each of the old clusters.
4. Repeat steps 2 and 3 until all items are clustered into a single cluster of size N. (*)

Step 3 can be done in different ways, which is what distinguishes single-linkage from complete-linkage and average-linkage clustering.

In single-linkage clustering (also called the connectedness or minimum method), we consider the distance between one cluster and another cluster to be equal to the shortest distance from any member of one cluster to any member of the other cluster. If the data consist of similarities, we consider the similarity between one cluster and another cluster to be equal to the greatest similarity from any member of one cluster to any member of the other cluster.

In complete-linkage clustering (also called the diameter or maximum method), we consider the distance between one cluster and another cluster to be equal to the greatest distance from any member of one cluster to any member of the other cluster.

In average-linkage clustering, we consider the distance between one cluster and another cluster to be equal to the average distance from any member of one cluster to any member of the other cluster.

A variation on average-link clustering is the UCLUS method, which uses the median distance, which is much more outlier-proof than the average distance.

This kind of hierarchical clustering is called agglomerative because it merges clusters iteratively. There is also a divisive hierarchical clustering which does the reverse by starting with all objects in one cluster and subdividing them into smaller pieces. Divisive methods are not generally available, and rarely have been applied. Of course there is no point in having all the N items grouped in a single cluster but, once you have got the complete hierarchical tree, if you want k clusters you just have to cut the $k-1$ longest links.

8.5.3 Single-Linkage Clustering: The Algorithm

Let's now take a deeper look at how Johnson's algorithm works in the case of single-linkage clustering.

The algorithm is an agglomerative scheme that erases rows and columns in the proximity matrix as old clusters are merged into new ones.

The N*N proximity matrix is $D = [d(i, j)]$. The clusterings are assigned sequence numbers 0, 1,……, $(n-1)$ and $L(k)$ is the level of the kth clustering. A cluster with sequence number m is denoted (m) and the proximity between clusters (r) and (s) is denoted $d[(r), (s)]$.

The algorithm is composed of the following steps:

1. Begin with the disjoint clustering having level $L(0) = 0$ and sequence number $m = 0$.
2. Find the least dissimilar pair of clusters in the current clustering, say pair (r), (s), according to
$$d[(r), (s)] = \min d[(i), (j)]$$
where the minimum is over all pairs of clusters in the current clustering.
3. Increment the sequence number : $m = m + 1$. Merge clusters (r) and (s) into a single cluster to form the next clustering m. Set the level of this clustering to
$$L(m) = d[(r), (s)]$$
4. Update the proximity matrix, D, by deleting the rows and columns corresponding to clusters (r) and (s) and adding a row and column corresponding to the newly formed cluster. The proximity between the new cluster, denoted (r, s) and old cluster (k) is defined in this way:
$$d[(k), (r, s)] = \min d[(k), (r)], d[(k), (s)]$$
5. If all objects are in one cluster, stop. Else, go to step 2.

8.5.4 Birch Clustering Algorithm

Birch (balanced iterative reducing and clustering using hierarchies) is an incremental and hierarchical clustering algorithm for large databases. The strongest point of the birch algorithm its support for very large databases (main memory is lower than the size of the DB).

There are two main building components in the birch algorithm:

1. hierarchical clustering component,
2. main memory structure component,

We will revisit every component in detail and give an conceptual idea how the birch clustering works

The idea of a hierarchical clustering is illustrated in Figure 8.3. The algorithm starts with single point clusters (every point in a database is a cluster, c_f Figure 8.3(*a*)). Then it groups the closest points into separate clusters (Figure 8.3(*b*)), and continues, until only one cluster remains (Figure 8.3(*c*)). The computation of the clusters is done with a help of distance matrix ($O(n_2)$ large) and $O(n_2)$ time.

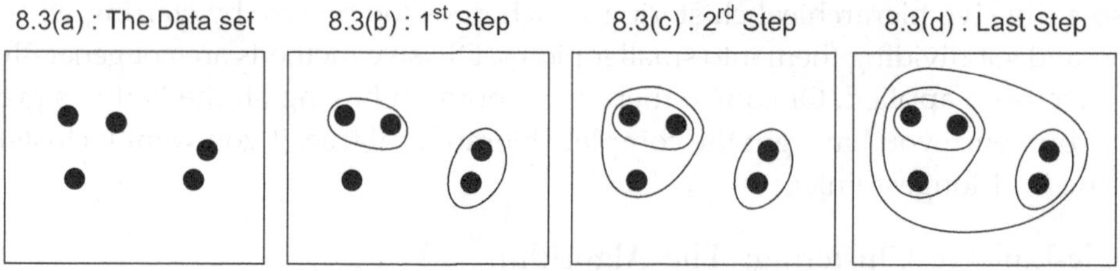

Fig. 8.3 The Idea of Hierarchical Clustering

Birch uses a main memory (of limited size) data structure called CF tree. The tree is organized in such a way that (*i*) the leave contain actual clusters, and (*ii*) the size of any cluster in a leaf is not large than R. An example of the CF tree is illustrated in Figure 8.4. Initially, the data points in one cluster. As the data arrives, a check is made whether the size of the cluster does not exceed R (c_f. Figures 8.4(*a*)-(*b*)).

If the cluster size grows too big, the cluster is split into two clusters, and the points are redistributed (Figure 8.4(*c*)). The points are then continuously inserted to the cluster which enlarges less (c_f. Figure 8.4(*d*)). At each node of the tree the CF tree keeps information about the mean of the cluster, and the mean of the sum of squares to compute the size of the clusters efficiently. The tree structure also depends on the branching parameter T, which determines the maximum number of children each node can have.

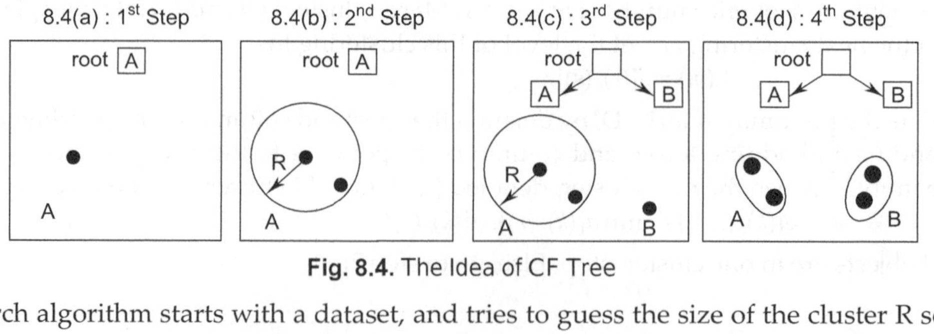

Fig. 8.4. The Idea of CF Tree

The birch algorithm starts with a dataset, and tries to guess the size of the cluster R so the tree can fit in the main memory. If the tree does not fit into the main memory, it reduces the R and rebuilds the tree. The process is repeated until the tree fits into main memory. The birch algorithm can also include a number of post processing phrases to remove outliers and improve clustering.

8.5.5 CURE: Clustering Using Representatives

Most clustering algorithms either favor clusters with spherical shape and similar sizes, or are fragile in the presence of outliers. To avoid the problems with non-uniform sized or shaped clusters, CURE employs a novel hierarchical clustering algorithm that adopts a middle ground between the centroid based and all point extremes. In CURE, a constant number c of well scattered points of a cluster are chosen and they are shrunk towards the centroid of the cluster by a fraction α. The scatterd points aftyre shrinking are used as representatives of the cluster. The clusters with the closest pair of representatives are the clusters that are merged at each step of CURE's hierarchical clustering algorithm. This enables CURE to correctly identify the clusters and makes it less sensitive to outliers.

The main strong points of the CURE algorithm differentiating it from others are recognition of arbitrary shaped clusters, and its robustness to the presence of outliers. Input data for the implemented algorithm are dataset with n points, desired number of clusters, and desired number of representatives. Such data structure as heap is used to organize selection of two closest clusters (step 3 in the following algorithm) therefore improving computing time.

The steps of CURE algorithm are:

1. Put each dataset point into a separate cluster
2. For each cluster u calculate its closest cluster u. closest
3. Identify two clusters u_1 and u_2 which are located closest to each other and merge them, replace two recently merged clusters by the new one
4. Select new representatives for the merged cluster:
    - choose a certain number of representative points in the cluster which are farthest away from each other
    - move the points towards the center of the cluster

Despite the fact that CURE algorithm features make it very effective clustering algorithm, sometimes it faces difficulties.

First of all, almost all the data contain outliers, which do not belong to any cluster and are typically points of non-agglomerative behavior.

The second problem is about the shrinking depends on a hidden assumption of spherical shape of cluster and CURE has difficulties in dealing with datasets having specific shapes.

The algorithm cannot be directly applied to large databases. So for this purpose we do the following enhancements

- **Random sampling:** To handle large data sets, we do random sampling and draw a sample data set. Generally the random sample fits in main memory. Also because of the random sampling there is a trade off between accuracy and efficiency.
- **Partitioning for speed up:** The basic idea is to partition the sample space into p partitions. Then in the first pass partially cluster each partition until the final number of clusters reduces to np/q for some constant $q \geq 1$. Then run a second clustering pass on n/q partial clusters for all the partitions. For the second pass we only store the representative points since the merge procedure only requires representative points of previous clusters before

computing the new representative points for the merged cluster. The advantage of partitioning the input is that we can reduce the execution times.

- **Labeling data on disk:** Since we only have representative points for k clusters, the remaining data points should also be assigned to the clusters. For this a fraction of randomly selected representative points for each of the k clusters is chosen and data point is assigned to the cluster containing the representative point closest to it.

The pseudo code algorithm is given below.

The running time of the algorithm is $O(n_2 \log n)$ and space complexity is $O(n)$.

Input : A set of points S

Output : k clusters

1. For every cluster u (each input point), in u.mean and u-represents store the mean of the points in the cluster and a set of c representative points of the cluster (initially $c = 1$ since each cluster has one data point). Also u.closest stores the cluster closest to u.
2. All the input points are inserted into a k-d tree T
3. Treat each input point as separate cluster, compute u.closest for each u and then insert each cluster into the heap Q. (clusters are arranged in increasing order of distances between u and u.closest).
4. While size(Q) $\geq k$
5. Remove the top element of Q(say u) and merge it with its closest cluster u.closest (say v) and compute the new representative points for the merged cluster w. Also remove u and v from T and Q.
6. Also for all the clusters x in Q, update x.closest and relocate x
7. insert w into Q
8. repeat

8.5.6 ROCK: A Hierarchical Clustering Algorithm for Categorical Attributes

ROCK (RObust Clustering using linKs) is a hierarchical clustering algorithm that explores the concept of links (the number of common neighbors between two objects) for data with categorical attributes. Traditional clustering algorithms for clustering data with Boolean and categorical attributes use distance functions. However, experiments show that such distance measures cannot lead to high-quality clusters when clustering categorical data. Furthermore, most clustering algorithms assess only the similarity between points when clustering; that is, at each step, points that are the most similar are merged into a single cluster. This "localized" approach is prone to errors. For example, two distinct clusters may have a few points or outliers that are close; therefore, relying on the similarity between points to make clustering decisions could cause the two clusters to be merged. ROCK takes a more global approach to clustering by considering the neighborhoods of individual pairs of points. If two similar points also have similar neighborhoods, then the two points likely belong to the same cluster and so can be merged.

More formally, two points, p_i and p_j, are neighbors if sim $(p_i, p_j) - q$, where sim is a similarity function and q is a user-specified threshold. We can choose sim to be a distance metric or even a non metric that is normalized so that its values fall between 0 and 1, with larger values indicating that the points are more similar. The number of links between p_i and p_j is defined as the number of common neighbors between p_i and p_j. If the number of links between two points is large, then it is more likely that they belong to the same cluster. By considering neighboring data points in the relationship between individual pairs of points, ROCK is more robust than standard clustering methods that focus only on point similarity.

8.5.7 CHAMELEON: Clustering Using Dynamic Modeling

Chameleon is a new agglomerative hierarchical clustering algorithm that overcomes the limitations of existing clustering algorithms. The Chameleon algorithm's key feature is that it accounts for both interconnectivity and closeness in identifying the most similar pair of clusters.

CHAMELEON operates on a sparse graph in which nodes represent data items, and weighted edges represent similarities among the data items. This sparse graph representation of the data set allows CHAMELEON to scale to large data sets and to operate successfully on data sets that are available only in similarity space and not in metric spaces. CHAMELEON finds the clusters in the data set by using a two phase algorithm. During the first phase, CHAMELEON uses a graph partitioning algorithm to cluster the data items into a large number of relatively small sub-clusters. During the second phase, it uses an agglomerative hierarchical clustering algorithm to find the genuine clusters by repeatedly combining together these sub-clusters.

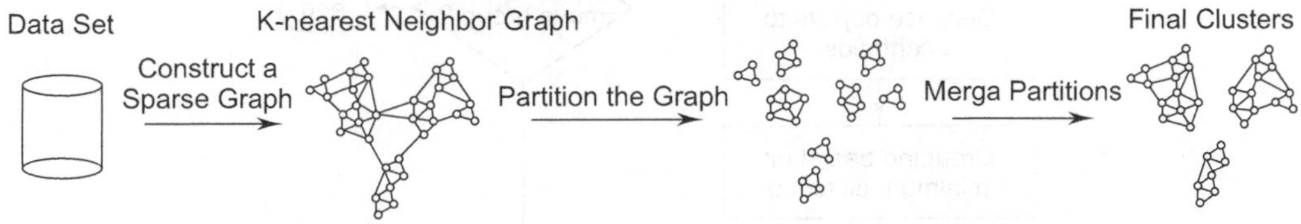

Fig. 8.5 Overall frame work of CHAMELEON algorithm

8.5.8 Difficulties with Hierarchical Clustering

The hierarchical clustering method, though simple, often encounters difficulties regarding the selection of merge or split points. Such a decision is critical because once a group of objects is merged or split, the process at the next step will operate on the newly generated clusters. It will neither undo what was done previously nor perform object swapping between clusters. Thus merge or split decisions, if not well chosen at some step, may lead to low-quality clusters. Moreover, the method does not scale well, because each decision to merge or split requires the examination and evaluation of a good number of objects or clusters. One promising direction for improving the clustering quality of hierarchical methods is to integrate hierarchical clustering with other clustering techniques, resulting in multiple-phase clustering.

8.6 PARTITION METHODS

Given a database of *n* objects and *k*, the number of clusters to form, a partitioning algorithm organizes the objects into *k* partitions (K<=*n*), where each partition represents a cluster. The clusters are formed to optimize an objective partitioning criterion, often called a similarity function, such as distance, so that the objects within the cluster are similar, whereas the objects of different clusters are dissimilar in terms of the database attributes.

8.6.1 K-Means Algorithm

The K-means clustering technique is simple. The *k*-mean algorithm takes the input parameter, *k* where *k* is a user specified parameter, and partitions a set of *n* objects into *k* clusters so that the resulting intracluster similarity is high but the intercluster similarity is low. Cluster similarity is measured in regard to the mean value of the objects in a cluster, which can be viewed as the cluster's center of gravity.

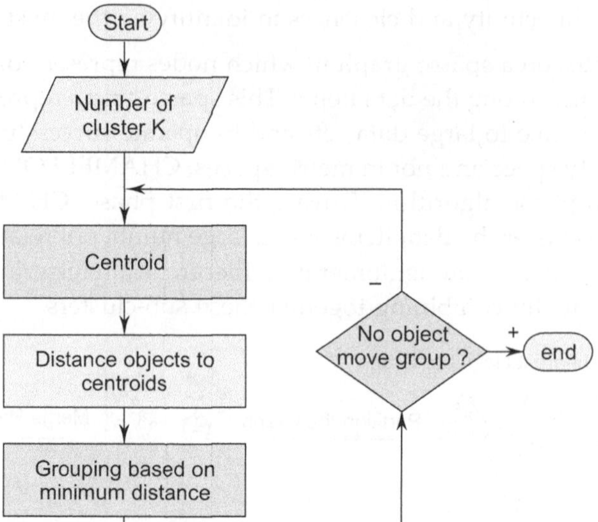

Flow chart 8.1 for K-Mean algorithm

Step 1: Begin with a decision on the value of k = number of clusters

Step 2 : Put any initial partition that classifies the data into *k* clusters, we may assign the training samples randomly, or systematically as the following:

Take the first *k* training sample as single-element clusters

Assign each of the remaining (N-K) training sample to the cluster with the nearest centroid after each assignment, recomputed the centroid of the gaining cluster.

Step 3: Take each sample in sequence and compute its distance from the centroid of each of the clusters. If a sample is not currently in the cluster with closet centroid, switch this sample to that cluster and update the centroid of the cluster gaining the new sample and the cluter losing the sample.

Step 4: Repeat step 3 until convergence is achieved, that is until a pass through the training sample causes no new assignments.

The algorithm attempts to determine *k* partitions that minimize the squared error function. It works well when the clusters are compact clouds that are rather well separated from one another. The method is relatively scalable and efficient in processing large data sets because the computational complexity of the algorithm is O(*nkt*), where *n* is the total number of objects, *k* is the number of clusters, and *t* is the number of iterations. Normally, $k \ll n$ and $t \ll n$. The method often terminates at a local optimum.

The *k*-mean method, however, can applied only when the mean of a cluster is defined. This may not be the case in some applications, such as when data with categorical attributes are involved. The necessity for users to specify *k*, the number clusters, in advance can be seen as disadvantage. The k-mean method is not suitable for discovering clusters with nonconvex shapes of clusters of very different size. Moreover, it is sensitive to noise and outlier data points since a small number of such data can substantially influence the mean value.

8.6.2 K-medoid Algorithm

Unfortunately, K-means clustering is sensitive to the outliers and a set of objects closest to a centroid may be empty, in which case centroids cannot be updated. For this reason, K-medoids clustering are sometimes used, where representative objects called medoids are considered instead of centroids. Because it uses the most centrally located object in a cluster, it is less sensitive to outliers compared with the K-means clustering.

The basic strategy of K-medoids clustering algorithms is to find K clusters in *n* objects by first arbitrarily finding a representative object (the medoid) for each cluster. Each remaining object is clustered with the mediod to which it is the most similar. The strategy then iteratively replaces one of the mediods by one of the nonmedoids as long as the quality of the resulting clustering is improved.

Basic k-medoid algorithm

1. Select K points as a initial medoids
2. Assign all points to the closet medoids
3. See if any other point is "better" medoid (*i.e.*, has the lowest average distance to all other points) Finding a better mediod involves comparing all pairs of medoid and non mediod points and is relatively inefficient
4. Repeat step 2 and 3 until the mediod does not change

The *k*-medoids method is more robust than *k*-means in the presence of noise and outliers, because a medoid is less influenced by outliers or other extreme values than a mean. However, its processing is more costly than the *k* means method. Both methods require the user to specify *k*, the number of clusters. Aside from using the mean or the medoid as a measure of cluster center, other alternative measures are also commonly used in partitioning clustering methods. The median can be used, resulting in the *k* median method, where the median or "middle value" is taken for each ordered attribute. Alternatively, in the *k*-modes method, the most frequent value for each attribute is used.

PAM (Partitioning Around Medoids) was one of the first *k*-medoids algorithms introduced. It attempts to determine *k* partitions for *n* objects. After an initial random selection of *k* mediods, the algorithm repeatedly tries to make a better choice of medoids. All of the possible pairs of objects are analyzed, where one object in each pair is considered a medoid and the other is not.

8.6.3 CLARA (Clustering LARge Applications)

This algorithm improves on the time complexity of PAM by using samples of the dataset. The basic idea is to applies PAM to a sample of the underlying database and then uses the medoids found as the mediods for the complete clustering. Each item from the complete database is then assigned to the cluster with the mediod to which it is closest. To improve the CLARA accuracy, several samples can be drawn with PAM applied to each. The sample chosen as the final clustering is the one that performs the best. Because of the sampling, CLARA is more efficient than PAM for large databases.

CLARA Algorithm
Input: Database of D objects
repeat

for n times draw a sample S subset of D randomly from D. Call PAM(s, k) to get a k medoids.

classify the entire data set D to $C_1, C_2, \ldots C_k$.

calculate the quality of clustering as the average dissimilarity

end.

8.6.4 CLARANS (Clustering Large Applications Based upon RANdomized Search)

It is similar to PAM and CLARA, but it applies a randomized Iterative-Optization for the determination of medoids. It is easy to see that in PAM, at every iteration we examine k(N-k) swaps to determine the pair corresponding to the minimum cost. On the other hand, CLARA tries to examine fewer elements by restricting its search to a smaller sample of the database. Thus, if the sample size is S<=N, it examines at most k(S-k) pairs at every iteration. Thus, in CLARA, an object can be a medoid only if it is in the randomly selected sample. But CLARANS does not restrict the search to any particular subset of objects. Neither does it search the entire data set. It begins with PAM and randomly selects few fairs(I, h), instead of examining all pairs, for swapping at the current state.

CLARANS like PAM starts with a randomly selected set of k-medoids. CLARANS requires two additional parameters: maxneighbour and numlocal. Maxneighbour is the number of neighbours of a node to which any specific node can be compared. It checks at most the "maxneighbour" number of pairs for swapping and, if a pair with negative cost is found, it updates the medoid set and continues. Otherwise, it records the current selection of medoids as a local optimum and restarts with a new randomly selected medoid, set to search for another local optimum. CLARANS stops after the "numlocal" numbers of local optimal medoid sets are determined and returns the best among these. As maxneighbour increases, CLARANS looks more and more like PAM because all nodes will be examined. Numlock indicates the number of samples to be taken. Since a new clustering is performed on each sample, this also indicates the number of clustering to be made.

CLARANS is a medoid-based method, which is more efficient than the earlier medoid-based methods, but suffers from two major drawbacks: it assumes that all objects fit into the main memory, and the result is very sensitive to input order. In addition, it may not find a real local minimum due to the trimming of its searching , controlled by "maxneighbor". Focusing technique is a way to improve CLARANS's ability to deal with disk-resident data sets, by focusing only on relevant parts of the database using R* trees.

Comparing *k*-means and PAM

Compared to the well-known k-means algorithm, Pam has the following features:

- It operates on the dissimilarity matrix of the given data set or when it is presented with an $n \times p$ data matrix, the algorithm first computes a dissimilarity matrix.
- It is more robust, because it minimizes a sum of dissimilarities instead of a sum of squared Euclidean distances.
- It provides a novel graphical display, the silhouette plot, which allows the user to select the optimal number of clusters.

In many clustering problems, one is interested in the characterization of the clusters by means of typical objects, which represent the various structural features of objects under investigation. The algorithm Pam first computes k representative objects, called medoids. A medoid can be defined as that object of a cluster, whose average dissimilarity to all the objects in the cluster is minimal. In the classification literature, such representative objects are called centrotypes. After finding the set of medoids, each object of the data set is assigned to the nearest medoid. That is, object i is put into cluster v_i, when medoid mv_i is nearer than any other medoid m_w.

$$d(i, mv_i) \leq d(i, m_w) \quad \text{for all} \quad w = 1, \ldots, k.$$

The k representative objects should minimize the objective function, which is the sum of the dissimilarities of all objects to their nearest medoid:

$$\text{Objective function} = \Sigma d(i, mv_1)$$

The algorithm proceeds in two steps:

- **BUILD-step:** This step sequentially selects k "centrally located" objects, to be used as initial medoids.
- **SWAP-step:** If the objective function can be reduced by interchanging (swapping) a selected object with an unselected object, then the swap is carried out. This is continued till the objective function can no longer be decreased.

Isolated clusters

The program considers two types of isolated clusters. L-clusters and L* clusters. Cluster C is an L-cluster, if for each object i belonging to C:

$$\max d_{ij} < \min d_{ih}, \; j \in C \; h \notin C$$

Cluster C is an L* – cluster, if

$$\max d_{ij} < \min d_{lh}, \; ij \; C, \; l \in C, \; h \notin C$$

It is clear that L*-clusters are also L-clusters. It should be noted that the property of being isolated depends on the internal structure of a cluster as well as on its position relative to other clusters.

Diameter of a cluster

The diameter of Cluster C is defined as the largest dissimilarity between objects belonging to the Cluster C.

$$\text{Diameter}_C = \max d_{ij}, \; i, j \in C$$

Separation of a cluster

The separation of Cluster C is defined as the smallest dissimilarity between two objects; one of which belong to Cluster C and the other does not.

$$\text{Separation}_C = \min d_{lh}, \; l \in C, \; h \notin C$$

Average distance to a medoid

If j is the medoid of Cluster C, the average distance of all objects of C to j is calculated as follows:

$$\text{Average distance}_j = \frac{\sum_{i \in C} d_{ij}}{N_j}$$

where N is the number of object minus other than j.

Maximum distance to medoid

If object j is the medoid of cluster C, the maximum distance of objects of C to j is calculated as follows:

$$\text{Maximum distance}_j = \max d_{ij},\ i \in C$$

Graphical display

Two of the most difficult tasks in cluster analysis are: How to decide the appropriate number of clusters and how to distinguish a bad cluster from a good one. The module Clusfind computes a set of values called silhouettes that provide key information about these tasks. First, we will explain how these are calculated and then we will show how they are used.

Each cluster is represented by one silhouette, showing which objects lie within the cluster and which objects merely hold an intermediate position. The entire clustering is displayed by plotting all silhouettes into a single diagram, from which the quality of the clusters can be compared.

Silhouettes are constructed in the following way. Consider any object i of the data set, and let A denote the cluster to which it is assigned, and then calculate

$$a(i) = \text{average dissimilarity of } i \text{ to all other objects of A}$$

Now consider any cluster C different from A and define

$$d(i, C) = \text{average dissimilarity of } i \text{ to all objects of C}$$

Compute $d\,(i, C)$ for all clusters $C \neq A$, and then select the smallest of those

$$b = \min d(i, C), C \neq A$$

Let B denote the cluster which attains the minimum *i.e.*, $d(i, B) = b(i)$ is called the neighbour of object i. The value $s(i)$ can now be defined as:

$$s(i) = \frac{b(i) - a(i)}{\max\{a(i), b(i)\}}$$

It can be easily seen that $s(i)$ lies between – 1 and + 1. The value of $s(i)$ may be interpreted as follows:

$S(i) = 1$	'within' dissimilarity $a(i)$ is much smaller than the smallest 'between' dissimilarity. In other words, object i has been assigned to an appropriate cluster. The second best cluster B is not nearly as close as the actual cluster A.
$S(i) = 0$	$a(i)$ and $b(i)$ are approximately equal. Hence, it is not clear whether i should be assigned to A or B. It can be considered as an 'intermediate' case.
$S(i) = -1$	Object i is badly classified. When s is close to negative one, the object is poorly classified. Its dissimilarity with other objects in its cluster is much greater than its dissimilarity with objects in the nearest cluster. Why isn't it in the neighboring cluster?

Hence, the silhouette value summarizes how appropriate each object's cluster is.

The silhouette of a cluster is a plot of the $s(i)$ ranked in decreasing order of all the objects i. The plot is a horizontal line, whose length is proportioned to $s(i)$. The silhouette shows which objects lie well within the cluster and which ones are merely somewhere in between clusters. A wide silhouette indicates large $s(i)$ values and hence a pronounced cluster. The height of a cluster is simply equal to the number of objects in the cluster.

The entire silhouette plot shows the silhouettes of all clusters next to each other, so that the quality of clusters can be compared. The overall average silhouette width of the silhouette plot is the average of $s(i)$ over all object in the data set.

The silhouette plot is quite useful for deciding the number of clusters. One can run Pam several times, each times for different values of k and then compare the resulting silhouette plots. The average silhouette width can be used to select the 'best' number of clusters, by choosing that k which yields the highest silhouette width.

$$SC = \max \bar{s}(k)$$

where the maximum is taken over all k, for which the silhouette can be constructed, which means $k = 2, 3,\text{–..}, n$. This coefficient is a dimensionless measure of the extent of clustering structuring that has been discovered by the clustering algorithm. The SC can be interpreted as follows:

Range of SC	*Interpretation*
0.71 – 1.0	A strong structure has been found
0.51 – 0.70	A reasonable structure has been found
0.26 – 0.50	The structure is weak and could be artificial. Try additional methods of data analysis.
≤ 0.25	No substantial structure has been found

8.7 DENSITY-BASED CLUSTERING

Most partitioning methods cluster objects based on the distance between objects. Such methods can find only spherical-shaped clusters and encounter difficulty at discovering clusters of arbitrary shapes. Other clustering methods have been developed based on the notion of density. Their general idea is to continue growing the given cluster as long as the density (number of objects or data points) in the "neighborhood" exceeds some threshold; that is, for each data point within a given cluster, the neighborhood of a given radius has to contain at least a minimum number of points. Such a method can be used to filter out noise (outlier) and discover clusters of arbitrary shape.

8.7.1 DBSCAN (Density-Based Spatial Clustering of Applications with Noise)

It is a density based clustering algorithm. The algorithm grows regions with sufficiently high density into clusters and discovers clusters of arbitrary shape in spatial databases with noise. It defines a cluster as a maximal set of density-connected points.

Two global parameters for DBSCAN algorithms are:

- **Eps:** Maximum radius of the neighborhood
- **MinPts:** Minimum number of points in an Eps-neighborhood of that point

Core Object: Object with at least MinPts objects within a radius 'Eps neighborhood'

Border Object: Object that on the border of a cluster

NEps(p): {q belongs to D | dist(p, q) <= Eps}

Directly Density-Reachable: A point p is directly density-reachable from a point q w.r.t Eps, MinPts if *p* belongs to *NEps(q)*

|*NEps (q)*| >= *MinPts*

Density-Reachable: A point p is density-reachable from a point q w.r.t Eps, MinPts if there is a chain of points $p_1, \ldots, p_n, p_1 = q, p_n = p$ such that $p_i + 1$ is directly density-reachable from p_i

Density-Connected: A point p is density-connected to a point q w.r.t Eps, MinPts if there is a point o such that both, p and q are density-reachable from o w.r.t Eps and MinPts.

Algorithm: The algorithm of DBSCAN is as follows (M. Ester, H. P. Kriegel, J. Sander, 1996)

- Arbitrary select a point p
- Retrieve all points density-reachable from p w.r.t Eps and MinPts.
- If p is a core point, a cluster is formed.
- If p is a border point, no points are density-reachable from p and

DBSCAN visits the next point of the database.

- Continue the process until all of the points have been processed.

Complexity

DBSCAN visits each point of the database, possibly multiple times (*e.g.*, as candidates to different clusters). For practical considerations, however, the time complexity is mostly governed by the number of getNeighbors queries. DBSCAN executes exactly one such query for each point, and if an indexing structure is used that executes such a neighborhood query in O(logn), an overall runtime complexity of $O(n \cdot \log n)$ is obtained.

Advantages

1. DBScan does not require you to know the number of clusters in the data a priori, as opposed to *k*-means
2. DBScan can find arbitrarily shaped clusters. It can even find clusters completely surrounded by (but not connected to) a different cluster. Due to the MinPts parameter, the so-called single-link effect (different clusters being connected by a thin line of points) is reduced.
3. DBScan has a notion of noise.
4. DBScan requires just two parameters and is mostly insensitive to the ordering of the points in the database. (Only points sitting on the edge of two different clusters might swap cluster membership if the ordering of the points is changed, and the cluster assignment is unique only up to isomorphism.)

Disadvantages

1. DBSCAN can only result in a good clustering as good as its distance measure is in the function getNeighbors(P,epsilon). The most common distance metric used is the euclidean distance measure. Especially for high-dimensional data, this distance metric can be rendered almost useless.
2. DBScan does not respond well to data sets with varying densities (called hierarchical data sets).

8.7.2 OPTICS: Ordering Points To Identify the Clustering Structure

OPTICS is an algorithm for finding cluster in spatial data. It was presented by Mihael Ankerst, Markus M. Breunig, Hans-Peter Kriegel and Jörg Sander. In its basic idea, it is similar to DBSCAN, but addresses one of DBSCAN's major weaknesses: the problem to detect meaningful cluster in data of varying density. In order to do so, the points of the database are (linearly) ordered such that points which are spatially closest become neighbors in the ordering. Additionally, a special distance is stored for each point that represents the density that needs to be accepted for a cluster in order to have both points belong to the same cluster.

Like DBSCAN, OPTICS requires two parameters: Eps, which describes the lowest density we want to consider, and MinPts, describing the number of points required to form a cluster. A point p is a core point if at least MinPts points are found within its Eps -neighborhood N $\varepsilon(p)$. Contrary to DBSCAN, OPTICS also considers points that are part of a more densely packed cluster, so each point is assigned a core distance that basically describes the distance to its MinPtsth point:

In DBSCAN, we can easily see that for a constant MinPts value, density based clusters with respect to a higher density (*i.e.*, a lower value for *e*) are completely contained in density-connected sets obtained with respect to a lower density. We use the parameter *e* is a distance—it is the neighborhood radius. Therefore, in order to produce a set or ordering of density-based clusters, we can extend the DBSCAN algorithm to process a set of distance parameter values at the same time. To construct the different clusterings simultaneously, the objects should be processed in a specific order. This order selects an object that is density-reachable with respect to the lowest e value so that clusters with higher density (lower e) will be finished first. Based on this idea, two values need to be stored for each object—core-distance and reachability-distance:

- The core-distance of an object p is the smallest ε value that makes $\{p\}$ a core object. If p is not a core object, the core-distance of p is undefined.
- The reachability-distance of an object q with respect to another object p is the greater value of the core-distance of p and the Euclidean distance between p and q. If p is not a core object, the reachability-distance between p and q is undefined.

The OPTICS algorithm creates an ordering of the objects in a database, additionally storing the core-distance and a suitable reachability-distance for each object. An algorithm was proposed to extract clusters based on the ordering information produced by OPTICS. Such information is sufficient for the extraction of all density-based clustering with respect to any distance ε' that is smaller than the distance ε used in generating the order.

Like DBSCAN, OPTICS process each point once, and performs one ε – neighborhood query during this processing. Given a spatial index that grants a neighborhood query in O(log n) runtime, an overall runtime of O(n log n) is obtained .

8.8 GRID BASED METHODS

In general, spatial data mining, or knowledge discovery in spatial databases, is the extraction of implicit knowledge, spatial relations and discovery of interesting characteristics and patterns that are not explicitly represented in the databases. Spatial data mining has wide applications in many fields, including GIS systems, image database exploration, medical imaging, etc.

Spatial data may be thought of as features located on or referenced to the Earth's surface, such as roads, streams, political boundaries, schools, land use classifications, property ownership parcels, drinking water intakes, pollution discharge sites - in short, anything that can be **mapped**.

Geographic features are stored as a series of coordinate values. Each point along a road or other feature is defined by positional coordinate value, such as longitude and latitude. The GIS stores and manages the data not as a map but as a series of layers or, as they are sometimes called, themes.

The amount of spatial data obtained from satellite, medical imagery and other sources has been growing tremendously in recent years. A crucial challenge in spatial data mining is the efficiency of spatial data mining algorithms due to the often huge amount of spatial data and the complexity of spatial data types and spatial accessing methods.

Spatial database systems aim at storing, retrieving, manipulating, querying, and analyzing geometric data. Special data types are necessary to model geometry and to suitably represent geometric data in database systems. These data types are usually called spatial data types, such as point, line, and region but also include more complex types like partitions and graphs (networks).

Data type understanding is a prerequisite for an effective construction of important components of a spatial database system (like spatial index structures, optimizers for spatial data, spatial query languages, storage management, and graphical user interfaces) and for cooperation with extensible DBMS providing spatial type extension packages (like spatial data blades and cartridges).

Grid-based methods quantize the object space into a finite number of cells that form a grid structure. All of the clustering operations are performed on the grid structure. The main advantage of this approach is its fast processing time, which is typically independent of the number of data objects and dependent only on the number of cells in each dimension in the quantized space.

8.8.1 STING: STatistical INformation Grid

STING is a grid-based multi resolution clustering technique in which the spatial area is divided into rectangular cells as shown in the figure 8.6. There are usually several levels of such rectangular cells corresponding to different levels of resolution, and these cells form a hierarchical structure: each cell at a high level is partitioned to form a number of cells at the next lower level. Statistical information regarding the attributes in each grid cell (such as the mean, maximum, and minimum values) is calculated and stored beforehand and is used to answer queries. These statistical parameters are useful for query processing.

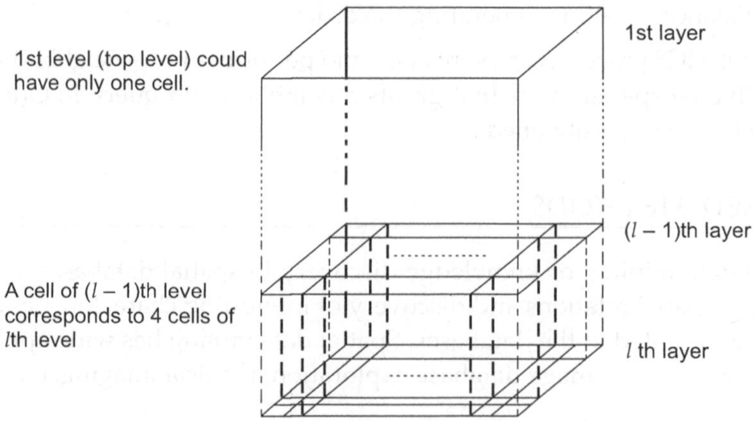

Fig. 8.6 Hierarchical Structure of grid

In Fig. 8.6 each cell at $(i-1)$th level has 4 children at ith level (can be changed). The size of leaf cell is dependent on the density of objects. Generally it should be from several dozens to thousands. Statistical parameters of higher-level cells can easily be computed from the parameters of the lower-level cells.

These parameters include the following: the attribute-independent parameter, count; the attribute-dependent parameters, mean, stdev (standard deviation), min (minimum), max (maximum); and the type of distribution that the attribute value in the cell follows, such as normal, uniform, exponential, or none (if the distribution is unknown).

When the data are loaded into the database, the parameters count, mean, stdev, min, and max of the bottom-level cells are calculated directly from the data. The value of distribution may either be assigned by the user if the distribution type is known beforehand or obtained by hypothesis tests such as the χ_2 test.

The type of distribution of a higher-level cell can be computed based on the majority of distribution types of its corresponding lower-level cells in conjunction with a threshold filtering process. If the distributions of the lower-level cells disagree with each other and fail the threshold test, the distribution type of the high-level cell is set to none.

Parameter generation:

$$n = \sum_i n_i$$

$$m = \frac{\sum_i m_i n_i}{n}$$

$$s = \sqrt{\frac{\sum_i \left(s_i^2 + m_i^2\right) n_i}{n} - m^2}$$

$$\min = \min_i \left(\min_i\right)$$

$$\max = \max_i \left(\max_i\right)$$

The determination of dist parameter is as follows

First the dist is set to distribution followed by most point

An estimate is made on number of conflicting points confl according to following rules

1. if disti is not equal to dist, $m = m_i$ and $s = s_i$ then confl is increased by amount n_i.
2. if disti is not equal to dist, $m = m_i$ or $s = s_i$ but not both then confl is set to n.
3. if disti = dist and $m = m_i$ and $s = s_i$ then confl is not changed
4. if disti = dist, $m = m_i$ or $s = s_i$ but not both then confl is set to n.

Finally if confl/n is greater than a threshold (say 0.05) then dist is set to none or Original dist is retained

I	1	2	3	4
N_i	100	50	60	10
M_i	20.1	19.7	21	20.5
S_i	2.3	2.2	2.4	2.1
Mini	4.5	5.5	3.8	7
Maxi	36	34	37	40
Disti	Normal	Normal	Normal	None

The parameters of the current cell are

$$N = 220$$
$$m = 20.27$$
$$s = 2.37$$
$$\min = 3.8$$
$$\max = 40$$

dist = NORMAL

This is so because there are 220 data points out of which 10 are not NORMAL

So confl/n = 10/220 = 0.045 < 0.05 hence it is still NORMAL.

The parameters are calculated only once so overall compilation time is O(N)

But querying requires much less time as we only scan the number of grid cells K *i.e.*, O(K)

STING offers several advantages:

1. the grid-based computation is query-independent, because the statistical information stored in each cell represents the summary information of the data in the grid cell, independent of the query.
2. the grid structure facilitates parallel processing and incremental updating.
3. the method's efficiency is a major advantage: STING goes through the database once to compute the statistical parameters of the cells, and hence the time complexity of generating clusters is O(n), where n is the total number of objects.

After generating the hierarchical structure, the query processing time is O(g), where g is the total number of grid cells at the lowest level, which is usually much smaller than n.

8.8.2 WaveCluster: Clustering Using Wavelet Transformation

Wave Cluster is a multiresolution clustering algorithm that first summarizes the data by imposing a multidimensional grid structure onto the data space. It then uses a wavelet transformation to transform the original feature space, finding dense regions in the transformed space.

In this approach, each grid cell summarizes the information of a group of points that map into the cell. This summary information typically fits into main memory for use by the multiresolution wavelet transform and the subsequent cluster analysis.

A wavelet transform is a signal processing technique that decomposes a signal into different frequency subbands. The wavelet model can be applied to d-dimensional signals by applying one-dimensional wavelets transform d times. In applying a wavelet transform, data are transformed so as to preserve the relative distance between objects at different levels of resolution.

- Function $f(x)$ is scaling function if it can be expressed as a liner combination of $f(2x - k)$

  Example: Haar function: 1 on [0,1), 0 -elsewhere

$$f(x) = f(2x) + f(2x - 1)$$

- For each j let V_j be a vector space of 2_j function f_{ji} defined as $f(2_{jx} - i)$
- $V_0 \{f(x)\}$, $V_1\{f(2x), f(2x - 1)\}$, $V_2 \{f(4x), f(4x - 1), f(4x - 2), f(4x - 3)\}$
- $V_0 (V_1 (V_2 \ldots (V_j$

Wavelet space W_j defined as an orthogonal complement of V_j in V_{j+1}

Lets $w(x)$ be defined as 1 on [0,1/2), -1 on [1/2,1), 0 - elsewhere

$V_1 = \{f(2x), f(2x - 1)\} = V_0 \times W_0$, were $V_0 = \{f(x)\}$ and $W_0 = \{w(x)\}$, because $<f, w>=0$ and every element of V_1 space can be represented as a liner combination of elements from V_0 and W_1 space:

$$f(2x) = 1/2f(x) + 1/2w(x), f(2x - 1) = 1/2f(x) - 1/2w(x)$$

Given a set of spatial objects o_i, $1<=i<=$ N detect cluster and assign labels to the objects based on the cluster they belong to

- Quantize feature space, then assign object to the units
- Apply wavelet transform on the feature space
- Find connected components in the transformed feature space at different levels
- Assign labels to the units
- Make the lookup table
- Map each object to the clusters

WaveCluster Clustering Algorithm: Quantization

- Divide each dimension d into m equal intervals, let s_i be the size of each unit in i dimension.
- An object o_k corresponding to the feature vector $F_k = (f_1, f_2, \ldots f_d)$ will be assign to the unit $M_j = (v_1, v_2, \ldots v_d)$ if for all $i : 1<=i<=d$ $(v_i - 1)s_i <= f_i < v_i s_i$

WaveCluster Clustering Algorithm: Transform

- Applying wavelet transform on each unit M_i result in new transformed feature space T_k
- Each connected component is a set of units from T_k and is considered a cluster
- Corresponding to each resolution level r there will be a set of clusters C_r
- Use some other well-know algorithms to find connected components in transformed feature space

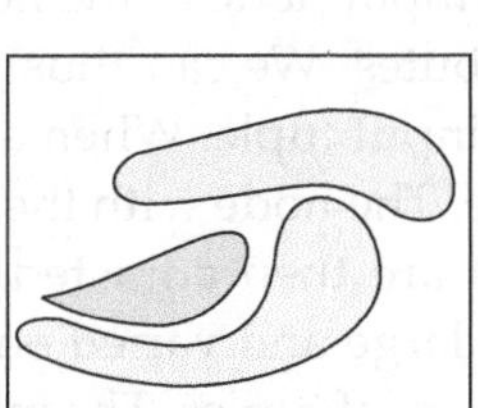

Fig. 8.7 Clustering arbitrary shapes

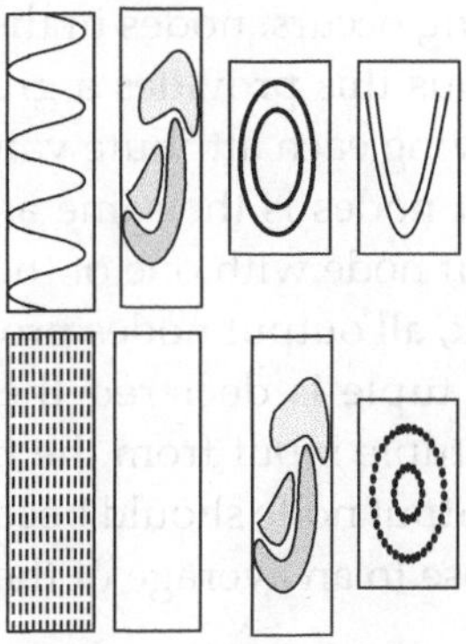

Fig. 8.8 Synthetic data sets

WaveCluster is a grid-based and density-based algorithm. It conforms with many of the requirements of a good clustering algorithm: It handles large data sets efficiently, discovers clusters with arbitrary shape, successfully handles outliers, is insensitive to the order of input parameters such as the number of clusters or a neighborhood radius.

8.9 MODEL-BASED CLUSTERING METHODS

Model based clustering approach was popularized by Banfield and Raftery (1993). This approach is one of the most advanced in clustering. Model based clustering approach usually assumes stochastic approach and the appropriate model is simply the particular multivariate distribution. Model based clustering methods attempts to optimize the fit between the given data and some mathematical model. Such methods are often based on the assumption that the data are generated by the mixture of underlying probability distributions.

Model-based clustering methods are follow two major approaches in the following:

1. Statistical approach
2. Neural Network approach

Statistical Approach: In a statistical approach that uses probability measurements in determining the concepts or clusters. Probabilistic descriptions are typically used to represent each derived concept.

Neural Network approach: The neural network approach to clustering tends to represent each cluster as an exemplar. An exemplar acts as a "prototype" of the cluster and does not necessarily have to correspond to a particular data example or objects.

Neural Networks that use unsupervised learning attempts to find features in the data that characterize the desired output. They look for clusters like data. These types of neural network are often called self-organizing neural networks. These are two basic types of unsupervised learning:

- Noncompetitive
- Competitive

Noncompetitive learning, the weight between two nodes is changed to be proportional to both output values.

Competitive learning, nodes are allowed to compete and the winner takes all. This approach usually assumes a two-layer NN in which all nodes from one layer are connected to all nodes in the other layer. As training occurs, nodes in the output layer become associated with certain tuples in the input dataset. Thus this provides a grouping of these tuples together into a cluster. Imagine every input tuple having each attribute value input to a specific input node in the neural network. The number of input nodes is the same as the number of attributes. We can thus associate each weight to each output node with one of the attributes from the input tuple. When a tuple is input to the neural network, all output nodes produce an output value. The node with the weights more similar to the input tuple is declared the winner. Its weights are then adjusted. This process continues with each tuple input from the training set. With the large and varied enough training set, over time each output node should become associated with a set of tuples. The input weights to the node are then close to an average of the tuples in this cluster.

8.10 OUTLIER ANALYSIS

Outliers, or commonly referred to as exceptional cases, exist in many real-world databases. Very often, there exist data objects that do not comply with the general behavior or model of the data. Outlier objects are objects that "are grossly different from or inconsistent with the remaining set of data are called outliers.

As per the above discussion outliers are sample points with values much different from those of the remaining set of data. Outliers represent errors in the data or could be correct data values that are simply much different from the remaining data. A person who is 4.5 meters tall is exceptionally tall this value probably would be viewed as an outlier.

Some clustering algorithms do not perform well with the presence of outliers. Clustering algorithms may actually searches and remove outliers to ensure that they perform better. However, care must be taken in actually removing outliers. For example, suppose that the data mining problem is to predict flooding. Extremely high water level values occur very infrequently, and when compared with the normal water level values may seem to be outliers. However, removing these values may not allow the data mining algorithms to work effectively because there would be no data that showed that floods ever actually occurred.

Some outlier detection techniques are based on statistical techniques. These usually assume that the set of data follows a known distribution and that outliers can be detected by well-known tests such as discordancy tests. However, these tests are not very realistic for real-world data because real-world data values may not follow well-defined data distributions. Also, most of these tests assume a single attribute value, and many attributes are involved in real-world datasets. Alternative detection techniques may be based on distance measures.

Detection of outliers is important for many applications and has attracted much attention from the data mining research community recently. Outlier detection is encompasses aspects of broad spectrum of techniques.

8.11 COMPARISON OF CLUSTERING ALGORITHMS

The different clustering algorithms discussed in this chapter are compared in the given Table 8.1

Table 8.1 Comparison of Clustering Algorithms

Algorithm	*Type*	*Space*	*Time*
Single link	Hierarchical	O(n2)	$O(kn^2)$
Average link	Hierarchical	O(n2)	$O(kn^2)$
K-means	Partition	O(n)	O(tkn)
Nearest neighbours	Partition	O(n)	O(tkn)
PAM	Partition	O(n2)	$O(tk(n-k)^2)$
BIRCH	Partition	O(n)	O(n)
CURE	Mixed	O(n)	O(n)
ROCK	Agglomerative	O(n2)	$O(n^2 \log n)$
DBSCAN	Density Based	O(n2)	$O(n^2)$

SUMMARY

- Clustering is technique for combining observed objects into groups or clusters. The process of grouping a set of physical or abstract objects into classes of seminal objects is called clustering.
- Cluster analysis has been widely used in numerous applications, including pattern recognition, data analysis, image processing, and market research.
- Clustering is a challenging field of research in which its potential applications pose their own special requirements like Scalability, Ability to deal with different types of attributes, Discovery of clusters with arbitrary shape, Minimal requirements for domain knowledge to determine input parameters, Ability to deal with noisy data, Incremental clustering and insensitivity to the order of input records, High dimensionality, Constraint-based clustering, Interpretability and usability.
- Clustering is a dynamic field of research in data mining. Many clustering algorithms have been developed. These can be categorized into partitioning methods, hierarchical methods, density-based methods, grid-based methods, model-based methods, methods for high-dimensional data (including frequent pattern-based methods), and constraint based methods. Some algorithms may belong to more than one category.
- Hierarchical clustering builds a cluster hierarchy or, in other words, a tree of clusters, also known as a *dendrogram*. Every cluster node contains child clusters; sibling clusters partition the points covered by their common parent. Such an approach allows exploring data on different levels of granularity.
- Partitioning method first creates an initial set of k partitions, where parameter k is the number of partitions to construct. It then uses an iterative relocation technique that attempts to improve the partitioning by moving objects from one group to another.
- Density-based method clusters objects based on the notion of density. It either grows clusters according to the density of neighborhood objects (such as in DBSCAN) or according to some density function (such as in DENCLUE). OPTICS is a density based method that generates an augmented ordering of the clustering structure of the data.
- Model based clustering approach usually assumes stochastic approach and the appropriate model is simply the particular multivariate distribution. Model based clustering methods attempts to optimize the fit between the given data and some mathematical model.
- Outliers, or commonly referred to as exceptional cases, exist in many real-world databases. Some clustering algorithms do not perform well with the presence of outliers. Clustering algorithms may actually searches and remove outliers to ensure that they perform better.

REVIEW QUESTIONS

1. Write algorithms for *k*-Means and *k*-Medoids. Explain.
2. Given the following measurement for the variable age: 18, 22, 25, 42, 28, 43, 33, 35, 56, 28 Standardize the variable by the following:
   (*i*) Compute the mean absolute deviation of age.
   (*ii*) Compute the Z-score for the first four measurements.
3. What are the categories of major clustering methods? Explain.
4. What are different types of hierarchical methods? Explain.
5. Explain about outlier analysis.
6. Explain about grid-based methods.
7. Discuss about density-based methods.

8. What is a distance-based outlier? What are efficient algorithms for mining distance-based algorithm? How are outliers determined in this method?
9. What major advantages does DENCLUE have in comparison with other clustering algorithms?
10. What advantages does STING offer over other clustering methods?
11. Why wavelet transformation useful for clustering?
12. Given two objects represented by the tuples (22, 1, 42, 10) and (20, 0, 36, 8):
    (*i*) Compute the Euclidean distance between the two objects.
    (*ii*) Compute the Manhanttan distance between the two objects.
    (*iii*) Compute the Minkowski distance between the two objects, using $q = 3$.
13. Explain about Statistical-based outlier detection and Deviation-based outlier detection.

9

DATA MINING FOR UNSTRUCTURED TYPES OF DATA

9.1 INTRODUCTION

So far we focused on data mining techniques on relational databases, transactional databases and data warehouse formed by the transformation and integration of structured data. Large amount of data in various complex forms like hypertext, multimedia, geographical, time series and text data have been growing rapidly for industrial transactions.

Therefore, an increasingly important task in data mining is to mine complex types of data, including complex objects, spatial data, multimedia data, time-series data, text data, and the World Wide Web.

In this chapter, we study only some preliminary issues, how to further develop the essential data mining techniques (such as characterization, association, classification and clustering) to extract knowledge from complex and unstructured types of data.

9.2 SPATIAL DATA MINING

Spatial data mining is the process of discovering interesting and previously un-known, but potentially useful patterns from large spatial datasets. Extracting interesting and useful patterns from spatial datasets is more difficult than extracting the corresponding patterns from traditional numeric and categorical data due to the complexity of spatial data types, spatial relationships, and spatial autocorrelation.

Fig. 9.1 Sea surface temperature

A spatial database stores a large amount of space-related data, such as maps, preprocessed remote sensing or medical imaging data, and VLSI chip layout data. Spatial databases have many features distinguishing them from relational databases.

The explosive growth of spatial data and widespread use of spatial databases emphasize the need for the automated discovery of spatial knowledge.

The complexity of spatial data and intrinsic spatial relationships limits the usefulness of conventional data mining techniques for extracting spatial patterns. Efficient tools for extracting information from geo-spatial data are crucial to organizations which make decisions based on large spatial datasets, including NASA, the National Imagery and Mapping Agency (NIMA), the National Cancer Institute (NCI), and the United States Department of Transportation (USDOT). These organizations are spread across many application domains including ecology and environmental management, public safety, transportation, Earth science, epidemiology, and climatology.

Specific features of geographical data that preclude the use of general purpose data mining algorithms are:

(*i*) Rich data types (*e.g.*, extended spatial objects)

(*ii*) Implicit spatial relationships among the variables

(*iii*) Observations that are not independent,

(*iv*) Spatial autocorrelation among the features.

The data inputs of spatial data mining are more complex than the inputs of classical data mining because they include extended objects such as points, lines, and polygons. The data inputs of spatial data mining have two distinct types of attributes:

1. Non-spatial attribute
2. Spatial attribute.

Non-spatial attributes are used to characterize non-spatial features of objects, such as name, population, and unemployment rate for a city. They are the same as the attributes used in the data inputs of classical data mining. Spatial attributes are used to define the spatial location and extent of spatial objects. The spatial attributes of a spatial object most often include information related to spatial locations, *e.g.*, longitude, latitude and elevation, as well as shape.

9.2.1 Statistical Foundations

Statistical models are often used to represent observations in terms of random variables. These models can then be used for estimation, description, and prediction based on probability theory.

Statistical spatial data analysis has been a popular approach to analyzing spatial data. The approach handles numerical data well and usually proposes realistic models of spatial phenomena. However, it typically assumes statistical independence among the spatially distributed data, although in reality, spatial objects are often inter-related. Moreover, experts having a fair amount of domain knowledge and statistical expertise can only perform most statistical modeling.

Furthermore, statistical methods do not work well with symbolic values, or incomplete or inconclusive data, and are computationally expensive in large databases. Spatial data allows the extension of traditional spatial analysis methods by placing minimum emphasis on efficiency, scalability, cooperation with database systems, improved interaction with the user, and the discovery of new types of knowledge.

One of the fundamental assumptions of statistical analysis is that the data samples are independently generated: like successive tosses of coin, or the rolling of a die. However, in the analysis of spatial data, the assumption about the independence of samples is generally false. In fact, spatial data tends to be highly self correlated. For example, people with similar characteristics, occupation and background tend to cluster together in the same neighborhoods. The economies of a region tend to be similar. Changes in natural resources, wildlife, and temperature vary gradually over space. The property of like things to cluster in space is so fundamental that geographers have elevated it to the status of the first law of geography: "Everything is related to everything else but nearby things are more related than distant things" [Tobler1979]. In spatial statistics, an area within statistics devoted to the analysis of spatial data, this property is called spatial autocorrelation.

Knowledge discovery techniques which ignore spatial autocorrelation typically perform poorly in the presence of spatial data. Often the spatial dependencies arise due to the inherent characteristics of the phenomena under study, but in particular they arise due to the fact that the spatial resolutions of imaging sensors are finer than the size of the object being observed.

With efficient implementation of spatial data cubes and spatial OLAP, generalization-based descriptive spatial mining, such as spatial characterization and discrimination, can be performed efficiently.

9.2.2 Spatial Association Analysis

Association analysis is applied to the transaction and relational databases, similarly spatial association rules can be mined in spatial databases. A spatial association rule is of the form

A =>B [*s*%, *c*%].

Where A and B are sets of spatial or nonspatial predicates, *s*% is the support of the rule, and *c*% is the confidence of the rule. For example, the following is a spatial association rule: is a (X, "school") A close to (X, "sports center") => close to(X, "park") [0.5%, 80%). This rule states that 80% of schools that are close to sports centers are also close to parks and 0.5% of the data belongs to such a case.

Different types of spatial predicates can constitute a spatial association rule mining. Examples include distance information (such as close to and far-away) topological relations (like intersect, overlap, and disjoint), and spatial orientations (like left of and west of).

Since spatial association mining needs to evaluate multiple spatial relationships among a large number of spatial objects, the process could be quite costly. An interesting mining optimization method called progressive refinement can be adopted in spatial association analysis. The method first mines large data sets roughly using a fast algorithm and then improves the quality of mining in a pruned data set using a more expensive algorithm.

To ensure that the pruned data set covers the complete set of answers when applying the high-quality data mining algorithms at a later stage, an important requirement for the rough mining algorithm applied in the early stage is the superset coverage property: that is, it preserves all of the potential answers. In other words, it should allow a false positive test, which might include some data sets that do not belong to the answer sets, but it should not allow a false negative test, which might exclude some potential answers.

For mining spatial associations related to the spatial predicate close to, we can first collect the candidates that pass the minimum support threshold by applying certain rough spatial evaluation algorithm for example, using a minimum bounding rectangle structure (which registers only two spatial points rather than a set of complex polygons). Then evaluating the relaxed spatial predicate, g close to, which is a generalized c close to covering a broader context that includes close to, touch, and intersect.

If two spatial objects are closely located, their enclosing minimum bounding rectangles must be closely located, matching *g* close to. However, the reverse is not always true: it the enclosing minimum bounding rectangles are closely located, the two spatial objects may or may not be located so closely. Thus, the minimum bounding rectangle pruning is a false positive testing tool for closeness: only those that pass the rough test need to be further examined using more expensive spatial computation algorithms. With this preprocessing, only the patterns that are frequent at the approximation level will need to be examined by more detailed and finer, yet more expensive, spatial computation.

9.2.3 Spatial Clustering

For spatial clustering straightway apply the clustering methods which we discussed in the chapter 8. Spatial data clustering identifies clusters, or densely populated regions, according to some distance measurement in a large, multidimensional data set.

9.2.4 Spatial Classification

Spatial classification analyzes spatial objects to derive classification schemes in relevance to certain spatial properties, such as the neighborhood of a district, highway, or river.

Suppose that you would like to classify regions in a province into rich versus poor according to the average family income. In doing so, you would like to identify the important spatial-related factors that determine a region's classification. There are many properties associated with spatial objects, such as hosting a university, containing interstate highways, being near a lake or ocean, and so on. These properties can be used for relevance analysis and to find interesting classification schemes. Such classification schemes may be represented in the form of decision trees or rules.

Spatial trend analysis deals with another issue the detection of changes and trends along a spatial dimension. Typically, trend analysis detects changes with time, such as the changes of temporal patterns in time-series data. Spatial trend analysis replaces time with space and studies the trend of non spatial or spatial data changing with space. For example, we may observe the trend of changes in economic situation when moving away from the center of a city, or the trend of changes of the climate or vegetation with the increasing distance from an ocean. For such analyses, regression and correlation analysis methods are often applied by utilization of spatial data structures and spatial access methods.

There are also many applications where patterns are changing with both space and time. For example, traffic flows on highways and in cities are both time and space related. Weather patterns are also closely related to both time and space. Although there have been a few interesting studies on spatial classification and spatial trend analysis, the investigation of spatiotemporal data mining is still in its infancy. More methods and applications of spatial classification and trend analysis, especially those associated with time, need to be explored in the future.

9.3 TEMPORAL DATA MINING

Temporal data mining is a rapidly evolving area of research that is at the intersection of several disciplines, including statistics (*e.g.*, time series analysis), temporal pattern recognition, temporal databases, optimization, visualization, high performance computing, and parallel computing.

Temporal data mining is concerned with data mining of large sequential data sets. By sequential data, we mean data that is ordered with respect to some index. For example, time series constitute a popular class of sequential data, where records are indexed by time. Other examples of sequential data could be text, gene sequences, protein sequences, lists of moves in a chess game etc. Here, although there is no notion of time as such, the ordering among the records is very important and is central to the data description/modeling.

Time series analysis has quite a long history. Techniques for statistical modeling and spectral analysis of real or complex-valued time series have been in use for more than fifty years. Weather forecasting, financial or stock market prediction and automatic process control have been some of the oldest and most studied applications of such time series analysis. Time series matching and classification have received much attention since the days speech recognition research saw heightened activity. These applications saw the advent of an increased role for machine learning techniques like Hidden Markov Models and time-delay neural networks in time series analysis.

Temporal data mining, however, is of a more recent origin with somewhat different constraints and objectives. One main difference lies in the size and nature of data sets and the manner in which the data is collected. Often temporal data mining methods must be capable of analyzing data sets that are prohibitively large for conventional time series modeling techniques to handle efficiently. Moreover, the sequences may be nominal-valued or symbolic (rather than being real or complex-valued), rendering techniques such as autoregressive moving average (ARMA) or autoregressive integrated moving average (ARIMA) modeling inapplicable. Also, unlike in most applications of statistical methods, in data mining we have little or no control over the data gathering process, with data often being collected for some entirely different purpose. For example, customer transaction logs may be maintained from an auditing perspective and data mining would then be called upon to analyze the logs for estimating customer buying patterns.

The second major difference (between temporal data mining and classical time series analysis) lies in the kind of information that we want to estimate or unearth from the data. The scope of temporal data mining extends beyond the standard forecast or control applications of time series analysis. Very often, in data mining applications, one does not even know which variables in the data are expected to exhibit any correlations or causal relationships. Furthermore, the exact model parameters (*e.g.*, coefficients of an ARMA model or the weights of a neural network) may be of little interest in the data mining context. Of greater relevance may be the unearthing of useful (and often unexpected) trends or patterns in the data which are much more readily interpretable by and useful to the data owner. For example, a time stamped list of items bought by customers lends itself to data mining analysis that could reveal which combinations of items tend to be frequently consumed together, or whether there has been some particularly skewed or abnormal consumption pattern this year (as compared to previous years), etc.

9.3.1 Temporal Data Mining Tasks

A relevant and important question is how to apply data mining techniques on a temporal database. According to techniques of data mining and theory of statistical time series analysis, the theory of temporal data mining may involve the following areas of investigation since a general theory for this purpose is yet to be developed

1. Temporal data mining tasks include
   Temporal data characterization and comparison

Temporal clustering analysis
Temporal Classification
Temporal Association rules
Temporal Pattern Analysis
Temporal Prediction and Trend Analysis.

2. A new temporal data model may need to be developed based on
   Temporal data structure
   Temporal semantics
3. A new temporal data mining concept may need to be developed based on the following issues.

The task of temporal data mining can be seen as a problem of extracting an interesting part of the logical theory of a model and

The theory of a model may be formulated in a logical formalism able to express quantitative knowledge and approximate truth. In addition, temporal data mining needs to include an investigation of tightly related issues such as temporal data warehousing, temporal OLAP , computing temporal measures, and so on.

9.4 MULTIMEDIA DATABASE MINING

Subfield of data mining that deals with an extraction of implicit knowledge, multimedia data relationships, or other patterns. A multimedia database system stores and manages a large collection of multimedia objects, such as audio data, image data, video data, sequence data, and hypertext data, which contain text, text markups and linkages. Multimedia database systems are increasingly common owing to the popular use of audio-video equipment, CD-ROMs and the Internet. Typical multimedia database systems include NASA's EOS (Earth Observation System), various kinds of image and audio-video databases, human genome databases, and Internet databases.

9.4.1 Multidimensional Analysis of Multimedia Data

To facilitate the multidimensional analysis of large multimedia databases, multimedia data cubes can be designed and constructed in a manner similar to that for traditional data cubes from relational data. A multimedia data cube can contain additional-dimensions and measures for multimedia information, such as color, texture, and shape.

Let's examine a multimedia data mining system prototype called Multi Media Miner, which extends the DBMiner system by handling multimedia data. The example database tested in the MultiMediaMiner system is constructed as follows: Each image contains two descriptors: a feature descriptor and a layout descriptor. The original image is not stored directly in the database; only its descriptors are stored. The description information encompasses fields like image file name, image URL, image type (*e.g.*, gif, jpeg, bmp, avi, mpeg, etc.), a list of all known Web pages referring to the image (*i.e.*, parent URLs), a list of keywords, and a thumbnail used by the user interface for image and video browsing. The feature descriptor is a set of vectors for each visual characteristic. The main vectors are a color vector containing the color histogram quantized to 512 colors ($8 \times 8 \times 8$ for $R \times G \times B$), a MFC (Most Frequent Color) vector, and a MFO (Most Frequent Orientation) vector. The MFC and MFO contain five color centroids and five edge orientation centroids for the five most frequent colors and five most frequent orientations, respectively. The edge orientations used are 0°, 22.5°, 45°, 67.5°, 90°, and so on. The layout descriptor contains a color layout vector and an edge layout vector. Regardless of their original size, all images are assigned an 8×8 grid. The most frequent color for each of the 64 cells is stored in the color layout vector, and the number of edges for each orientation in each of the cells is stored in the edge layout vector. Other sizes of grids, like 4×4, 2×2 and 1×1, can easily be derived.

The Image Excavator component of MultiMediaMiner uses image contextual information, like HTML tags in Web pages, to derive keywords. By traversing on-line directory structures, like the Yahoo! directory, it is possible to create hierarchies of keywords mapped onto the directories in which the image was found. These graphs are used as concept hierarchies for the dimension keyword in the multimedia data cube.

A multimedia data cube can have many dimensions. The following are some examples: the size of the image or video in bytes; the width and height of the frames (or picture), constituting two dimensions; the date on which the image or video was created (or last modified); the format type of the image or video; the frame sequence duration in seconds; the image or video Internet domain; the Internet domain of pages referencing the image or video (parent URL); the keywords; a color dimension; an edge-orientation dimension; and so on. Concept hierarchies for many numerical dimensions may be automatically defined. For other dimensions, such as for Internet domains or color, predefined hierarchies may be used.

The construction of a multimedia data cube will facilitate multiple dimensional analyses of multimedia data primarily based on visual content, and the mining of multiple kinds of knowledge, including summarization, comparison, classification, association, and clustering.

The multimedia data cube seems to be an interesting model for multidimensional analysis of multimedia data. However, we should note that it is difficult to implement a data cube efficiently given a large number of dimensions. This curse of dimensionality is especially serious in the case of multimedia data cubes. We may like to model color, orientation, texture, keywords, and so on, as multiple dimensions in a multimedia data cube. However, many of these attributes are set-oriented instead of single-valued. For example, one image may correspond to a set of keywords. It may contain a set of objects, each associated with a set of colors. If we use each keyword as a dimension or each detailed color as a dimension in the design of the data cube, it will create a huge number of dimensions. On the other hand, not doing so may lead to the modeling of an image at a rather rough, limited, and imprecise scale. More research is needed on how to design a multimedia data cube that may strike a balance between efficiency and the power of representation.

9.4.2 Classification and Prediction Analysis of Multimedia Data

Classification and predictive modeling have been used for mining multimedia data, especially in scientific research, such as astronomy, seismology, and geo-scientific research. Decision tree classification is an essential data mining method in reported image data mining applications.

Example Taking sky images that have been carefully classified by astronomers as the training set, we can construct models for the recognition of galaxies, stars, and other stellar objects, based on properties like magnitudes, areas, intensity, image moments, and orientation. A large number of sky images taken by telescopes or space probes can then be tested against the constructed models in order to identify new celestial bodies. Similar studies have successfully been performed to identify volcanoes on Venus.

Data preprocessing is important when mining such image data and can include data cleaning, data focusing, and feature extraction. Aside from standard methods used in pattern recognition such as edge detection and Hough transformations, techniques can be explored such as the decomposition of images to eigenvectors or the adoption of probabilistic models to deal with uncertainty. Since the image data are often in huge volumes and may require substantial processing power, parallel and distributed processing are useful. Image data mining classification and clustering are closely linked to image analysis and scientific data mining, and thus many image analysis techniques and scientific data analysis methods can be applied to image data mining.

9.4.3 Mining Associations in Multimedia Data

Association rules involving multimedia objects can be mined in image and video databases— At least three categories can be observed:

Associations between image content and non-image content features: A rule like "if at least 50% of the upper part of the picture is blue, it is likely to represent sky" belongs to this category since it links the image content to the keyword sky.

Associations among image contents that are not related to spatial relationships: A rule like "a picture contains two blue squares, it is likely to contain one red circle as well" belongs to this category since the associations are all regarding image contents.

Associations among image contents related to spatial relationships: A rule like "a red triangle is in between two yellow squares, it is likely there is a big oval-shaped object underneath" belongs to this category since it associates objects in the image with spatial relationships.

To mine associations among multimedia objects, we can treat each image as a transaction and find frequently occurring patterns among different images.

First, an image may contain multiple objects, each with many features such as color, shape, texture, keyword, and spatial location, so that there could be a large number of possible associations. In many cases, a feature may be considered as the same in, two images at a certain level of resolution, but different at a finer resolution level. Therefore, it is essential to promote a progressive resolution refinement approach. That is, we can first mine frequently occurring patterns at a relatively rough resolution level, and then focus only on those that have passed the minimum support threshold when mining at a finer resolution level. This is because the patterns that are not frequent at a rough level cannot be frequent at finer resolution levels. Such a multi-resolution mining strategy substantially reduces the overall data mining cost without loss of the quality and completeness of data mining results. This leads to an efficient methodology for mining frequent itemsets and associations in large multimedia databases.

Second, since a picture containing multiple recurrent objects is an important feature in image analysis, recurrence of the same objects should not be ignored in association analysis. For example, a picture containing two golden circles is treated quite differently from that containing only one. This is quite different from that in a transaction database, where the fact that a person buys one gallon of milk or two may often be treated the same as "buys_milk". Therefore, the definition of multimedia association and its measurements, such as support and confidence, should be adjusted accordingly.

Third, there often exist important relative spatial relationships among multimedia objects, such as above, beneath, between, nearby, left-of, and so on. These features are very useful for exploring object associations and correlations. Spatial relationships together with other content-based multimedia features, such as color, shape, texture, and keywords, may form interesting associations. Thus, spatial data mining methods and properties of topological spatial relationships become quite important for multimedia mining.

9.5 WEB MINING

The World Wide Web, has grown in the past few years from a small research community to the biggest and most popular way of communication and information dissemination. Every day, the WWW grows by roughly a million electronic pages, adding to the hundreds of millions already on line. WWW serves as a platform for exchanging various kinds of information, ranging from research papers, and educational content, to multimedia content and software.

The continuous growth in the size and the use of the WWW imposes new methods for processing these huge amounts of data. Because of its rapid and chaotic growth, the resulting network of information lacks of organization and structure. Moreover, the content is published in various diverse formats. Due to this fact, users are feeling sometimes disoriented, lost in that information overload that continues to expand.

Data mining is the technology used to discover non-obvious, potentially useful and previously unknown information from data sources. The potential of **web mining** is in the application of existing and new data mining algorithms to Internet data, which include Internet server logs, as well as external data on customer, sales, and products.

9.5.1 Web Mining Taxonomy

Web Mining can be broadly divided into three distinct categories, according to the kinds of data to be mined. We provide a brief overview of the three categories. A figure depicting the taxonomy is shown in Fig. 9.2.

1. **Web Content Mining:** Web Content Mining is the process of extracting useful information from the contents of Web documents. Content data corresponds to the collection of facts a Web page was designed to convey to the users. It may consist of text, images, audio, video, or structured records such as lists and tables. Application of text mining to Web content has been the most widely researched. Issues addressed in text mining are, topic discovery, extracting association patterns, clustering of web documents and classification of Web Pages. Research activities on this topic have drawn heavily on techniques developed in other disciplines such as Information Retrieval (IR) and Natural Language Processing (NLP). While there exists a significant body of work in extracting knowledge from images in the fields of image processing and computer vision, the application of these techniques to Web content mining has been limited.
2. **Web Structure Mining:** The structure of a typical Web graph consists of Web pages as nodes, and hyperlinks as edges connecting related pages. Web Structure Mining is the process of discovering structure information from the Web. This can be further divided into two kinds based on the kind of structure information used.
   - **Hyperlinks:** A Hyperlink is a structural unit that connects a location in a Web page to different location, either within the same Web page or on a different Web page. A hyperlink that connects to a different part of the same page is called an Intra-Document Hyperlink, and a hyperlink that connects two different pages is called an Inter-Document Hyperlink. There has been a significant body of work on hyperlink analysis, of which provide an up-to-date survey.
   - **Document Structure:** In addition, the content within a Web page can also be organized in a tree-structured format, based on the various HTML and XML tags within the page. Mining efforts here have focused on automatically extracting document object model (DOM) structures out of documents.

3. **Web Usage Mining:** Web usage mining is the mining of log files and associated data from a particular web site to discover knowledge on browser and buyer behaviour on that site. In short, Web Mining can be seen to apply existing analysis techniques together with cutting edge technology to the plethora of data that the internet is generating.

Web Usage Mining is the application of data mining techniques to discover interesting usage patterns from Web data, in order to understand and better serve the needs of Web-based applications. Usage data captures the identity or origin of Web users along with their browsing behavior at aWeb site. Web usage mining itself can be classified further depending on the kind of usage data considered:

- **Web Server Data:** The user logs are collected by Web server. Typical data includes IP address, page reference and access time.
- **Application Server Data:** Commercial application servers such a have significant features to enable E-commerce applications to be built on top of them with little effort. A key feature is the ability to track various kinds of business events and log them in application server logs.
- **Application Level Data:** New kinds of events can be defined in an application, and logging can be turned on for them — generating histories of these specially defined events.

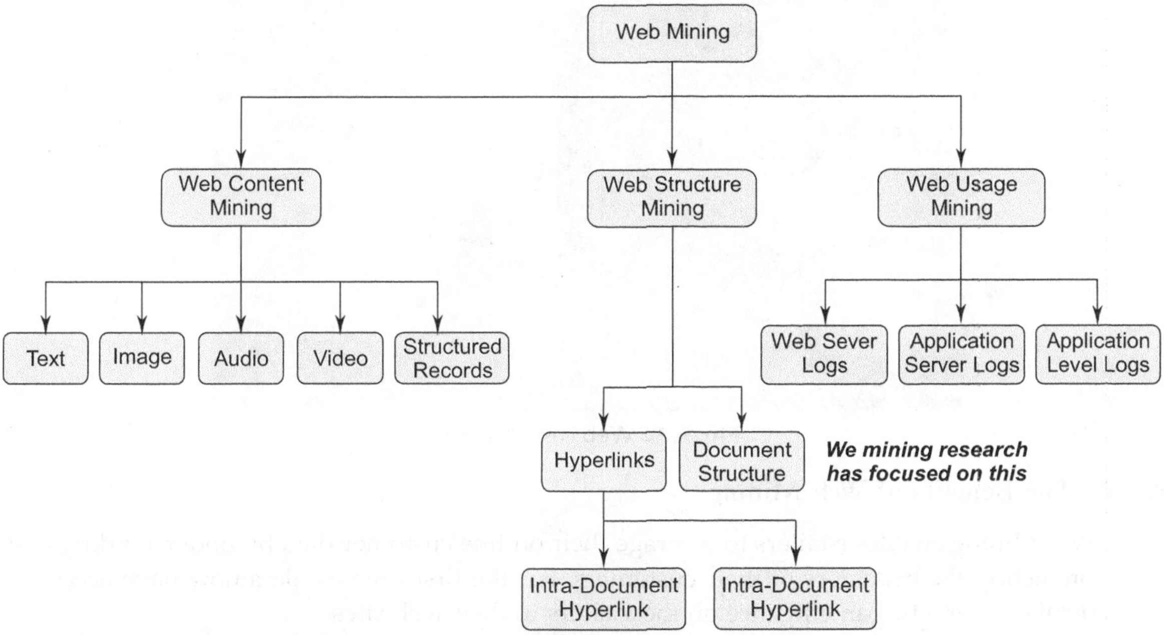

Fig. 9.2 Web mining taxonomy

9.5.2 Ranking Metrics — for Page Quality and Relevance

Searching the Web involves two main steps: Extracting the relevant pages to a query and ranking them according to their quality. Ranking is important as it helps the user look for "quality" pages that are relevant to the query. Different metrics have been proposed to rank Web pages according to their quality. We briefly discuss two of the prominent metrics.

PageRank: PageRank is a metric for ranking hypertext documents based on their quality. Page developed this metric for the popular search engine Google. The key idea is that a page has a high rank if it is pointed to by many highly ranked pages. So, the rank of a page depends upon the ranks of the pages pointing to it. This process is done iteratively till the rank of all the pages is determined. The rank of a page p can thus be written as:

$$\mathrm{PR}(p) = d/n + (1-d) \sum_{(q,p)\in G} \left(\frac{\mathrm{PR}(q)}{\mathrm{Outdegree}(q)} \right)$$

Here, n is the number of nodes in the graph and outdegree(q) is the number of hyperlinks on page q. Intuitively, the approach can be viewed as a stochastic analysis of a random walk on the Web graph. The first term in the right hand side of the equation corresponds to the probability that a random Web surfer arrives at a page p by typing the URL or from a bookmark, or may have a particular page as his/her homepage. Here, d is the probability that a random surfer chooses a URL directly, rather than traversing a link and $1 - d$ is the probability that a person arrives at a page by traversing a link. The second term in the right hand side of the equation corresponds to the probability of arriving at a page by traversing a link.

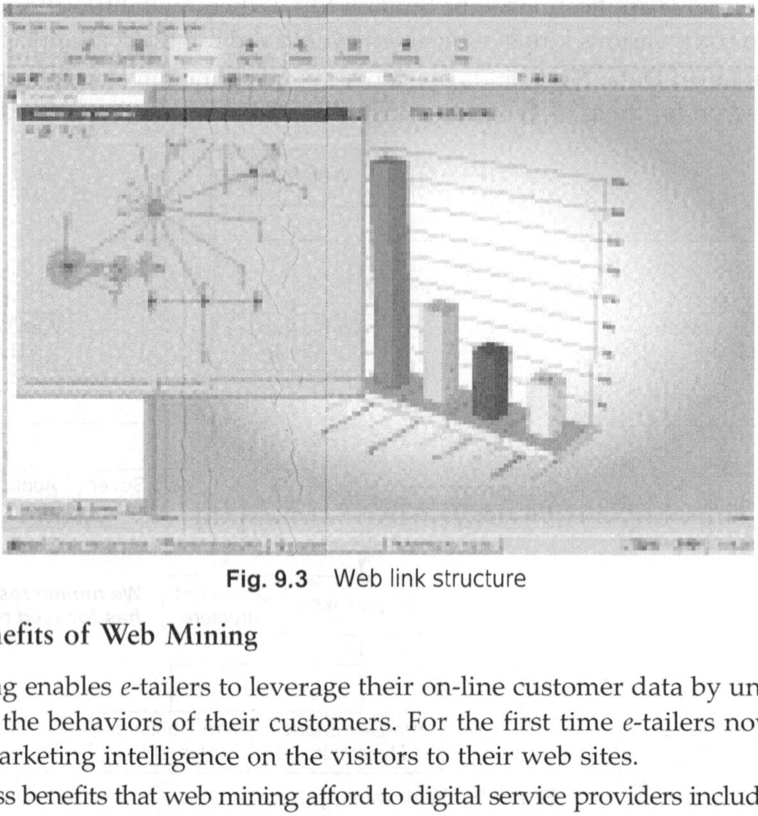

Fig. 9.3 Web link structure

9.5.3 The Benefits of Web Mining

- Web Mining enables *e*-tailers to leverage their on-line customer data by understanding and predicting the behaviors of their customers. For the first time *e*-tailers now have access to detailed marketing intelligence on the visitors to their web sites.
- The business benefits that web mining afford to digital service providers include personalization, collaborative filtering, enhanced customer support, product and service strategy definition, particle marketing and fraud detection.

In short, the ability to understand their customers' needs and to deliver the best and most appropriate service to those individual customers at any given moment.

9.6 TEXT MINING

Text databases (or document databases), which consist of large collections of documents from various sources, such as news articles, research papers, books, digital libraries, *e*-mail messages, and Web pages. Text databases are rapidly growing due to the increasing amount of information available in electronic forms, such as electronic publications, *e*-mail, CD-ROMs and the World Wide Web (which can also be viewed as a huge, interconnected, dynamic text database).

General definition includes all types of text processing that deal with finding, organizing and analyzing information.

A more formal definition restricts text mining to mean the creation of new information that is not obvious in a collection of documents.

New information is defined as a pattern trend, or relationship that cannot be easily gleaned by reading individual documents.

Text collection, in general, lacks the imposed structure of traditional database. The text expresses a huge range of information, but encodes the information in a form that is difficult to decipher automatically.

The nature of the text data normally unstructured characteristics, that deploys the development of separate text mining techniques. One way is to impsose a structure on the textual database and use any of the known data mining techniques meant for structured databases. The other approach would be to develop a very specific technique for mining that exploits the inherent characteristics of textual databases. Irrespective of the approach chosen for text mining, one cannot ignore the close interactions of other related subjects, such as computational linguistics, Natural Language Processing (NLP) and Information Retrieval (IR).

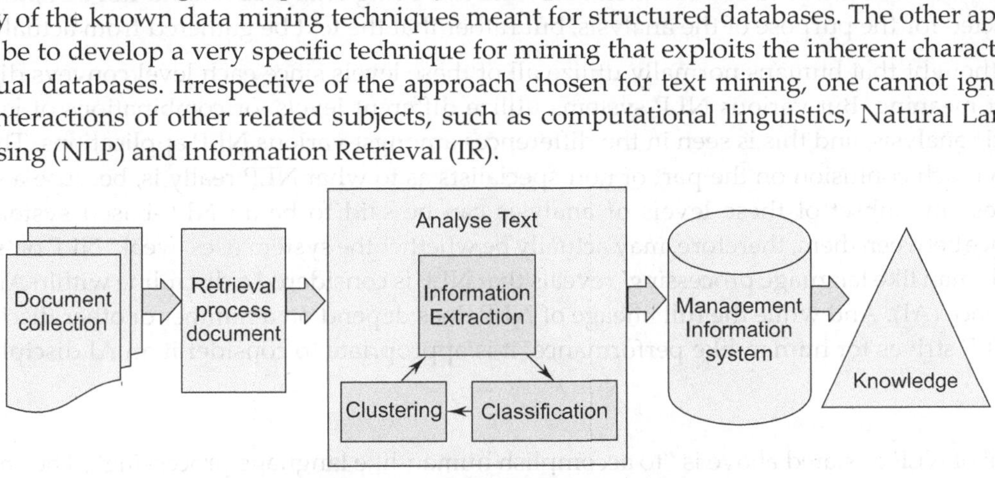

Fig. 9.4 Example of text mining

9.6.1 Origins of Text Mining

Information Retrieval: Search usually begin with a need for information. This information need could be a search for a fact, a procedural explanation or a list of references. Searches for facts are relatively easy to state in the form of a question.

Ex "what is the capital of Iceland?

"who is the president of India?

For the above example a simple keyword search – "capital and Iceland" – is sufficient to fetch references that contain the answer to the first question.

Second question the query "India president" would work as well

This assumes that the IR system contains the answer in one or more documents.

In most cases, procedural questions are not answered in a single sentence.

Natural Language Processing

Natural Language processing has come to mean the analysis or synthesis of natural text and not necessarily the understanding of text.

Natural Language Processing (NLP) is the computerized approach to analyzing text that is based on both a set of theories and a set of technologies. And, being a very active area of research and development, there is not a single agreed upon definition that would satisfy everyone, but there are some aspects, which would be part of any knowledgeable person's definition.

Definition: Natural Language Processing is a theoretically motivated range of computational techniques for analyzing and representing naturally occurring texts at one or more levels of linguistic analysis for the purpose of achieving human like language processing for a range of tasks or applications.

Several elements of this definition can be further detailed. Firstly the imprecise notion of 'range of computational techniques' is necessary because there are multiple methods or techniques from which to choose to accomplish a particular type of language analysis. 'Naturally occurring texts' can be of any language, mode, genre, etc.

The texts can be oral or written. The only requirement is that they be in a language used by humans to communicate to one another. Also, the text being analyzed should not be specifically constructed for the purpose of the analysis, but rather that the text be gathered from actual usage.

It is thought that humans normally utilize all of these levels since each level conveys different types of meaning. But various NLP systems utilize different levels, or combinations of levels of linguistic analysis, and this is seen in the differences amongst various NLP applications. This also leads to much confusion on the part of non-specialists as to what NLP really is, because a system that uses any subset of these levels of analysis can be said to be an NLP-based system. The difference between them, therefore, may actually be whether the system uses 'weak' NLP or 'strong' NLP. 'Human like language processing' reveals that NLP is considered a discipline within Artificial Intelligence (AI). And while the full lineage of NLP does depend on a number of other disciplines, since NLP strives for human-like performance, it is appropriate to consider it an AI discipline.

Goal

The goal of NLP as stated above is "to accomplish human-like language processing". The choice of the word 'processing' is very deliberate, and should not be replaced with 'understanding'. For although the field of NLP was originally referred to as Natural Language Understanding (NLU) in the early days of AI, it is well agreed today that while the goal of NLP is true NLU, that goal has not yet been accomplished. A full NLU System would be able to:

1. Paraphrase an input text
2. Translate the text into another language
3. Answer questions about the contents of the text
4. Draw inferences from the text

While NLP has made serious inroads into accomplishing goals 1 to 3, the fact that NLP systems cannot, of themselves, draw inferences from text, NLU still remains the goal of NLP.

9.6.2 Text Mining Observations

Unstructured documents are free texts, such as news stories. Traditionally, most of research uses bag of words to represent unstructured documents and extract different features form it

For an unstructured document, features are extracted to convert it to a structured form. Some of the important features are listed on next page.

- **Word Occurrence:** The bag of words or vector representation takes single words found in the training corpus as features ignoring the sequence in which the words occur. This representation is based on the statistic about single words in isolation. Such a feature is said to be Boolean, if we consider whether a word either occurs or does not occur in a document. The feature is said to be frequency based if the frequency of the word in a document is taken into consideration.
- **Stop Words:** The feature selection includes removing the case, punctuation, in frequent words, and stop words. A Good site for the set of stop-words for the English language www.dos.gla.alc.UK.
- **Latent Semantic Indexing:** Latent semantic indexing (LSI) transforms the original document vectors to a lower dimensional space by analyzing the correlational structure of terms in the document collection, such that similar documents that do not share terms are placed in the same topic.
- **Stemming:** Stemming is a process which reduces words to their morphological roots. For example, the words "informing", "informer", and "informed" would be stemmed to their common root " inform", and only the latter word is used as the feature instead of the former four.
- ***n*-GRAM:** Other feature representations are also possible, such as using information about word positions in the document, or using n-grams representation (word sequences of length up to n) (In WEBSOM)
- **Part-of Speech (POS):** One important feature is the POS. There can be 25 possible, values for POS tags. Most common tags are noun, verb, adjective and adverb. Thus, we can assign a number 1, 2, 3, 4, or 5, depending on whether the word is a noun, verb, adjective, adverb or any other, respectively.
- **Positional Collocations:** The values of this type of feature are the words that occur one or two position to the right or left of the given word.
- **Higher Order Feature:** Other features include phrases, document concept categories, terms, hypernyms, named entities, dates, email addresses, locations, organizations, or URLs. Theses features could be reduced further by applying some other feature selection techniques, such as information gain, mutual information, cross entropy, or odd ratio.

Once the features are extracted, the text is represented as structured data, and traditional data mining techniques can be used. The techniques include discovering frequent sets, frequent sequences and episode rules. We describe below the preprocessing stage to fund frequent episodes.

9.6.3 Measures for Text Retrieval

"Suppose that a text retrieval system has just retrieved a number of documents for me based on my input in the form of a query. How can we assess how 'accurate' or 'correct' the system was?" Let the set of documents relevant to a query be denoted as [Relevant], and the set of documents retrieved be denoted as [Retrieved]. There are two basic measures for assessing the quality of text retrieval:

Precision:

This is the percentage of retrieved documents that are in fact relevant to the query (i.e., "correct" responses). It is formally defined as

$$\text{Precision} = \frac{|\{\text{Relevant}\} \cap \{\text{Retrieved}\}|}{|\{\text{Retrieved}\}|}$$

Recall:

This is the percentage of documents that are relevant to the query and were in fact, retrieved. It is formally defined as

$$\text{Recall} = \frac{|\{\text{Relevant}\} \cap \{\text{Retrieved}\}|}{|\{\text{Retrieved}\}|}$$

9.6.4 Text Mining Tasks

On a collection of text database we will apply the techniques like association analysis, cluster analysis and other data mining techniques to discover the knowledge. The technique which will apply on the text database discussed below.

Keyword-Based Association Analysis

"What is keyword-based association analysis?" Such analysis collects sets of keywords or terms that occur frequently together and then finds the association or correlation relationships among them.

Like most of the analyses in text databases, association analysis first preprocesses the text data by parsing, stemming, removing stop words, and so on, and then evokes association-mining algorithms. In a document database, each document can be viewed as a transaction, while a set of keywords in the document can be considered as a set of items in the transaction. That is, the database is in the format

[document_id, a_set_of_keywords].

The problem of keyword association mining in document databases is thereby mapped to item association mining in transaction databases, where many interesting methods have been developed.

Notice that a set of frequently occurring consecutive or closely located keywords may form a term or a phrase. The association mining process can help detect compound associations, that is, domain-dependent terms or phrases, such as [Stanford, University] or [U.S. President, Barik, Obama], or non-compound associations, such as [dollars, shares, exchange, total, commission, stake, securities].

Mining based on these associations is referred to as "term level association mining" (as opposed to mining on individual words). Term recognition and term level association mining enjoy two advantages in text analysis:

1. Terms and phrases are automatically tagged so that there is no need for human effort in tagging documents.
2. The number of meaningless results is greatly reduces, as is the execution time of the mining algorithms.

With such term and phrase recognition, term level mining can be evoked to find associations among a set of detected terms and keywords. Some users may like to find associations between pairs of keywords or terms from a given set of keywords or phrases, whereas others may wish to find the maximal set of terms occurring together. Therefore, based on user mining requirements, standard association mining or max-pattern mining algorithms may be evoked.

Document Classification Analysis

Automated document classification is an important text-mining task since, with the existence of a tremendous number of on-line documents, it is tedious yet essential to be able to automatically organize such documents into classes so as to facilitate document retrieval and subsequent analysis.

A general procedure for performing document classification is as follows: First, a set of pre-classified documents is taken as the training as the training set. The training set is then analyzed in order to derive a classification scheme. Such a classification scheme often needs to be refined with a testing process. The so-derived classification scheme can be used for classification of other on-line documents.

This process appears similar to the classification of relational data. However, there is a fundamental difference. Relational data are well structured: each tuple is defined by a set of attribute-value pairs. For example, in the tuple [*sunny, warm, dry, not_windy, play_tennis*], the value "sunny" corresponds to the attribute weather_outlook, "warm" corresponds to the attribute temperature, and so on. The classification analysis decides which set of attribute-value pairs has the greatest discriminating power in determining whether or not a person is going to play tennis. On the other hand, document databases are not structured according to attribute-value pairs. That is, a set of keywords associated with a set of documents is not organized into a fixed set of attributes or dimensions. Therefore, commonly used relational data-oriented classification methods, such as decision tree analysis, cannot be used to classify document databases.

An effective method for document classification is to explore association-based classification, which classifies documents based on a set of associated, frequently occurring text patterns. Such an association -based classification method proceeds as follows: First, keywords and terms can be extracted by information retrieval and simple association analysis techniques. Second, concept hierarchies of keywords and terms can be obtained using available term classed, such as WordNet, or relying on expert knowledge, or some keyword classification systems. Documents in the training set can also be classified into class hierarchies. A term association mining method can then be applied to discover sets of associated terms that can be used to maximally distinguish one class of documents from others. This derives a set of association rules associated with each document class. Such classification rules can be ordered based on their occurrence frequency and discriminative power, and used to classify new documents. Such a kind of association-based document classifier has been proven effective. For Web document classification of document classes. Web linkage analysis methods are discussed in the next section.

Document clustering

It is a method of grouping the documents using clustering. Text clustering is another important task of text mining. Once the features of an unstructured text are identified or the structured data of the text is available, text clustering can be done by employing any of the clustering techniques discussed in the chapter cluster analysis.

Scatter/Gather

Clustering is not popular in large document collections because of its long run-time to build clusters. In smaller collections, it is effective in improving recall. Instead of merely providing a list of matching clusters in response to a query, an alternate use of clustering was proposed (cutting92). Clustering was used to iteratively assist the end user to find relevant documents.

Two operations-a scatter and gather — are executed alternately in every iteration. The scatter operation is viewed as a broad grouping of documents that are currently of interest. In contrast, the gather operation is the selection of a few specific clusters. The concepts for these two operations are modeled on the organization of a book.

The table of contents (TOC) can be viewed as list of clusters created from the text. Each cluster (chapter) gives a broad overview of the contents of a subtopic. An index at the end of the book is a more specific organization by keyword. If we know the right keywords, we can quickly locate information in a book using the index.

This is somewhat reminiscent of the organization of the web. Search engines allow researchers to quickly find information provided the keywords are accurate. Web directories are like a TOC to broadly search the web. Of course, unlike the web, the TOC of most books is less than two or three levels deep.

This modified approach alternates between the broad and specific models of search. The steps to use scatter/Gather are as follows.

1. Initially cluster all documents in the collection
2. Use a keyword-based query to fetch a list of clusters or specify a list of initial clusters.
3. Repeat in a loop

   3.1 Scatter: Cluster the documents from the selected clusters.

   3.2 Gather: Select a few clusters from the results.

   3.3 Terminate: Terminate if there are too few documents or too few clusters.

We begin by clustering all documents in the algorithm. Since this operation is performed prior to a search, an accurate clustering method can be used and run time is not a high priority, for simplicity, we will assume a flat cluster organization. But, this same algorithm will work for hierarchical cluster organizations as well.

9.6.5 Applications of Text Mining

The main Test Mining applications are most often used in the following sectors:

- Publishing and media.
- Telecommunications, energy and other services industries.
- Information technology sector and internet.
- Banks, insurance and financial markets.
- Political institutions, political analysts, public administration and legal documents.
- Pharmaceutical and research companies and healthcare.

SUMMARY

- Large amount of data in various complex forms like hypertext, multimedia, geographical, time series and text data have been growing rapidly for industrial transactions.
- Data mining is to mine complex types of data, including complex objects, spatial data, multimedia data, time-series data, text data, and the World Wide Web.
- Spatial data mining is the process of discovering interesting and previously un-known, but potentially useful patterns from large spatial datasets. Spatial data cubes that contain spatial dimensions and measures can be constructed.

- Temporal data mining is concerned with data mining of large sequential data sets. Time series database consists of sequence of value or events changing with time, such as stock market data, business transaction sequences, dynamic production process.
- Multimedia database system stores and manages a large collection of multimedia objects, such as audio data, image data, video data, sequence data, and hypertext data, which contain text, text markups and linkages.
- The World Wide Web has grown in the past few years from a small research community to the biggest and most popular way of communication and information dissemination. Everyday, the WWW grows by roughly a million electronic pages, adding to the hundreds of millions already on line.
- Web contains a rich and dynamic collection of hyperlink information, and access and usage information, providing rich source for data mining.
- Text mining is a relatively new practice derived from Information Retrieval (IR) and Natural Language Processing (NLP). Text mining covers more general text-processing techniques such as searching, extracting, and categorizing.

REVIEW QUESTIONS

1. Explain spatial data cube construction and spatial OLAP.
2. Design a spatial data warehouse that stores the highway traffic information so that people can easily see the average and peak time traffic flow by highway, by time of day, and by weekdays, and the traffic situation when a major accident occurs.
3. This data warehouse contains both spatial and temporal data. Propose one mining technique that can efficiently mine interesting patterns from such a spatial-temporal data warehouse.
4. Define web mining. What are the observations made in mining the Web for?
5. What is web usage mining? Explain with suitable example.
6. How to mine Multimedia databases? Explain.
7. What is sequential pattern mining? Explain.
8. Explain the construction of a multilayered web information base.
9. Discuss about mining text databases.
10. Explain the following:
    (*a*) Constriction and mining of object cubes
    (*b*) Mining associations in multimedia data
    (*c*) Periodicity analysis
    (*d*) Latent semantic indexing.

10

Introduction to Soft Computing Techniques

10.1 WHAT IS SOFT COMPUTING?

Soft computing differs from conventional (hard) computing in that, unlike hard computing, it is tolerant of imprecision, uncertainty, partial truth, and approximation. In effect, the role model for soft computing is the human mind. The guiding principle of soft computing is: Exploit the tolerance for imprecision, uncertainty, partial truth, and approximation to achieve tractability, robustness and low solution cost.

The basic ideas underlying soft computing in its current incarnation have links to many earlier influences, among them Zadeh's 1965 paper on fuzzy sets; the 1973 paper on the analysis of complex systems and decision processes; and the 1979 report (1981 paper) on possibility theory and soft data analysis. The inclusion of neural computing and genetic computing in soft computing came at a later point.

At this juncture, the principal constituents of Soft Computing (SC) are Fuzzy Logic (FL), Neural Computing (NC), Evolutionary Computation (EC) Machine Learning (ML) and Probabilistic Reasoning (PR), with the latter subsuming belief networks, chaos theory and parts of learning theory. What is important to note is that soft computing is not a mélange (combination). Rather, it is a partnership in which each of the partners contributes a distinct methodology for addressing problems in its domain. In this perspective, the principal constituent methodologies in Soft Computing are complementary rather than competitive. Furthermore, soft computing may be viewed as a foundation component for the emerging field of conceptual intelligence.

- Neural Networks
- Fuzzy Systems
- Evolutionary Computation
- Machine Learning
- Probabilistic Reasoning

10.2 IMPORTANCE OF SOFT COMPUTING

The complementarity of FL, NC, and PR has an important consequence: in many cases a problem can be solved most effectively by using FL, NC, and PR in combination rather than exclusively. A striking example of a particularly effective combination is what has come to be known as "neurofuzzy systems." Such systems are becoming increasingly visible as consumer products ranging from air conditioners and washing machines to photocopiers and camcorders. Less visible but perhaps even more important are neurofuzzy systems in industrial applications. What is particularly significant is that in both consumer products and industrial systems, the employment of soft computing techniques leads to systems which have high MIQ (Machine Intelligence Quotient).

In large measure, it is the high MIQ of SC-based systems that accounts for the rapid growth in the number and variety of applications of soft computing. In many ways, soft computing represents a significant paradigm shift in the aims of computing — a shift which reflects the fact that the human mind, unlike present day computers, possesses a remarkable ability to store and process information which is pervasively imprecise, uncertain and lacking in categoricity.

10.3 FUZZY LOGIC

The concept of Fuzzy Logic (FL) was conceived by Lotfi Zadeh, a professor at the University of California at Berkley, and presented not as a control methodology, but as a way of processing data by allowing partial set membership rather than crisp set membership or non-membership.

This approach to set theory was not applied to control systems until the 70's due to insufficient small-computer capability prior to that time. Professor Zadeh reasoned that people do not require precise, numerical information input, and yet they are capable of highly adaptive control. If feedback controllers could be programmed to accept noisy, imprecise input, they would be much more effective and perhaps easier to implement.

Fuzzy logic is a superset of conventional (Boolean) logic that has been extended to handle the concept of partial truth — truth values between "completely true" and "completely false".

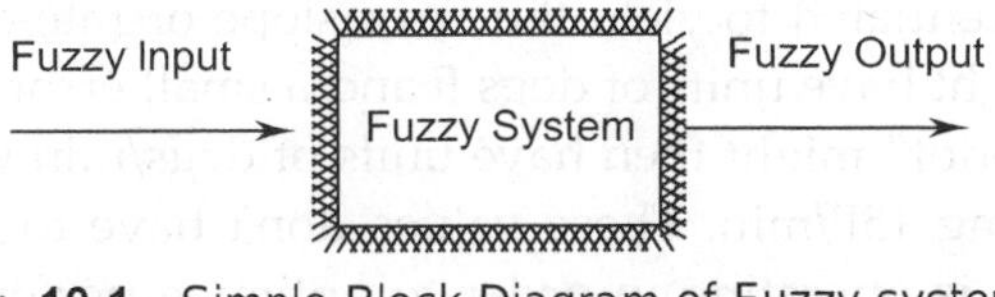

Fig. 10.1 Simple Block Diagram of Fuzzy systems

Fuzzy Logic is a problem-solving control system methodology that lends itself to implementation in systems ranging from simple, small, embedded micro-controllers to large, networked, multi-channel PC or workstation-based data acquisition and control systems. It can be implemented in hardware, software, or a combination of both. FL provides a simple way to arrive at a definite conclusion based upon vague, ambiguous, imprecise, noisy, or missing input information. FL's approach to control problems mimics how a person would make decisions, only much faster.

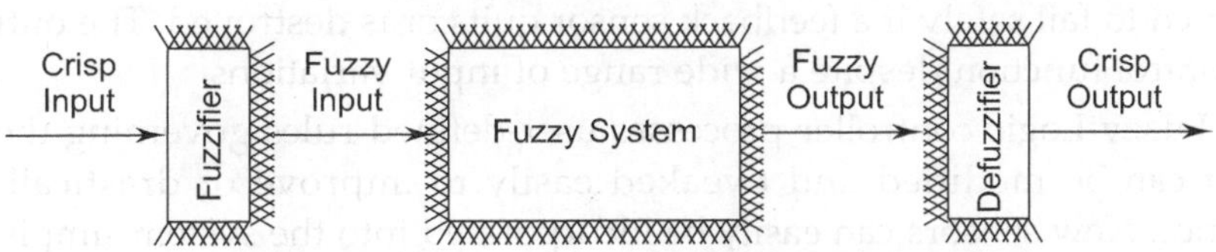

Fig. 10.2 Simple Fuzzy crisp inputs to get the fuzzy inputs

10.3.1 Fuzzy Logic v/s Conventional Control Methods

Fuzzy Logic incorporates a simple, rule-based IF X AND Y THEN Z approach to a solving control problem rather than attempting to model a system mathematically. The FL model is empirically-based, relying on an operator's experience rather than their technical understanding of the system.

For example, rather than dealing with temperature control in terms such as "SP =500F", "T <1000F", or "210C <TEMP <220C", terms like "IF (process is too cool) AND (process is getting colder) THEN (add heat to the process)" or "IF (process is too hot) AND (process is heating rapidly) THEN (cool the process quickly)" are used. These terms are imprecise and yet very descriptive of what must actually happen. Consider what you do in the shower if the temperature is too cold: you will make the water comfortable very quickly with little trouble. FL is capable of mimicking this type of behavior but at very high rate.

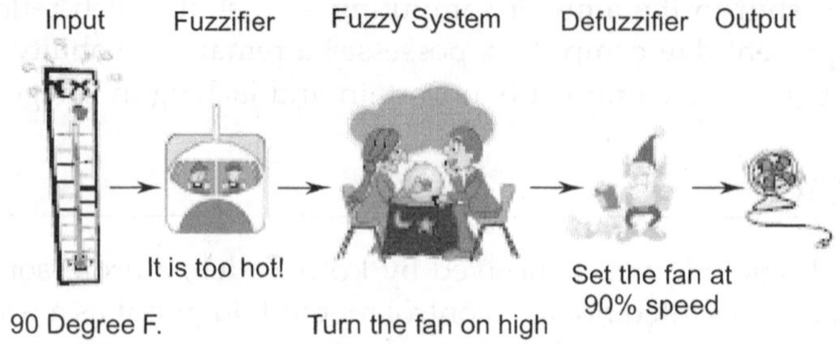

Fig. 10.3 Example Fuzzy Systems

10.3.2 How Does Fuzzy Logic Works

Fuzzy Logic requires some numerical parameters in order to operate such as what is considered significant error and significant rate-of-change-of-error, but exact values of these numbers are usually not critical unless very responsive performance is required in which case empirical tuning would determine them. For example, a simple temperature control system could use a single temperature feedback sensor whose data is subtracted from the command signal to compute "error" and then time-differentiated to yield the error slope or rate-of-change-of-error, hereafter called "error-dot". Error might have units of degs F and a small error considered to be 2F while a large error is 5F. The "error-dot" might then have units of degs/min with a small error-dot being 5F/min and a large one being 15F/min. These values don't have to be symmetrical and can be "tweaked" once the system is operating in order to optimize performance. Generally, FL is so forgiving that the system will probably work the first time without any tweaking.

10.3.3 Uses of Fuzzy-Logic

Fuzzy Logic offers several unique features that make it a particularly good choice for many control problems.

1. It is inherently robust since it does not require precise, noise-free inputs and can be programmed to fail safely if a feedback sensor quits or is destroyed. The output control is a smooth control function despite a wide range of input variations.
2. Since the Fuzzy Logic controller processes user-defined rules governing the target control system, it can be modified and tweaked easily to improve or drastically alter system performance. New sensors can easily be incorporated into the system simply by generating appropriate governing rules.

3. Fuzzy Logic is not limited to a few feedback inputs and one or two control outputs, nor is it necessary to measure or compute rate-of-change parameters in order for it to be implemented. Any sensor data that provides some indication of a system's actions and reactions is sufficient. This allows the sensors to be inexpensive and imprecise thus keeping the overall system cost and complexity low.
4. Because of the rule-based operation, any reasonable number of inputs can be processed (1–8 or more) and numerous outputs (1–4 or more) generated, although defining the rulebase quickly becomes complex if too many inputs and outputs are chosen for a single implementation since rules defining their interrelations must also be defined. It would be better to break the control system into smaller chunks and use several smaller FL controllers distributed on the system, each with more limited responsibilities.
5. Fuzzy Logic can control nonlinear systems that would be difficult or impossible to model mathematically. This opens doors for control systems that would normally be deemed unfeasible for automation.

10.3.4 How Fuzzy Logic Used

1. Define the control objectives and criteria: What am I trying to control? What do I have to do to control the system? What kind of response do I need? What are the possible (probable) system failure modes?
2. Determine the input and output relationships and choose a minimum number of variables for input to the FL engine (typically error and rate-of-change-of-error).
3. Using the rule-based structure of FL, break the control problem down into a series of IF X AND Y THEN Z rules that define the desired system output response for given system input conditions. The number and complexity of rules depends on the number of input parameters that are to be processed and the number fuzzy variables associated with each parameter. If possible, use at least one variable and its time derivative. Although it is possible to use a single, instantaneous error parameter without knowing its rate of change, this cripples the system's ability to minimize overshoot for a step inputs.
4. Create FL membership functions that define the meaning (values) of Input/Output terms used in the rules.
5. Create the necessary pre-and post-processing FL routines if implementing in software, otherwise program the rules into the FL hardware engine.
6. Test the system, evaluate the results, tune the rules and membership functions, and retest until satisfactory results are obtained.

Linguistic Variables

In 1973, Professor Lotfi Zadeh proposed the concept of linguistic or "fuzzy" variables. Think of them as linguistic objects or words, rather than numbers. The sensor input is a noun, *e.g.*, "temperature", "displacement", "velocity", "flow", "pressure", etc. Since error is just the difference, it can be thought of the same way. The fuzzy variables themselves are adjectives that modify the variable (*e.g.*, "large positive" error, "small positive" error ,"zero" error, "small negative" error, and "large negative" error). As a minimum, one could simply have "positive", "zero", and "negative" variables for each of the parameters. Additional ranges such as "very large" and "very small" could also be added to extend the responsiveness to exceptional or very nonlinear conditions, but aren't necessary in a basic system.

10.3.5 The Rule Matrix

The fuzzy parameters of error (command-feedback) and error-dot (rate-of-change-of-error) were modified by the adjectives "negative", "zero", and "positive". To picture this, imagine the simplest practical implementation, a 3-by-3 matrix. The columns represent "negative error", "zero error", and "positive error" inputs from left to right. The rows represent "negative","zero", and "positive" "error-dot" input from top to bottom. This planar construct is called a rule matrix. It has two input conditions, "error" and "error-dot", and one output response conclusion (at the intersection of each row and column). In this case there are nine possible logical products (AND) output response conclusions.

Although not absolutely necessary, rule matrices usually have an odd number of rows and columns to accommodate a "zero" center row and column region. This may not be needed as long as the functions on either side of the center overlap somewhat and continuous dithering of the output is acceptable since the "zero" regions correspond to "no change" output responses the lack of this region will cause the system to continually hunt for "zero". It is also possible to have a different number of rows than columns. This occurs when numerous degrees of inputs are needed. The maximum number of possible rules is simply the product of the number of rows and columns, but definition of all of these rules may not be necessary since some input conditions may never occur in practical operation. The primary objective of this construct is to map out the universe of possible inputs while keeping the system sufficiently under control.

Starting the Process

The first step in implementing FL is to decide exactly what is to be controlled and how. For example, suppose we want to design a simple proportional temperature controller with an electric heating element and a variable-speed cooling fan. A positive signal output calls for 0–100 percent heat while a negative signal output calls for 0–100 percent cooling. Control is achieved through proper balance and control of these two active devices.

SIMPLE FL CONTROL SYSTEM

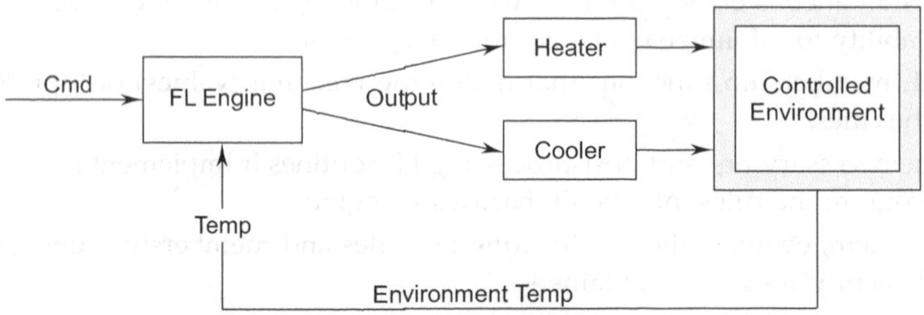

Cmd: Targettemperature
Temp: Feedback sensor in controlled environment
Error: Cmd-Temp (+ = too cold, – = too hot)
Error-dot: Time derivation or Error (+ = getting hotter, - = getting cooler)
Output: HEAT or NO CHANGE or COOL

Fig. 10.4 A simple block diagram of the control system.

It is necessary to establish a meaningful system for representing the linguistic variables in the matrix. For this example, the following will be used:

"N" = "negative" error or error-dot input level
"Z" = "zero" error or error-dot input level
"P" = "positive" error or error-dot input level

"H" = "Heat" output response
"-" = "No Change" to current output
"C" = "Cool" output response

Define the minimum number of possible input product combinations and corresponding output response conclusions using these terms. For a three-by-three matrix with heating and cooling output responses, all nine rules will need to be defined. The conclusions to the rules with the linguistic variables associated with the output response for each rule are transferred to the matrix.

10.3.6 What is Being Controlled and How

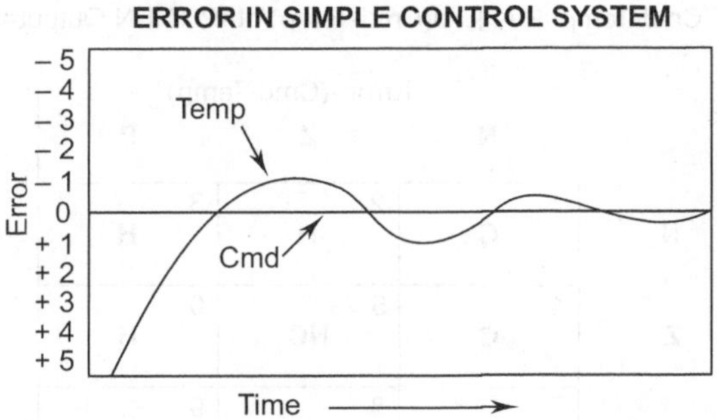

Fig. 10.5 Typical control system response

Figure 10.5 shows what command and error look like in a typical control system relative to the command set point as the system hunts for stability. Definitions are also shown for this example.

DEFINITIONS:

INPUT#1: ("Error", positive (P), zero (Z), negative (N))

INPUT#2: ("Error-dot", positive (P), zero (Z), negative (N))

CONCLUSION: ("Output", Heat (H), No Change (-), Cool (C))

INPUT#1 System Status

Error = Command-Feedback

P=Too cold, Z=Just right, N=Too hot

INPUT#2 System Status

Error-dot = d(Error)/dt

P=Getting hotter Z=Not changing N=Getting colder

OUTPUT Conclusion & System Response

Output H = Call for heating - = Don't change anything C = Call for cooling

SYSTEM OPERATING RULES

Linguistic rules describing the control system consist of two parts; an antecedent block (between the IF and THEN) and a consequent block (following THEN). Depending on the system, it may not be necessary to evaluate every possible input combination (for 5-by-5 & up matrices) since some may rarely or never occur. By making this type of evaluation, usually done by an experienced operator, fewer rules can be evaluated, thus simplifying the processing logic and perhaps even improving the FL system performance.

RULE STRUCTURE & RULE MATRIX

Antecedent Block | Consequent Block

1. IF Cmd-Temp=N AND d(Cmd-Temp)/dt=N THEN Output=C
2. IF Cmd-Temp=Z AND d(Cmd-Temp)/dt=N THEN Output=H
3. IF Cmd-Temp=P AND d(Cmd-Temp)/dt=N THEN Output=H
4. IF Cmd-Temp=N AND d(Cmd-Temp)/dt=Z THEN Output=C
5. IF Cmd-Temp=Z AND d(Cmd-Temp)/dt=Z THEN Output=NC
6. IF Cmd-Temp=P AND d(Cmd-Temp)/dt=Z THEN Output=H
7. IF Cmd-Temp=N AND d(Cmd-Temp)/dt=P THEN Output=C
8. IF Cmd-Temp=Z AND d(Cmd-Temp)/dt=P THEN Output=C
9. IF Cmd-Temp=P AND d(Cmd-Temp)/dt=P THEN Output=H

Error-dot-d(cmd-Temp)(dt) \ Error -(Cmd-Temp)	N	Z	P
N	1 C	2 H	3 H
Z	4 C	5 NC	6 H
P	7 C	8 C	9 H

Fig. 10.6 The rule structure

After transferring the conclusions from the nine rules to the matrix there is a noticeable symmetry to the matrix. This suggests (but doesn't guarantee) a reasonably well-behaved (linear) system. This implementation may prove to be too simplistic for some control problems, however it does illustrate the process. Additional degrees of error and error-dot may be included if the desired system response calls for this. This will increase the rule base size and complexity but may also increase the quality of the control. Figure 9.6 shows the rule matrix derived from the previous rules.

10.3.7 Membership Functions

The membership function is a graphical representation of the magnitude of participation of each input. It associates a weighting with each of the inputs that are processed, define functional overlap between inputs, and ultimately determines an output response. The rules use the input membership values as weighting factors to determine their influence on the fuzzy output sets of the final output conclusion. Once the functions are inferred, scaled, and combined, they are defuzzified into a crisp output which drives the system. There are different membership functions associated with each input and output response. Some features to note are:

SHAPE — triangular is common, but bell, trapezoidal, haversine and, exponential have been used. More complex functions are possible but require greater computing overhead to implement. HEIGHT or magnitude (usually normalized to 1) WIDTH (of the base of function), SHOULDERING (locks height at maximum if an outer function. Shouldered functions evaluate as 1.0 past their center) CENTER points (center of the member function shape) OVERLAP (N&Z, Z&P, typically about 50% of width but can be less).

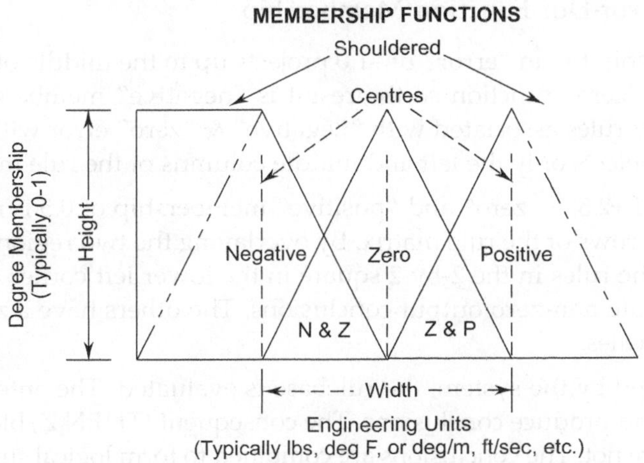

Fig. 10.7 The features of a membership function

Figure 10.7 illustrates the features of the triangular membership function which is used in this example because of its mathematical simplicity. Other shapes can be used but the triangular shape lends itself to this illustration.

The degree of membership (DOM) is determined by plugging the selected input parameter (error or error-dot) into the horizontal axis and projecting vertically to the upper boundary of the membership function(s).

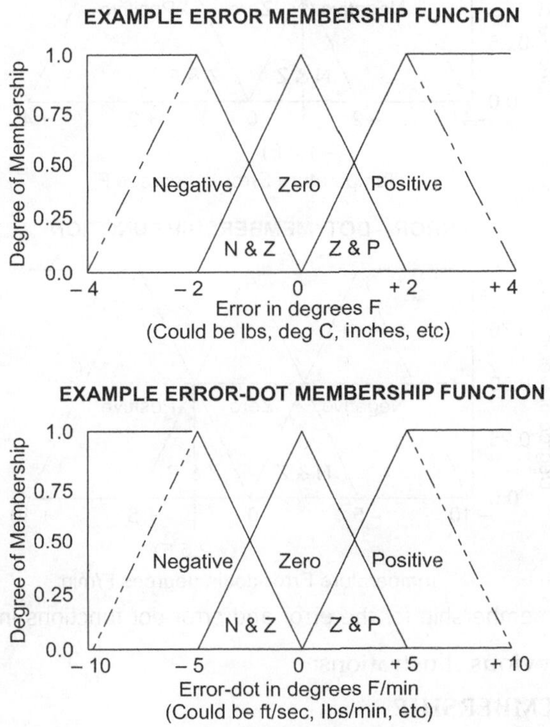

Fig. 10.8 A sample case

In Fig. 10.8, consider an "error" of –1.0 and an "error-dot" of +2.5. These particular input conditions indicate that the feedback has exceeded the command and is still increasing.

10.3.8 Error and Error-Dot Function Membership

The degree of membership for an "error" of –1.0 projects up to the middle of the overlapping part of the "negative" and "zero" function so the result is "negative" membership = 0.5 and "zero" membership = 0.5. Only rules associated with "negative" & "zero" error will actually apply to the output response. This selects only the left and middle columns of the rule matrix.

For an "error-dot" of +2.5, a "zero" and "positive" membership of 0.5 is indicated. This selects the middle and bottom rows of the rule matrix. By overlaying the two regions of the rule matrix, it can be seen that only the rules in the 2-by-2 square in the lower left corner (rules 4, 5, 7, 8) of the rules matrix will generate non-zero output conclusions. The others have a zero weighting due to the logical AND in the rules.

As inputs are received by the system, the rulebase is evaluated. The antecedent (IF X AND Y) blocks test the inputs and produce conclusions. The consequent (THEN Z) blocks of some rules are satisfied while others are not. The conclusions are combined to form logical sums. These conclusions feed into the inference process where each response output member function's firing strength (0 to 1) is determined.

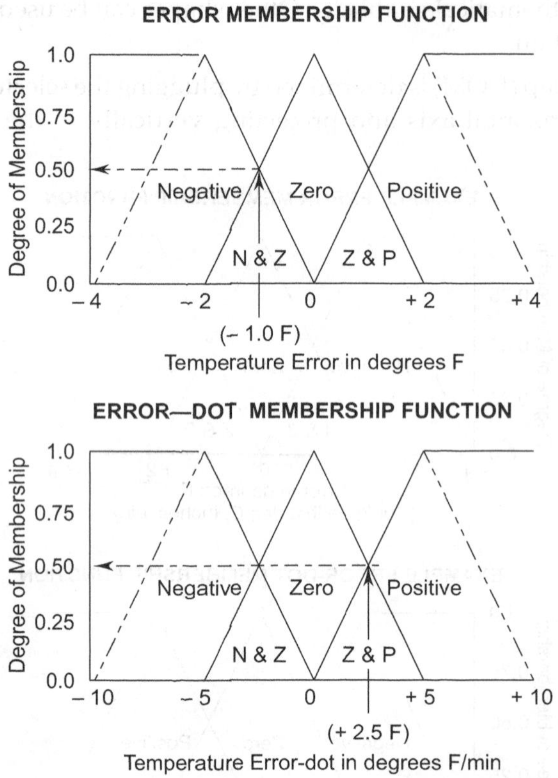

Fig. 10.9 Degree of membership for the error and error-dot functions in the current example

Data summary from previous illustrations:

INPUT DEGREE OF MEMBERSHIP

"error" = –1.0: "negative" = 0.5 and "zero" = 0.5

"error-dot" = +2.5: "zero" = 0.5 and "positive" = 0.5

ANTECEDENT & CONSEQUENT BLOCKS (e = error, er = error-dot or error-rate)

Now referring back to the rules, plug in the membership function weights from above. "Error" selects rules 1, 2, 4, 5, 7, 8 while "error-dot" selects rules 4 through 9. "Error" and "error-dot" for all rules are combined to a logical product (LP or AND, that is the minimum of either term). Of the nine rules selected, only four (rules 4, 5, 7, 8) fire or have non-zero results. This leaves fuzzy output response magnitudes for only "Cooling" and "No_Change" which must be inferred, combined, and defuzzified to return the actual crisp output. In the rule list below, the following definitions apply: (e)=error, (er)=error-dot

1. If (e < 0) AND (er < 0) then Cool 0.5 & 0.0 = 0.0
2. If (e = 0) AND (er < 0) then Heat 0.5 & 0.0 = 0.0
3. If (e > 0) AND (er < 0) then Heat 0.0 & 0.0 = 0.0
4. If (e < 0) AND (er = 0) then Cool 0.5 & 0.5 = 0.5
5. If (e = 0) AND (er = 0) then No_Chng 0.5 & 0.5 = 0.5
6. If (e > 0) AND (er = 0) then Heat 0.0 & 0.5 = 0.0
7. If (e < 0) AND (er > 0) then Cool 0.5 & 0.5 = 0.5
8. If (e = 0) AND (er > 0) then Cool 0.5 & 0.5 = 0.5
9. If (e > 0) AND (er > 0) then Heat 0.0 & 0.5 = 0.0

Fuzzy Logic provides a completely different, unorthodox way to approach a control problem. This method focuses on what the system should do rather than trying to understand how it works. One can concentrate on solving the problem rather than trying to model the system mathematically, if that is even possible. This almost invariably leads to quicker, cheaper solutions. Once understood, this technology is not difficult to apply and the results are usually quite surprising and pleasing.

10.4 EVOLUTIONARY COMPUTATIONS

Evolutionary computation is the study of computational systems that use ideas and get inspiration from natural evolution. Its techniques can be applied to optimization, learning and design.

Evolutionary Computing is a collection of 'nature-inspired' heuristic optimization techniques, *e.g.*,

- Genetic Algorithms
- Genetic Programming
- Evolutionary Strategies

10.4.1 History

1859 - publication of the 'Origin of Species' by one Charles Darwin

1865 - Gregor Mendel presents his work on 'Experiments in Plant Hybridisation' demonstrated the particulate nature of inheritance.

Evolutionary ideas were being applied in optimisation as early as the mid 20th century, e.g.

- Box (1957) Evolutionary operation: a method for increasing industrial productivity. Applied Statistics.
- Bremermann (1962) Optimization through evolution and recombination. In: Self-Organizing Systems.

In the 1970's Genetic Algorithms became a prominent research area

John Holland presented a mathematical definition of GAs, and theory explaining their performance.
Holland (1975) Adaptation in Natural and Artificial Systems

10.5 GENETIC ALGORITHMS

10.5.1 Foundations of Science

In the mid 1800s, 1859 to be exact, a British naturalist named Charles Darwin published a book that would change the way humans view the world. In this book, The Origin of Species, Darwin proposed that humans, and in fact all creatures, were not put on this planet by God and made unchanging, but rather that they evolved from other creatures. At the time, the idea sounded preposterous, but time and time again have we discovered that he may be correct. Advances in technology have made it possible for us to read our DNA and that of other creatures, and what it has shown us is that we aren't as different from other creatures as we think. Over time, creatures change to adapt to their environment to survive and thrive.

One of the most striking examples of this is the Galapagos Islands. Located in the Pacific Ocean, off the coast of Ecuador, this series of islands is one of the most prominent examples of evolution and adaptation. The island contains many species not found anywhere else on the planet, including several species of birds that share many characteristics; too many for it to be a coincidence. It is believed that many birds were blown to the islands by winds and were unable to get back. Over time, the birds spread throughout the islands and began to change to better survive in the differing environments of the islands. Some birds developed large, strong beaks suited to cracking nuts, others long, narrow beaks more suitable for digging bugs out of wood.

The birds that had these characteristics when blown to the island survived longer than other birds. This allowed them to reproduce more and therefore have more offspring that also had this unique characteristic. Those without the characteristic gradually died out from starvation. Eventually all of the birds had a type of beak that helped it survive on its island. This is the process of natural selection and evolution. The individuals themselves do not change, but those that survive better, or have a higher fitness, will survive longer and produce more offspring. This continues to happen, with the individuals becoming more suited to their environment every generation. It was this continuous improvement that inspired computer scientists, one of the most prominent being John Holland, to create genetic algorithms.

10.5.2 Introduction to Genetic Algorithms

Many human inventions were inspired by nature. An artificial neural network is one example. Another example is *Genetic Algorithms* (GA). GAs search is by simulating evolution, starting from an initial set of solutions or hypotheses, and generating successive "generations" of solutions. This particular branch of AI was inspired by the way living things evolved into more successful organisms in nature. The main idea is *survival of the fittest*, a.k.a. *natural selection*.

This is an introduction to genetic algorithm methods for optimization. Genetic algorithms were formally introduced in the United States in the 1970s by John Holland at University of Michigan. The continuing price/performance improvement of computational systems has made them attractive for some types of optimization. In particular, genetic algorithms work very well on mixed (continuous *and* discrete), combinatorial problems. They are less susceptible to getting 'stuck' at local optima than gradient search methods. But they tend to be computationally expensive.

To use a genetic algorithm, you must represent a solution to your problem as a *genome* (or *chromosome*). The genetic algorithm then creates a population of solutions and applies genetic operators such as mutation and crossover to evolve the solutions in order to find the best one(s).

This presentation outlines some of the basics of genetic algorithms. The three most important aspects of using genetic algorithms are:

1. Definition of the objective function
2. Definition and implementation of the genetic representation
3. Definition and implementation of the genetic operators.

Once these three have been defined, the generic genetic algorithm should work fairly well. Beyond that you can try many different variations to improve performance, find multiple optima (species—if they exist), or parallelize the algorithms.

Genetic algorithms are one of the best ways to solve a problem for which little is known. They are a very general algorithm and so will work well in any search space. All you need to know is what you need the solution to be able to do well, and a genetic algorithm will be able to create a high quality solution. Genetic algorithms use the principles of selection and evolution to produce several solutions to a given problem.

Genetic algorithms tend to thrive in an environment in which there is a very large set of candidate solutions and in which the search space is uneven and has many hills and valleys. True, genetic algorithms will do well in any environment, but they will be greatly outclassed by more situation specific algorithms in the simpler search spaces. Therefore you must keep in mind that genetic algorithms are not always the best choice. Sometimes they can take quite a while to run and are therefore not always feasible for real time use. They are, however, one of the most powerful methods with which to (relatively) quickly create high quality solutions to a problem. Now, before we start, I'm going to provide you with some key terms so that makes sense.

- Individual - Any possible solution.
- Search Space - All possible solutions to the problem.
- Trait - Possible aspect of an individual.
- Allele - Possible settings for a trait
- Locus - The position of a gene on the chromosome.
- Genome - Collection of all chromosomes for an individual.
- Chromosome - a solution to the problem the GA is solving, encoded as a fixed length string in some finite alphabet or Blueprint for an individual.
- Gene - a position on the chromosome which can take a particular value Locus - see gene.
- Allele - a value that a gene can take (*e.g.*, 0 or 1 in binary chromosomes).
- Population - the set of chromosomes the GA is acting on.
- Fitness - the objective value of the solution a chromosome encodes for a problem.
- Fitness/objective function - the function that returns the objective value of a given solution.
- Selection - the mechanism for choosing chromosomes to reproduce, based on their fitness.
- Parent - a chromosome selected for reproduction.

- Offspring - the chromosome resulting from reproduction of one or more Parents.
- Crossover - the process of recombining alleles from multiple parents during reproduction to produce offspring.
- Mutation - the process of randomly replacing offsprings' alleles with randomly chosen alternatives during reproduction.

10.5.3 Basics of Genetic Algorithms

The most common type of genetic algorithm works like this: a population is created with a group of individuals created randomly. The individuals in the population are then evaluated. The evaluation function is provided by the programmer and gives the individuals a score based on how well they perform at the given task. Two individuals are then selected based on their fitness, the higher the fitness, the higher and the chance of being selected. These individuals then "reproduce" to create one or more offspring, after which the offspring are mutated randomly. This continues until a suitable solution has been found or a certain number of generations have passed, depending on the needs of the programmer.

Selection

A key idea of the GA is that parents should be selected based on their fitness. While there are many different types of selection, here we will cover the most common type — roulette wheel selection. In roulette wheel selection, individuals are given a probability of being selected that is directly proportionate to their fitness.

Each chromosome i in the population P is assigned a probability of selection p_i based on its fitness f_i as a proportion of total population fitness:

$$p_i = \frac{f_i}{\sum_{j \in P} f_i}$$

Two individuals are then chosen randomly based on these probabilities and produce offspring. Pseudo-code for a roulette wheel selection algorithm is shown below.

```
for all members of population
  sum += fitness of this individual
end for
for all members of population
  probability = sum of probabilities + (fitness / sum)
  sum of probabilities += probability
end for
loop until new population is full
    do this twice
      number = Random between 0 and 1
    for all members of population
      if number > probability but less than next probability
          then you have been selected
```

```
    end for
  end
  create offspring
  end loop
```

While this code is very general and will obviously not compile, it illustrates the basic structure of a selection algorithm. Besides, you should write the code yourself, you learn better that way.

Having selected a parent we then reproduce that parent according to our operators, parameters, etc.

According to our parameters we may apply crossover, and/or mutation, and/or any other operators. Often crossover rate (probability of applying crossover during reproduction) is referred to as *x* Similarly mutation rate (per gene probability of mutation during reproduction) by μ

Crossover

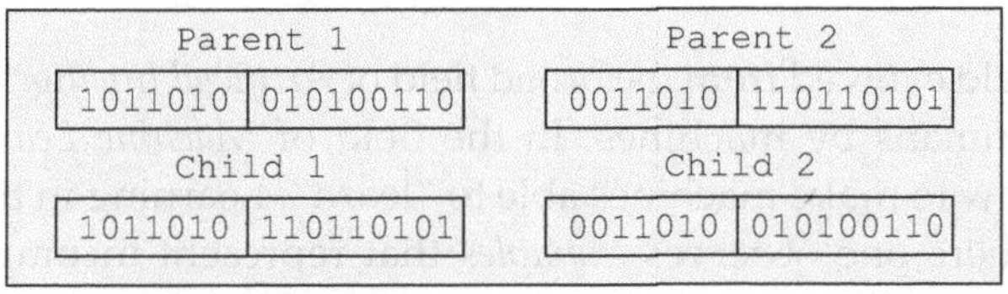

So now you have selected your individuals, and you know that you are supposed to somehow produce offspring with them, but how should you go about doing it? The most common solution is something called crossover, and while there are many different kinds of crossover, the most common type is single point crossover. In single point crossover, you choose a locus at which you swap the remaining alleles from on parent to the other.

This is complex and is best understood visually. As you can see, the children take one section of the chromosome from each parent. The point at which the chromosome is broken depends on the randomly selected crossover point. This particular method is called single point crossover because only one crossover point exists. Sometimes only child 1 or child 2 is created, but oftentimes both offspring are created and put into the new population. Crossover does not always occur, however. Sometimes, based on a set probability, no crossover occurs and the parents are copied directly to the new population. The probability of crossover occurring is usually 60% to 70%.

Mutation

```
Before: 1101101001101110
After:  1101100001101110
```

After selection and crossover, you now have a new population full of individuals. Some are directly copied, and others are produced by crossover. In order to ensure that the individuals are not all exactly the same, you allow for a small chance of mutation. You loop through all the alleles of all the individuals, and if that allele is selected for mutation, you can either change it by a small amount or replace it with a new value. The probability of mutation is usually between 1 and 2 tenths of a percent. A visual for mutation is shown below.

As you can easily see, mutation is fairly simple. You just change the selected alleles based on what you feel is necessary and move on. Mutation is, however, vital to ensuring genetic diversity within the population.

Applications

Genetic algorithms are a very effective way of quickly finding a reasonable solution to a complex problem. Granted they aren't instantaneous, or even close, but they do an excellent job of searching through a large and complex search space. Genetic algorithms are most effective in a search space for which little is known. You may know exactly what you want a solution to do but have no idea how you want it to go about doing it. This is where genetic algorithms thrive. They produce solutions that solve the problem in ways you may never have even considered. Then again, they can also produce solutions that only work within the test environment and flounder once you try to use them in the real world. Put simply: use genetic algorithms for everything you cannot easily do with another algorithm.

10.6 MACHINE LEARNING

10.6.1 Introduction

The Machine Learning field evolved from the broad field of *Artificial Intelligence*, which aims to mimic intelligent abilities of humans by machines. In the field of *Machine Learning* one considers the important question of how to make machines able to "learn". Learning in this context is understood as *inductive inference*, where one observes *examples* that represent incomplete information about some "statistical phenomenon".

In *unsupervised* learning one typically tries to uncover hidden regularities (*e.g.*, clusters) or to detect anomalies in the data (for instance some unusual machine function or a network intrusion). In *supervised learning*, there is a *label* associated with each example. It is supposed to be the answer to a question about the example. If the label is discrete, then the task is called *classification problem* — otherwise, for real valued labels we speak of a *regression problem*. Based on these examples (including the labels), one is particularly interested to *predict* the answer for other cases before they are explicitly observed. Hence, learning is not only a question of remembering but also of *generalization to unseen cases*.

An important task in Machine Learning is *classification*, also referred to as pattern recognition, where one attempts to build algorithms capable of automatically constructing methods for distinguishing between different exemplars, based on their differentiating patterns. We already discussed *classification* techniques in this book.

Machine learning is usually refers to the changes in systems that perform tasks associated with artificial intelligence (AI). Such tasks involve recognition, diagnosis, planning, robot control, prediction etc.

The "changes" might be either enhancements to already perform systems. There are several reasons why machine learning is important. Achievement of learning in machine might help us understand how animals and humans learn. But there are important engineering reasons as well. Some of these are:

- Some tasks cannot be defined well except by example; that is, we might be able to specify input/output pairs but not a concise relationships between inputs and desired outputs. We would like machines to be able to adjust their internal structure to produce correct outputs for a large number of sample inputs and thus suitable constraint their input/output function to approximate the relationship implicit in the example.

- It is possible that hidden among large piles of data are important relationships and correlations. Machine learning methods can often be used to extract these relationships (data mining).
- Human designers often produce machines that do not work as well as desired in the environments in which they are used. In fact certain characteristics of the working environment might not be completely known at design time. Machine learning methods can be used for on-the-job improvement of existing machine designs.
- The amount of knowledge available about certain tasks might be too large for explicit encoding by humans. Machines that learn this knowledge gradually might be able to capture more of its than humans would want to write down.
- Environment change over time. Machine that can be adapt to changing environment would reduce the need for constant design.
- New knowledge about tasks is constantly being discovered by humans. Continuing redesign of AI systems to conform to new knowledge is impractical, but machine learning methods might be able to track much of it.

Here is a brief listing of some of the separate disciplines that have contributed to machine learning.

- **Statistics:** A long standing problem in statistics is how best to use samples drawn from unknown probability distributions to help decide from which distributions to help decided from which distribution some new sample is drawn. A related problem is how to estimate the value of unknown function at a new point given the value of this function at a set of sample points. Statistical methods for dealing with these problems can be consider instances of machine learning because the decision and estimation rules depend on a corpus of samples drawn from the problem environment.
- **Brain Model:** Non-linear elements with weighted inputs have been suggested as simple model of biological neurons. Several important machine learning techniques are based on networks of non-linear elements often called neural network. Neural networks concepts already discussed in this book.
- **Adaptive Control Theory:** Control theorists study the problem of controlling a process having unknown parameters which must be established during operation. Often, the parameters change during the operation, and the control must track these changes. Some aspects of controlling a robot based on sensory inputs represent instances of this sort problem.
- **Psychological Models:** Psychologists have studied the performance of human in various learning tasks. Related to this work decision tress, and semantic network methods. More recent work of this sort has been influenced by activities in artificial intelligence.
- **Artificial Intelligence:** From the beginning, AI research has been concerned with machine learning. AI researchers have also explored the role of the analogies in learning and how future actions and decisions can be based on exemplary cases. Recent work has been directed at discovering rules for expert systems using decision—tree methods and inductive logical programming.
- **Evolutionary Models:** In nature, not only do individual animals learn to perform better, but species evolve to be better fit in their individual machines. Since the distinction between evolving and learning can be blurred in computer systems, techniques that model certain aspects of biological evaluations have been proposed as learning methods to improve the performance of computer programs.

SUMMARY

- Recently various soft computing methodologies have been applied to handle the different challenges posed by data mining. The main constituents of soft computing.
- Fuzzy logic, neural networks, genetic algorithms, and rough sets. Each of them contributes a distinct methodology for addressing problems in its domain. The intelligent and robust systems provide a human-interpretable, low cost, approximate solution, as compared to traditional techniques.
- In many ways, soft computing represents a significant paradigm shift in the aims of computing — a shift which reflects the fact that the human mind, unlike present day computers, possesses a remarkable ability to store and process information.
- Fuzzy logic is a superset of conventional (Boolean) logic that has been extended to handle the concept of partial truth — truth values between "completely true" and "completely false".
- Evolutionary computation is the study of computational systems that use ideas and get inspiration from natural evolution. Its techniques can be applied to optimization, learning and design.

REVIEW QUESTIONS

1. What is the difference between soft computing and conventional computing?
2. What are the various soft computing methodologies?
3. How to apply genetic algorithm concepts to data mining?
4. What is the relationship between soft computing techniques with Artificial Intelligence?
5. How to find optimized solution using fuzzy logic?

11 ARTIFICIAL NEURAL NETWORKS

11.1 INTRODUCTION

For many decades, it has been a goal of science and engineering to develop intelligent machines with a large number of simple elements. In 1940s, researchers desiring to duplicate the function of the human brain, have developed simple hardware (and later software) models of biological neurons and their interaction systems.

The interest in neural networks comes from the networks' ability to mimic human brain as well as its ability to learn and respond. As a result, neural networks have been used in a large number of applications and have proven to be effective in performing complex functions in a variety of fields. These include pattern recognition, classification, vision, control systems, and prediction.

Adaptation or learning is a major focus of neural net research that provides a degree of robustness to the NN model. In predictive modeling, the goal is to map a set of input patterns onto a set of output patterns. NN accomplishes this task by learning from a series of input/output data sets presented to the network.

Definition: The simplest definition of a neural network, more properly referred to as an 'artificial' neural network (ANN), is provided by the inventor of one of the first neurocomputers, Dr. Robert Hecht-Nielsen. He defines a neural network as: *"...a computing system made up of a number of simple, highly interconnected processing elements, which process information by their dynamic state response to external inputs"*.

Neural Networks (NNs) are networks of neurons, for example, as found in real (*i.e.*, biological) brains.

Artificial Neurons are crude approximations of the neurons found in brains. They may be physical devices, or purely mathematical constructs.

Artificial Neural Networks (ANNs) are networks of Artificial Neurons, and hence constitute crude approximations to parts of real brains. They may be physical devices, or simulated on conventional computers.

ANNs are processing devices (algorithms or actual hardware) that are loosely modeled after the neuronal structure of the mammalian cerebral cortex but on much smaller scales. A large ANN might have hundreds or thousands of processor units, whereas a mamalian brain has billions of neurons with a corresponding increase in magnitude of their overall interaction and emergent behavior. Although ANN researchers are generally not concerned with whether their networks accurately resemble biological systems, some have. For example, researchers have accurately simulated the function of the retina and modeled the eye rather well.

Although the mathematics involved with neural networking is not a trivial matter, a user can rather easily gain at least an operational understanding of their structure and function.

11.2 HOW DO NEURAL NETWORKS DIFFER FROM CONVENTIONAL COMPUTING?

To better understand artificial neural computing it is important to know first how a conventional 'serial' computer and it's software process information. A serial computer has a central processor that can address an array of memory locations where data and instructions are stored. Computations are made by the processor reading an instruction as well as any data the instruction requires from memory addresses, the instruction is then executed and the results are saved in a specified memory location as required.

In a serial system (and a standard parallel one as well) the computational steps are deterministic, sequential and logical, and the state of a given variable can be tracked from one operation to another.

In comparison, ANNs are not sequential or necessarily deterministic. There are no complex central processors, rather there are many simple ones which generally do nothing more than take the weighted sum of their inputs from other processors. ANNs do not execute programmed instructions; they respond in parallel (either simulated or actual) to the pattern of inputs presented to it. There are also no separate memory addresses for storing data. Instead, information is contained in the overall activation 'state' of the network. 'Knowledge' is thus represented by the network itself, which is quite literally more than the sum of its individual components.

11.2.1 Why Neural Networks?

- They are extremely powerful computational devices (Turing equivalent, universal computers).
- Massive parallelism makes them very efficient.
- They can learn and generalize from training data — so there is no need for enormous feats of programming.
- They are particularly fault tolerant — this is equivalent to the "graceful degradation" found in biological systems.
- They are very noise tolerant — so they can cope with situations where normal symbolic systems would have difficulty.
- In principle, they can do anything a symbolic/logic system can do, and more. (In practice, getting them to do it can be rather difficult…)

As with the field of AI in general, there are two basic goals for neural network research:

Brain modeling: The scientific goal of building models of how real brains work. This can potentially help us understand the nature of human intelligence, formulate better teaching strategies, or better remedial actions for brain damaged patients.

Artificial System Building: The engineering goal of building efficient systems for real world applications. This may make machines more powerful, relieve humans of tedious tasks, and may even improve upon human performance.

11.3 LEARNING IN NEURAL NETWORKS

There are many forms of neural networks. Most operate by passing neural 'activations' through a network of connected neurons.

One of the most powerful features of neural networks is their ability to learn and generalize from a set of training data. They adapt the strengths/weights of the connections between neurons so that the final output activations are correct.

The following lists the categories of learning

1. **Categories of learning**
   - Supervised, reinforcement and unsupervised
   - Off-line and on-line
   - Deterministic, stochastic and fuzzy
   - Discrete and continuous
   - Criteria for learning
2. **Hebbian learning**
   - Basic Hebbian learning
   - Differential Hebbian learning
   - Stochastic versions
3. **Competitive learning—learning without a teacher**
   - Linear competitive learning
   - Differential competitive learning
   - Linear differential competitive learning
   - Stochastic versions
4. **Error correction learning—learning with a teacher**
   - Perceptron learning
   - Delta Learning
   - LMS learning
5. **Reinforcement learning—learning with a critic**
   - Fixed credit assignment
   - Probabilistic credit assignment
   - Temporal credit assignment
6. **Stochastic learning**
   - In multilayer perceptron
   - In Boltzmann machine
7. **Other learning methods**
   - Sparse coding
   - Min-max learning

- Principal component learning
- Drive-reinforcement learning.

11.4 HISTORY OF NEURAL NETWORKS

The study of the human brain dates back thousands of years. But is has only been with the dawn of modern day electronics that man has begun to try and emulate the human brain and its thinking processes.

1943- The modern era of neural network research is credited with the work done by neuro-physiologist, Warren McCulloch and young mathematical prodigy Walter Pitts in 1943. McCulloch had spent 20 years of life thinking about the "event" in the nervous system that allowed to us to think, feel, etc. It was only until the two joined forces that they wrote a paper on how neurons might work, and they designed and built a primitive artificial neural network using simple electric circuits. They are credited with the McCulloch-Pitts Theory of Formal Neural Networks.

1949- The next major development in neural network technology arrived in 1949 with a book, The Organization of Behavior written by Donald Hebb. The book supported and further reinforced McCulloch-Pitts's theory about neurons and how they work. A major point bought forward in the book described how neural pathways are strengthened each time they were used. As we shall see, this is true of neural networks, specifically in training a network.

1950- During the 1950's traditional computing began, and as it did, it left research into neural networks in the dark. However certain individuals continued research into neural networks. In 1954 Marvin Minsky wrote a doctorate thesis, Theory of Neural-Analog Reinforcement Systems and its Application to the Brain-Model Problem, which was concerned with the research into neural networks. He also published a scientific paper entitled, "Steps Towards Artificial Intelligence" which was one of the first papers to discuss AI in detail. The paper also contained a large section on what nowadays is known as neural networks.

1956- In 1956 the Dartmouth Summer Research Project on Artificial Intelligence began researching AI, what was to be the primitive beginnings of neural network research.

1958- In 1958 Frank Rosenblatt, a neuron-biologist at Cornell University began working on the Perceptron. The perceptron was the first "practical" artificial neural network. It was built using the somewhat primitive and "ancient" hardware of that time. The perceptron is based on research done on a fly's eye. The processing which tells a fly to flee when danger is near is done in the eye. One major downfall of the perceptron was that it had limited capabilities and this was proven by Marvin Minsky and Seymour Papert's book of 1969 entitled, Perceptions.

1959-60- Between 1959 and 1960, Bernard Wildrow and Marcian Hoff of Stanford University, in the USA developed the ADALINE (ADAptive LINear Elements) and MADELINE (Multiple ADAptive LINear Elements) models. These were the first neural networks that could be applied to real problems. The ADALAINE model is used as a filter to remove echoes from telephone lines.

1969- In 1969 Minsky and Papert published several documents, including their book, 'Perceptron'. They showed how the neural networks of the time were severely limited, and due to the opinion of these two influencial men research into neural networks drastically decreased.

1970- The period between 1969 and 1981 resulted in much attention towards neural networks. The capabilities of artificial neural networks were completely blown out of proportion by writers and producers of books and movies. People believed that such neural networks could do anything, resulting in disappointment when people realized that this was not so. Asimov's television series on robots highlighted humanity's fears of robot domination as well as the moral and social implications if machines could do mankind's work. Writers of best-selling novels like 2001 created fictional sinister computers. These factors contributed to large-scale critique of AI and neural networks, and thus funding for research projects came to a near halt. An important aspect that did come forward in the 1970's was that of self-organizing maps (SOM's). Self-organizing maps will be discussed later in this project.

1982- In 1982 John Hopfield of Caltech presented a paper to the scientific community in which he stated that the approach to AI should not be to purely imitate the human brain but instead to use its concepts to build machines that could solve dynamic problems. He showed what such networks were capable of and how they would work. It was his articulate, likeable character and his vast knowledge of mathematical analysis that convinced scientists and researchers at the National Academy of Sciences to renew interest into the research of AI and neural networks. His ideas gave birth to a new class of neural networks that over time became known as the Hopfield Model.

At about the same time at a conference in Japan about neural networks, Japan announced that they had again begun exploring the possibilities of neural networks. The United States feared that they would be left behind in terms of research and technology and almost immediately began funding for AI and neural network projects.

1986- 1986 saw the first annual Neural Networks for Computing conference that drew more than 1800 delegates. In 1986 Rumelhart, Hinton and Williams reported back on the developments of the back-propagation algorithm. The paper discussed how back-propagation learning had emerged as the most popular learning set for the training of multi-layer perceptrons.

1990's and Beyond

With the dawn of the 1990's and the technological era, many advances into the research and development of artificial neural networks are occurring all over the world. Nature itself is living proof that neural networks do in actual fact work. The challenge today lies in finding ways to electronically implement the principals of neural network technology. Electronics companies are working on three types of neuro-chips namely, digital, analog, and optical. With the prospect that these chips may be implemented in neural network design, the future of neural network technology looks very promising.

11.5 APPLICATIONS OF NEURAL NETWORKS

Neural networks are universal approximators, and they work best if the system you are using them to model has a high tolerance to error. One would therefore not be advised to use a neural network to balance one's check book! However they work very well for: capturing associations or discovering regularities within a set of patterns; where the volume, number of variables or diversity of the data is very great; the relationships between variables are vaguely understood; or, the relationships are difficult to describe adequately with conventional approaches.

Brain Modeling

Models of human development — help children with developmental problems Simulations of adult performance — aid our understanding of how the brain works Neuropsychological models — suggest remedial actions for brain damaged patients

Real World Applications

Financial modeling –	predicting stocks, shares, currency exchange rates
Other time series prediction –	climate, weather, airline marketing tactician
Computer games –	intelligent agents, backgammon, first person shooters
Control systems –	autonomous adaptable robots, microwave controllers
Pattern recognition –	speech recognition, hand-writing recognition, sonar signals
Data analysis –	data compression, data mining, PCA, GTM
Noise reduction –	function approximation, ECG noise reduction
Bioinformatics –	protein secondary structure, DNA sequencing

11.6 BASIC STRUCTURE OF NEURON

11.6.1 Model of Biological Neurons

In general, the human nervous system is a very complex neural network. The brain is the central element of the human nervous system, consisting of near 10^{10} biological neurons that are connected to each other through sub-networks. Each neuron in the brain is composed of a body, one axon and multitude of dendrites.

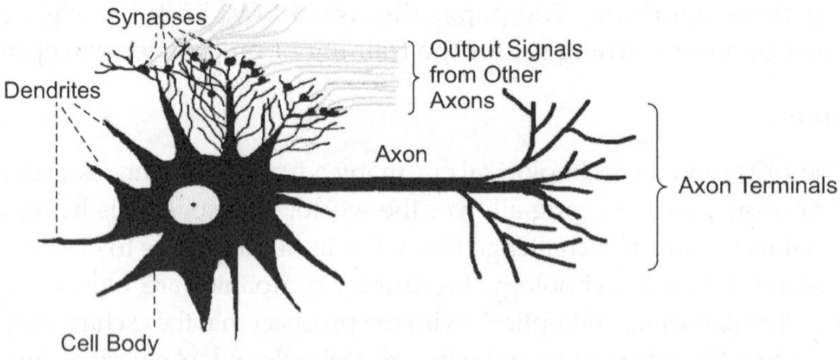

Fig. 11.1 A Biological Neuron

The neuron model shown in figure11.1 serves as the basis for the artificial neuron. The dendrites receive signals from other neurons. The axon can be considered as a long tube, which divides into branches terminating in little endbulbs. The small gap between an endbulb and a dendrite is called a synapse. The axon of a single neuron forms synaptic connections with many other neurons. Depending upon the type of neuron, the number of synapses connections from other neurons may range from a few hundreds to 10^4.

The cell body of a neuron sums the incoming signals from dendrites as well as the signals from numerous synapses on its surface. A particular neuron will send an impulse to its axon if sufficient input signals are received to stimulate the neuron to its threshold level. However, if the inputs do not reach the required threshold, the input will quickly decay and will not generate any action. The biological neuron model is the foundation of an artificial neuron as will be described in detail in the next section.

11.6.2 Basic Components of Biological Neurons

1. The majority of ***neurons*** encode their activations or outputs as a series of brief electrical pulses (*i.e.*, spikes or action potentials).
2. The neuron's ***cell body (soma)*** processes the incoming activations and converts them into output activations.
3. The neuron's ***nucleus*** contains the genetic material in the form of DNA. This exists in most types of cells, not just neurons.
4. ***Dendrites*** are fibres which emanate from the cell body and provide the receptive zones that receive activation from other neurons.
5. ***Axons*** are fibres acting as transmission lines that send activation to other neurons.
6. The junctions that allow signal transmission between the axons and dendrites are called ***synapses***. The process of transmission is by diffusion of chemicals called ***neurotransmitters*** across the synaptic cleft.

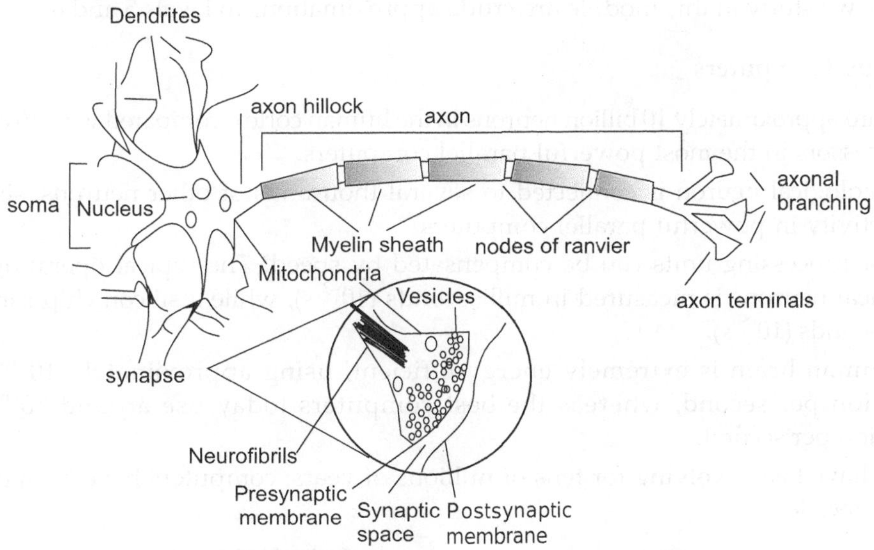

Fig. 11.2 Schematic diagram of a biological neuron

11.6.3 The Nervous System

The human nervous system can be broken down into three stages that may be represented in block diagram form as:

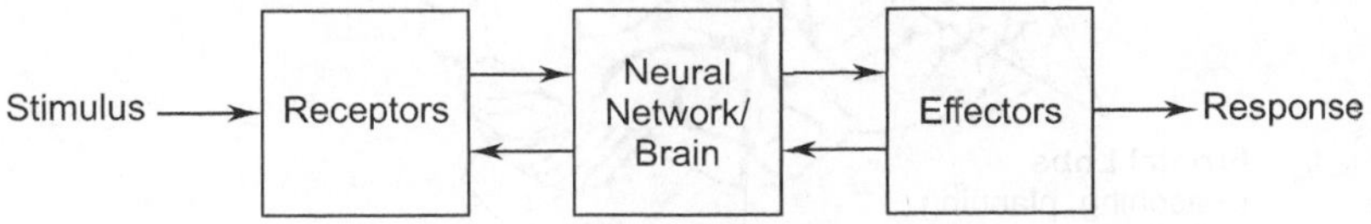

Fig. 11.3 Human nervous systems

The receptors collect information from the environment – *e.g.*, photons on the retina.

The effectors generate interactions with the environment – *e.g.*, activate muscles.

The flow of information/activation is represented by arrows – feedforward and feedback.

Naturally, in this module we will be primarily concerned with the neural network in the middle.

11.6.4 Levels of Brain Organization

The brain contains both large scale and small scale anatomical structures and different functions take place at higher and lower levels.

There is a hierarchy of interwoven levels of organization:

1. Molecules and Ions
2. Synapses
3. Neuronal microcircuits
4. Dendritic trees
5. Neurons
6. Local circuits
7. Inter-regional circuits
8. Central nervous system

The ANNs we study in this module are crude approximations to levels 5 and 6.

Brains Versus Computers

1. There are approximately 10 billion neurons in the human cortex, compared with 10 of thousands of processors in the most powerful parallel computers.
2. Each biological neuron is connected to several thousands of other neurons, similar to the connectivity in powerful parallel computers.
3. Lack of processing units can be compensated by speed. The typical operating speeds of biological neurons is measured in milliseconds (10^{-3} s), while a silicon chip can operate in nanoseconds (10^{-9} s).
4. The human brain is extremely energy efficient, using approximately 10^{-16} joules per operation per second, whereas the best computers today use around 10^{-6} joules per operation per second.
5. Brains have been evolving for tens of millions of years; computers have been evolving for tens of decades.

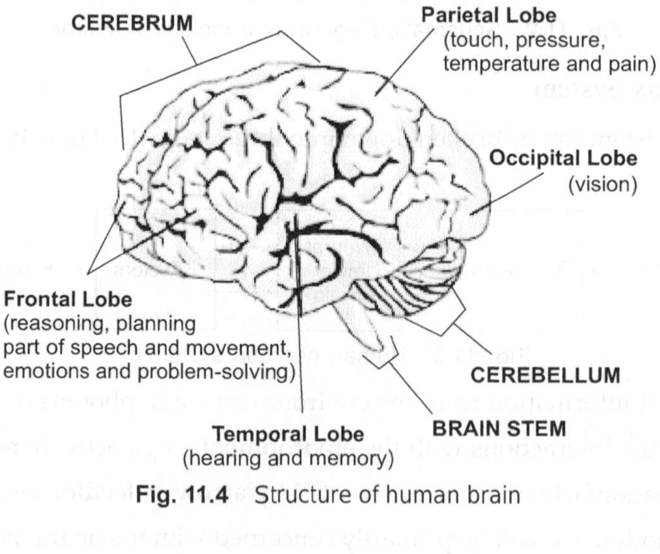

Fig. 11.4 Structure of human brain

11.7 MODELS OF ARTIFICIAL NEURON

In this section introduced three classical models of an artificial neuron or processing units.

11.7.1 Basic Elements of Neural Networks or McCulloch-Pitts Model

An artificial neuron is shown in the Fig. 11.5 is the basic element of a neural network or McCulloch-Pitts model. It consists of three basic components that include weights, thresholds, and a single activation function.

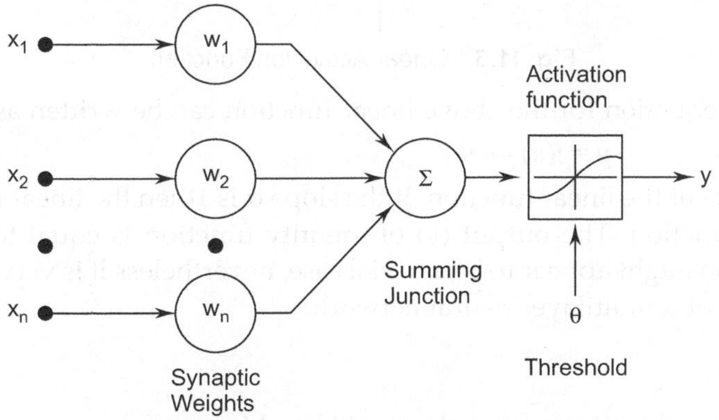

Fig. 11.5 Basic elements of an Artificial Neuron

Weighting Factors

The values W_1, W_2, W_3,....., W_n are weight factors associated with each node to determine the strength of input row vector $X = [x_1\ x_2\ x_3.....,x_n]^T$. Each input is multiplied by the associated weight of the neuron connection X^TW. Depending upon the activation function, if the weight is positive, X^TW commonly excites the node output; whereas, for negative weights, X^TW tends to inhibit the node output.

Threshold

The node's internal threshold θ is the magnitude offset that affects the activation of the node output y as follows:

$$y = \sum_{i=1}^{n} (X_i W_i) - \theta_k$$

Activation Function

Here five of the most common activation functions are presented. An activation function performs a mathematical operation on the signal output. More sophisticated activation functions can also be utilized depending upon the type of problem to be solved by the network.

Linear Function

As is known, a linear function satisfies the superposition concept. The function is shown in Fig. 11.6.

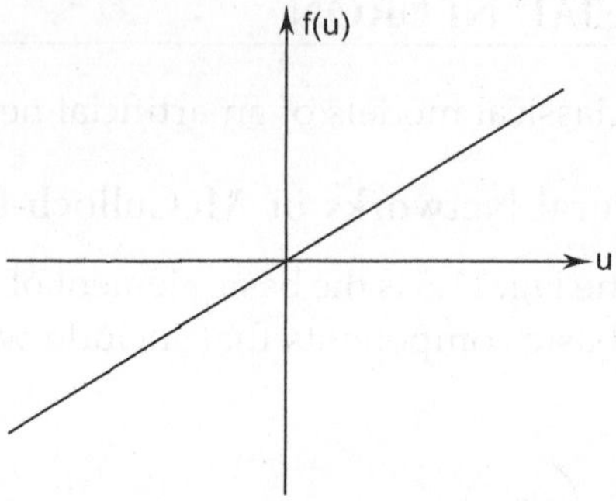

Fig. 11.6 Linear Activation Function

The mathematical equation for the above linear function can be written as

$$y = f(u) = a.u$$

where α is the slope of the linear function. If the slope α is 1then the linear activation function is called the identity function. The output (y) of identity function is equal to input function (u). Although this function might appear to be a trivial case, nevertheless it is very useful in some cases such as the last stage of a multilayer neural network.

Threshold Function

A threshold (hard-limiter) activation function is either a binary type or a bipolar type as shown in Figs. 11.7 and 11.8, respectively. The output of a *binary* threshold function can be written as:

$$y = f(u) = \begin{cases} 0 & \text{if} \quad u < 0 \\ 1 & \text{if} \quad u \geq 0 \end{cases}$$

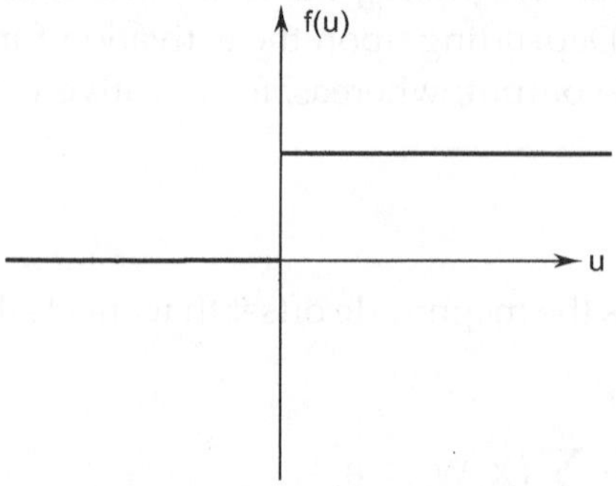

Fig. 11.7 Binary Threshold Activation Function

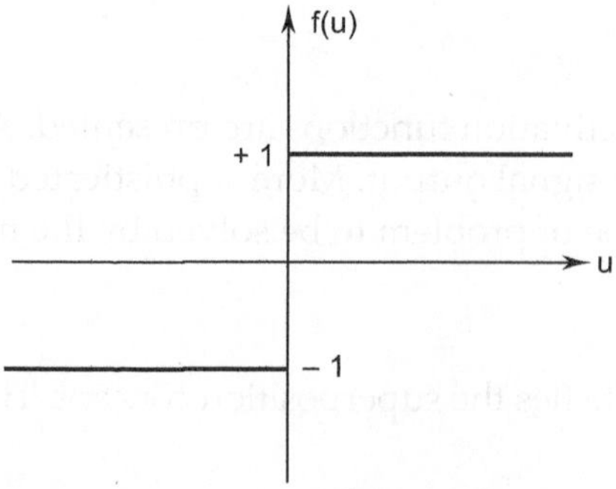

Fig. 11.8 Bipolar Threshold Activation Function

The neuron with the hard limiter activation function is referred to as the McCulloch-Pitts model.

Piecewise Linear Function

This type of activation function is also referred to as saturating linear function and can have either a binary or bipolar range for the saturation limits of the output. The mathematical model for a symmetric saturation function (Fig. 11.9) is described as follows:

$$y = f(u) = \begin{cases} -1 & \text{if} \quad u < -1 \\ u & \text{if} \quad -1 \geq u \geq 1 \\ 1 & \text{if} \quad u \geq 1 \end{cases}$$

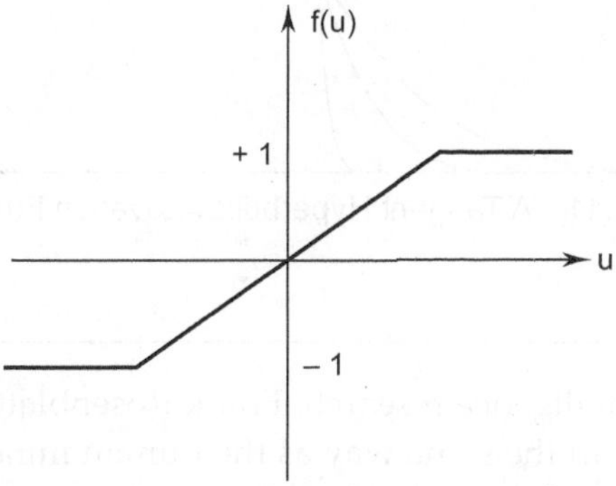

Fig. 11.9 Piecewise Linear Activation Function

Sigmoidal (S shaped) Function

This nonlinear function is the most common type of the activation used to construct the neural networks. It is mathematically well behaved, differentiable and strictly increasing function. A sigmoidal transfer function can be written in the following form:

$$f(x) = \frac{1}{1 + e^{-\alpha x}}, \; 0 \leq f(x) \leq 1$$

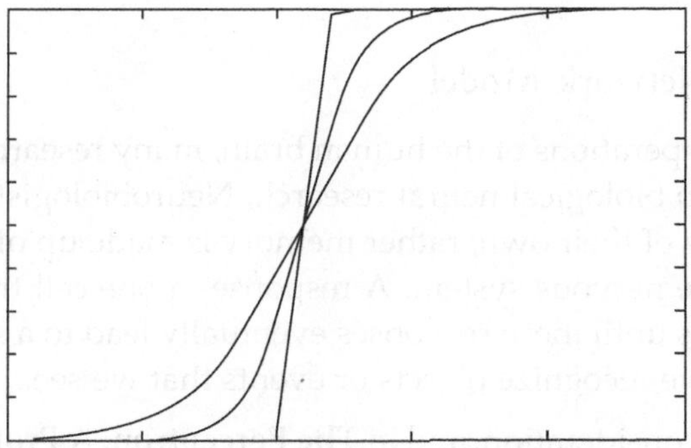

Fig. 11.10 A Sigmoid Activation Function

where α is the shape parameter of the sigmoid function. By varying this parameter, different shapes of the function can be obtained as illustrated in Fig. 11.10. This function is continuous and differentiable.

Tangent Hyperbolic Function

This transfer function is described by the following mathematical form:

$$f(x) = \frac{e^{\alpha x} - e^{-\alpha x}}{e^{\alpha x} + e^{-\alpha x}} \quad -1 \leq f(x) \leq 1$$

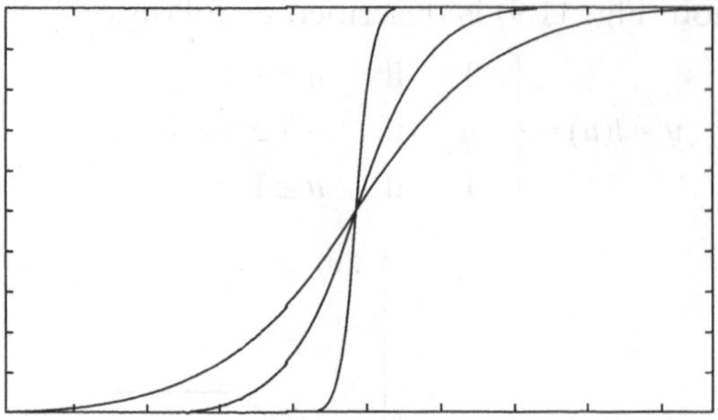

Fig. 11.11 A Tangent Hyperbolic Activation Function

11.8 PERCEPTRON

In the early days of artificial intelligence research, Frank Rosenblatt devised a machine called the perceptron that operated much in the same way as the human mind. Albeit, it did not have what could be called a "mental capacity", it could "learn" — and that was the breakthrough needed to pioneer today is current neural network technologies.

A perceptron is a connected network that simulates an associative memory. The most basic perceptron is composed of an input layer and output layer of nodes, each of which are fully connected to the other. Assigned to each connection is a weight which can be adjusted so that, given a set of inputs to the network, the associated connections will produce a desired output. The adjusting of weights to produce a particular output is called the "training" of the network which is the mechanism that allows the network to learn. Perceptrons are among the earliest and most basic models of artificial neural networks, yet they are at work in many of today is complex neural net applications.

11.8.1 An Associative Network Model

In order to understand the operations of the human brain, many researchers have chosen to create models based on findings in biological neural research. Neurobiologists have shown that human nerve cells have no memory of their own; rather memory is made up of a series of connections, or associations, throughout the nervous system. A response in one cell triggers responses in others which trigger more in others until these responses eventually lead to a so-called recognition of the input stimuli. This is how we recognize objects or events that we see.

Rosenblatt took this into consideration, and in **The Perceptron: A Probabilistic Model for Information Storage and Organization in the Brain**, published in 1958, he summarizes the basis of his work on perceptron theory in the following assumptions:

1. The physical connections of the nervous system which are involved in learning and recognition are not identical from one organism to another. At birth, the construction of the most important networks is largely random, subject to a minimum number of genetic constraints.

2. The original system of connected cells is capable of a certain amount of plasticity; after a period of neural activity, the probability that a stimulus applied to one set of cells will cause a response in some other set is likely to change, due to some relatively long-lasting changes in the neuron themselves.
3. Through exposure to a large sample of stimuli, those which are most "similar" (in some sense which must be defined in terms of the particular physical system) will tend to form pathways to the same sets of responding cells. Those which are markedly "dissimilar" will tend to develop connections to different sets of responding cells.
4. The application of positive and/or negative reinforcement (or stimuli which serve this function) may facilitate or hinder whatever formation of connections is currently in progress.
5. *Similarity*, in such a system, is represented at some level of the nervous system by a tendency of similar stimuli to activate the same sets of cells. Similarity ... depends on the physical organization of the perceiving system, an organization which evolves through interaction with a given environment. The structure of the system, as well as the ecology of the stimulus-environment, will affect, and will largely determine, the classes of things into which the perceptual world is divided.

With these basic assumptions, Rosenblatt was able to treat the workings of a learning device as "an intricate switching network, where retention takes the form of new connections". At this, he embarked on his remarkable invention of the perceptron.

11.8.2 Architecture

Using the simple two-layer perceptron as an example, there is one layer of input nodes (layer 1) and one layer of output nodes (layer 2). Each layer is fully connected between the other, but no connections exist between nodes in the same layer (See figure below). When layer 1 sends a signal to layer 2, the associated weights on the connections are applied and each receiving node on layer 2 sums up the incoming values. If the sum exceeds a given threshold, that node in turn fires an output signal.

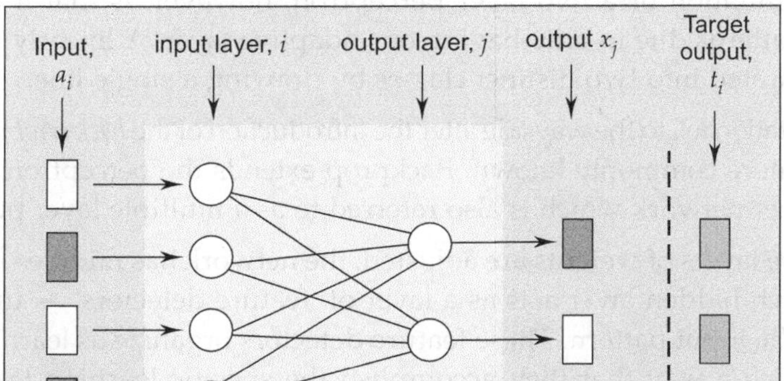

Fig. 11.12 A Simple Perceptron Diagram

The outputs are summed across all the inputs ($a[i]$) received by a node (j) in the output layer. The output of each node is determined as such:

Output are determined by: $S_j = \sum_{i=0}^{n} a_i w_{ij}$

If $S_j > \Theta$ then $x_j = 1$

If $S_j \leq \Theta$ then $x_j = 0$

where Θ is a predetermined threshold value

11.8.3 Training

By adjusting the weights on the connections between layers, the perceptronís output could be "trained" to match a desired output. Training is accomplished by sending a given set of inputs through the network and comparing the results with a set of target outputs. If there is a difference between the actual and the target outputs, the weights are adjusted on the adaptive layer to produce a set of outputs closer to the target values.

New weights are determined by adding an error correction value to the old weight. The amount of the correction is determined by multiplying the difference between the actual output ($x[j]$) and target ($t[j]$) values by a learning rate constant (C). If the input nodeís output ($a[i]$) is a 1, that connection weight is adjusted, and if it sends 0, it has no bearing on the output and subsequently, there is no need for adjustment. Thus, the process can be summed as follows:

Error Correction Formula: $\underset{new}{w_{ij}} = \underset{old}{w_{ij}} = C(t_j - x_j)a_i$

C = learning rate

This training procedure is repeated until the network is performance no longer improves. The network is then said to have "converged". At this point, it has either successfully learned the training set or it has failed to learn all of the answers correctly. If it is successful, it can then is given new sets of input and generally produce correct results on its own.

The functional limitation of a two-layer perceptron, however, is that it can only recognize linearly separable patterns due to only having one adaptive layer. A linearly separable pattern is one that can be separated into two distinct classes by drawing a single line.

However, this limitation fell to the wayside after the introduction of the *back error propagation* paradigm, or *backprop*, as it is more commonly known. Backprop extends the perceptron by implementing a multiple, hidden layer network which is also referred to as a multiple layer perceptron (MLP).

When two or more layers of weights are adjusted, the network has middle - or hidden - layers of processing units. Each hidden layer acts as a layer of 'feature detectors' — units that respond to specific features in the input pattern. These feature detectors organize as learning takes place, and are developed in such a way that they accomplish the specific learning task presented in the network.

Backprop first processes the inputs, checks for errors in the output set, and then proceed to *back propagate* (hence its name) the errors such that the hidden layers can adjust for the errors as well. Backprop is the most popular paradigm applied in neural nets today.

11.9 ADALINE

ADAptive LINear Element (ADALINE) is a computing model proposed by Windrow. The main distinction between the Perceptron model and the Adaline model is that, in the Adaline the analog activation value is compared with target output.

An ADAptive LINear Element (ADALINE) consists of a single neuron of the McCulloch-Pitts type, where its weights are determined by the normalized least mean square (LMS) training law. The LMS learning algorithm was originally proposed by Widrow and Hoff [6]. This learning rule is also referred to as delta rule. It is a well-established supervised training method that has been used over a wide range of diverse applications.

The architecture of a simple ADALINE is shown In Fig. 11.13. It is observed that the basic structure of an ADALINE is similar to a linear neuron.

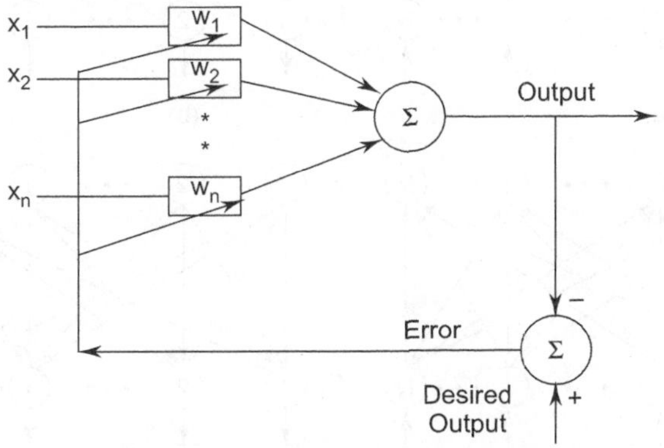

Fig. 11.13 ADALINE Model Network

During the training phase of ADALINE, the input vector $X = [x_1\ x_2\ x_3\ldots\ x_n]^T$ as well as desired output are presented to the network. The weights are adaptively adjusted based on delta rule. After the ADALINE is trained, an input vector presented to the network with fixed weights will result in a scalar output.

The activation function is not used during the training phase. Once the weights are properly adjusted, the response of the trained unit can be tested by applying various inputs, which are not in the training set. If the network produces consistent responses to a high degree with the test inputs, it said that the network could generalize. Therefore, the process of training and generalization are two important attributes of the network.

11.10 TOPOLOGY

Artificial neural networks are useful only when the processing units are organized in a suitable manner to accomplish a given pattern recognition task. This section presents a few basic structures which will assist in evolving new architectures. The arrangement of the processing units, connections, and pattern input/output is referred to as topology.

Artificial neural networks are normally organized into layers of processing units. Connections can be made either from units of one layer to units of another (interlayer connections) or from the units within the layer (intralayer connections) or both inter and intralayer connections. Further, the connections among the layers and among the units within a layer can be organized either in a feedforward manner or in a feedback manner. In a feedback network the same processing unit may be visited more than once.

We will discuss a few basic structures which form building blocks for complex neural network architectures. Let us consider two layers F, and F, with N and M processing units, respectively. By providing connections to the jth unit in F, from all the units in F,, as shown in Fig. 11.14, we get two network structures *instar* and *outstar*, which have fan-in and fan-out geometries, respectively.

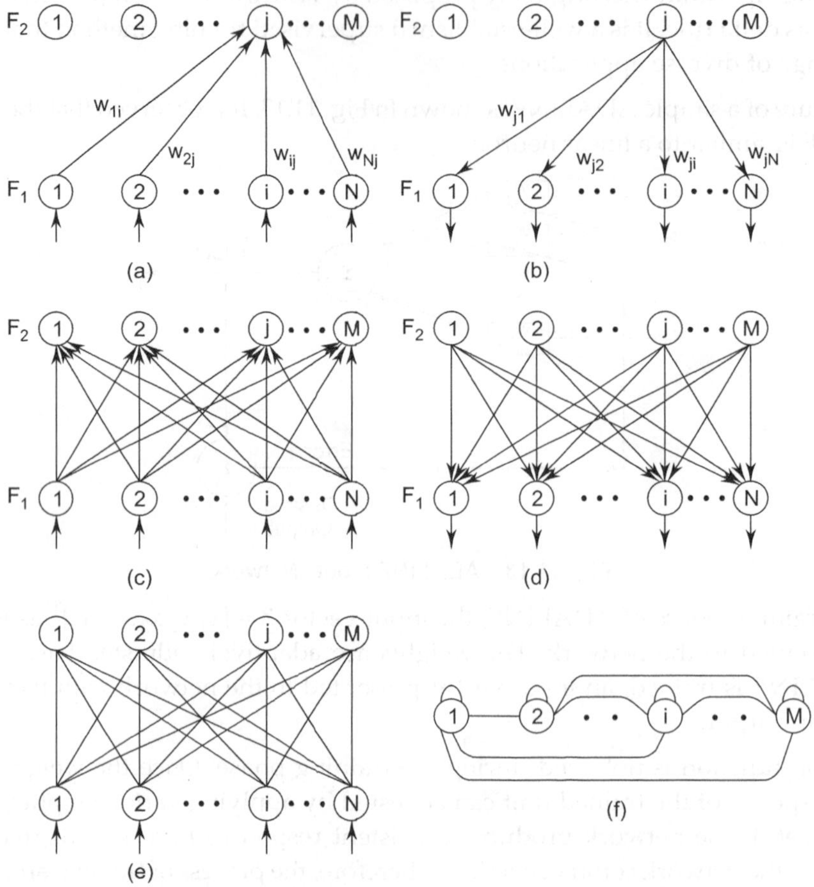

Fig. 11.14 Some Basic Structure of Artificial Neural Networks (a) Instar (b) Outstar (c) Group of instars (d) Group of outstars (e) Bidirectional Associate Memory (f) auto associate memory

The units in the F, layer are linear units, so that for each unit i in this layer the input $(a,)$ = activation $(x_i =)$ output signal$(s,)$. In instar, during learning, the weight vector w_j $(w_{j1}, w_{j2},..., w_{jN})$ is adjusted so as to approach the given input vector a at F_1, layer.

Therefore whenever the input is given to F_1, then the *j*th unit of F_2 will be activated to the maximum extent. Thus the operation of the **instar** can be viewed as content addressing the memory.

In the case of the outstar, during learning, the weight vector for the connections from the *j*th unit in F_2 approaches the activity pattern in F, when input vector a is present at F,. During recall, whenever the unit *j* is activated, the signal pattern (*sjwlj*, *sjwIj*,...*sjw*N*j*) will be transmitted to F,, which then produces the original activity pattern corresponding to the input vector a, although the input is absent. Thus the operation of the outstar can be viewed as memory addressing the contents.

11.11 BASIC LEARNING LAWS

The operation of a neural network is governed by neuronal dynamics. Neuronal dynamics consists of two parts:

1. Models of activation Dynamics
2. Dynamics of synaptic weights

The Short Term Memory(STM) in neural networks is modeled by the activation state of the network. The Long Term Memory (LTM) corresponds to the encoded pattern information in the synaptic weights due to learning.

Learning laws describe the weight vector for the ith processing unit at time instant $(t + 1)$ in terms of the weight vector at time instant (t) as follows

$$w_i(t+1) = w_i(t) + \Delta w_i(t),$$

There are different methods for implementing the synaptic dynamics. These methods are called learning laws. A few common discrete time learning laws are given below

1. **Hebb's law**

   Here $g(.) = f(w_i{}^{T} a)$, where f is the output function. Therefore

   $$\Delta w_{ij} = nf(w_i{}^{T} a)a_j$$
   $$= \eta\, s_i a_j, \quad \text{for} \quad j = 1,2\ldots N$$

   This law requires weight initialization $w_i \approx 0$ prior to learning.

2. **Perceptron learning law**

   Here $g(.) = b_i - s_i = b_i - sgn(w^r a)$. Therefore

   $$\Delta w_{ij} = \eta[b_i - sgn(w^r a)]a_j, \quad \text{for} \quad j = 1, 2 \ldots N.$$

   This rule is applicable for bipolar output function. The weights can be initialized to any values prior to learning.

3. **Delta learning law**

   Here $g(.) = [b_i - f(w_i{}^{T} a)]\, f'(w_i{}^{T} a)$. This is obtained by setting

   $$\Delta w_i = -\eta\, \nabla E$$

   where – VE is the negative gradient of the error $E = \frac{1}{2}\left[b_i - f\left(w_i^{T} a\right)\right]^2$. Therefore

   $$\Delta w_{ij} = \eta(b_i - s_i)\, f'(w_i{}^{T} a)a_j, \text{ for } j = 1, 2 \ldots N$$

   Here $f(.)$ is a continuous function. The weights may be initialized to any values.

4. **Widro-Hoff LMS learning law**

   Here $g(.) = b_i - w_i{}^{T} a$. Therefore

   $$Aw_{ij} = \eta(b_i - w_i{}^{T} a)a_j, \quad \text{for} \quad j = 1, 2 \ldots .N.$$

   This is a special case of the delta learning law where the output function is assumed to be linear, *i.e.*,

   $f(w_i{}^{T} a) = w_i{}^{T} a$ The weights may be initialized to any values.

5. **Correlation learning law:**

   $$\Delta w_{ij} = \eta b_i a_j, \quad \text{for} \quad j = 1, 2 \ldots N.$$

This is applicable for binary output units. This is a special case of Hebbian learning with output signal (s_i) = desired signal (b_i). The weights are initialized to zero prior to learning.

6. **Instar (winner-take-all) learning law:**

$$\Delta w_{mj} = \eta(a_j - w_{mj}), \quad \text{for} \quad j = 1, 2, \ldots N,$$

Where $w_m^T a = \max_t \left(w_i^T a\right)$. Here the weights are initialized to random values prior to learning and their lengths are normalized during learning.

7. **Outstar learning law:**

$$\Delta w_{kj} = \eta(b_k - w_{kj}), \quad \text{for} \quad k = 1, 2 \ldots k$$

where b is the desired response from the layer of K neurons. The weights are initialized to zero before learning.

SUMMARY

- We have seen the background and fundamental study of artificial neural networks. The interest in neural networks comes from the networks' ability to mimic human brain as well as its ability to learn and respond. As a result, neural networks have been used in a large number of applications and have proven to be effective in performing complex functions in a variety of fields. These include pattern recognition, classification, vision, control systems, and prediction.
- Neural networks are typically organized in layers. Layers are made up of a number of interconnected 'nodes' which contain an 'activation function'. Patterns are presented to the network via the 'input layer', which communicates to one or more 'hidden layers' where the actual processing is done via a system of weighted 'connections'.
- The most important issue for solving practical problems using the principles of ANN is still in evolving a suitable architecture to solve a problem. This continues to dominate this research area. ANN research may have to expand its scope to take into account the fuzzy nature of real world data and reasoning, and the complex (unknown) processing performed by the human perceptual mechanism through biological neural networks.

REVIEW QUESTIONS

1. Describe about characteristics of neural networks.
2. Explain briefly the terms cell body, axon, synapse, dendrite and neuron with reference to a biological neural network.
3. How do neural networks differ from conventional computing?
4. What are the basic learning laws?
5. What is meant by topology of artificial neural networks? Give a few basic topological structures of artificial neural networks.
6. Identify supervised and unsupervised basic learning laws.
7. Discuss about the artificial neural network and about activation functions in detail.

GLOSSARY

A

Accuracy: A measure of a predictive model that reflects the proportionate number of times that the model is correct when applied to data.

Activation function: A function used by a node in a neural net to transform input data from any domain of values into a finite range of values. The original idea was to approximate the way neurons fired, and the activation function took on the value 0 until the input became large and the value jumped to 1. The discontinuity of this 0-or-1 function caused mathematical problems, and sigmoid-shaped functions (*e.g.*, the logistic function) are now used.

Antecedent: When an association between two variables is defined, the first item (or left-hand side) is called the antecedent. For example, in the relationship "When a prospector buys a pick, he buys a shovel 14% of the time," "buys a pick" is the antecedent.

Application Programming Interface (API): This formally defined programming language interface between a program (system control program, licensed program) and its user.

Artificial Intelligence: The scientific field concerned with the creation of intelligent behavior in a machine.

Artificial Neural Network (ANN): ANN is networks of Artificial Neurons, and hence constitutes crude approximations to parts of real brains. They may be physical devices, or simulated on conventional computers.

Association Rule: A rule in the form of "if this then that" that associates events in a database. For example, association between purchases items at a supermarket.

B

Back Propagation: It is one of the most common learning algorithms for training neural networks.

Bias: In a neural network, bias refers to the constant terms in the model. (Note that bias has a different meaning to most data analysts.) Also see *precision*.

Binning: It is the process of break up continuous values into bins. Binning is usually done as a preprocessing step for some data mining algorithms. For example, break up age into bins for every ten years.

Bootstrapping: Training data sets are created by re-sampling with replacement from the original training set, so data records may occur more than once. In other words, this method treats a sample as if it were the entire population. Usually, final estimates are obtained by taking the average of the estimates from each of the bootstrap test sets.

Brute Force Algorithm: A computer technique that exhaustively uses the repetition of very simple steps repeated in order to find an optimal solution. They stand in contrast to complex techniques that are less wasteful in moving toward and optimal solution but are harder to construct and are more computationally expensive to execute.

Business Intelligence: Business Intelligence as a set of concepts and methodologies to improve decision-making in business through use of facts and facts based system.

C

Categorical Data: Categorical data fits into a small number of discrete categories (as opposed to continuous). Categorical data is either non-ordered (nominal) such as gender or city, or ordered (ordinal) such as high, medium, or low temperatures.

Cardinality: The number of different values a categorical predictor or OLAP dimension can have. High cardinality predictors and dimensions have large numbers of different values (*e.g.*, zip codes), low cardinality fields have few different values (*e.g.*, eye color).

CART: It is full form is Classification and Regression Trees. A decision tree algorithm is that automates the pruning process through cross validation and other techniques.

CHAID: Its archenemy is Chi-Square Automatic Interaction Detector. A decision tree is that uses contingency tables and the chi-square test to create the tree for classification. The process of learning to distinguish and discriminate between different input patterns using a supervised training algorithm. Classification is the process of determining that a record belongs to a group.

Chi-squared: A statistic that assesses how well a model fits the data. In data mining, it is most commonly used to find homogeneous subsets for fitting categorical trees as in CHAID.

Cleaning (cleansing): Refers to a step in preparing data for a data mining activity. Obvious data errors are detected and corrected (*e.g.*, improbable dates) and missing data is replaced.

Classification: Refers to the data mining problem of attempting to predict the category of categorical data by building a model based on some predictor variables.

Classification Tree: A decision tree that places categorical variables into classes.

Clustering: The process of grouping similar input patterns together using an unsupervised training algorithm.

(or)

The technique of grouping records together based on their locality and connectivity within the *n*-dimensional space. This is an unsupervised learning technique.

Collinearity: The property of two predictors showing significant correlation without a causal relationship between them.

Confidence: Confidence of rule "B given A" is a measure of how much more likely it is that B occurs when A has occurred. It is expressed as a percentage, with 100% meaning B always occurs if A has occurred. Statisticians refer to this as the conditional probability of B given A. When used with association rules, the term confidence is observational rather than predictive. (Statisticians also use this term in an unrelated way. There are ways to estimate an interval and the probability that the interval contains the true value of a parameter is called the interval confidence. So a 95% confidence interval for the mean has a probability of .95 of covering the true value of the mean.)

Conditional Probability: The probability of an event happening given that some event has already occurred. For example the chance of a person committing fraud is much greater given that the person had previously committed fraud.

Confusion Matrix: A confusion matrix shows the counts of the actual versus predicted class values. It shows not only how well the model predicts, but also presents the details needed to see exactly where things may have gone wrong.

Consequent: When an association between two variables is defined, the second item (or right-hand side) is called the consequent. For example, in the relationship "When a prospector buys a pick, he buys a shovel 14% of the time," "buys a shovel" is the consequent.

Continuous Data: Continuous data can have any value in an interval of real numbers. That is, the value does not have to be an integer. Continuous is the opposite of discrete or categorical.

Cross Validation: A method of estimating the accuracy of a classification or regression model. The data set is divided into several parts, with each part in turn used to test a model fitted to the remaining parts.

Coverage: A number that represents either the number of times that a rule can be applied or the percentage of times that it can be applied.

CRM: See Customer Relationship Management.

Cross Validation: (and Test Set Validation). The process of holding aside some training data which is not used to build a predictive model and to later use that data to estimate the accuracy of the model on unseen data simulating the real world deployment of the model.

Cube: A multi-dimensional representation of data in which the cells contain measures and the edges represent data dimensions by which the data can be sliced and diced.

Customer Relationship Management: The process by which companies manage their interactions with customers.

D

Data: Values collected through record keeping or by polling, observing, or measuring, typically organized for analysis or decision making. More simply, data is facts, transactions and figures.

Database: A database is a logically coherent collection of data with some inherent meaning, representing some aspect of real world and which is designed, built and populated with data for a specific purpose.

Database Management Systems: It is a collection of programs that enables user to create and maintain a database. In other words it is general-purpose software that provides the users with the processes of defining, constructing and manipulating the database for various applications.

Data Format: Data items can exist in many formats such as text, integer and floating-point decimal. Data format refers to the form of the data in the database.

Data Mart: Data mart is usually sponsored at the department level and developed with a specific issue or subject in mind, a Data Mart is a data warehouse with focused objective.

Data Mining: An information extraction activity whose goal is to discover hidden facts contained in databases. Using a combination of machine learning, statistical analysis, modeling techniques and database technology, data mining finds patterns and subtle relationships in data and infers rules that allow the prediction of future results. Typical applications include market segmentation, customer profiling, fraud detection, evaluation of retail promotions, and credit risk analysis.

Data Mining Method: Procedures and algorithms designed to analyze the data in databases.

Data Warehouse: It is a "Subject-oriented, Time-Variant, Nonvolatile collection of data in support of decision making"

Decision Trees: A class of data mining and statistical methods that form tree like predictive models.

(or)

A tree-like structure that represents collection of hierarchical rules that lead to a class or value.

Deduction: Deduction infers information that is a logical consequence of the data.

Degree of Fit: A measure of how closely the model fits the training data. A common measure is *r*-square.

Dependent Variable: The dependent variables (outputs or responses) of a model are the variables predicted by the equation or rules of the model using the independent variables (inputs or predictors).

Deployment: After the model is trained and validated, it is used to analyze new data and make predictions. This use of the model is called deployment.

Dimension: Each attribute of a case or occurrence in the data being mined. Stored as a field in a flat file record or a column of relational database table.

Discrete: A data item that has a finite set of values. Discrete is the opposite of continuous.

Discriminate Analysis: A statistical method based on maximum likelihood for determining boundaries that separate the data into categories.

E

Embedded Data Mining: An implementation of data mining where the data mining algorithms are embedded into existing data stores and information delivery processes rather than requiring data extraction and new data stores.

Entropy: A measure often used in data mining algorithms that measures the disorder of a set of data.

Error Rate: A number that reflects the rate of errors made by a predictive model. It is one minus the accuracy.

ETL: stands for Extract, Transform and Load

Expert System: A data processing system comprising a knowledge base (rules), an inference (rules) engine, and a working memory.

Exploratory Analysis: Looking at data to discover relationships not previously detected. Exploratory analysis tools typically assist the user in creating tables and graphical displays.

Exploratory Data Analysis: The processes and techniques for general exploration of data for patterns in preparation for more directed analysis of the data.

External Data: Data not collected by the organization, such as data available from a reference book, a government source or a proprietary database.

F

Factor Analysis: A statistical technique which seeks to reduce the number of total predictors from a large number to only a few "factors" that have the majority of the impact on the predicted outcome.

Feed-forward: A neural net in which the signals only flow in one direction, from the inputs to the outputs.

Field: The structural component of a database that is common to all records in the database. Fields have values. Also called features, attributes, variables, table columns, dimensions.

Front Office: The part of a company's computer system that is responsible for keeping track of relationships with customers.

Fuzzy Logic: Fuzzy logic is applied to fuzzy sets where membership in a fuzzy set is a probability, not necessarily 0 or 1. Non-fuzzy logic manipulates outcomes that are either true or false. Fuzzy logic needs to be able to manipulate degrees of "maybe" in addition to true and false.

Fuzzy Set: A set of items whose degree of membership is in the set may range from 0 to 1.

Fuzzy System: A set of rules using fuzzy linguistic variables described by fuzzy sets and processed using fuzzy logic operations.

G

Genetic Algorithm: A method of solving optimization problems using parallel search, based on Darwin's biological model of natural selection and survival of the fittest.

(or)

A computer-based method of generating and testing combinations of possible input parameters to find the optimal output. It uses processes based on natural evolution concepts such as genetic combination, mutation and natural selection.

Genetic Operator: An operation on the population member strings in a genetic algorithm which are used to produce new strings.

Gini Metric: A measure of the disorder reduction caused by the splitting of data in a decision tree algorithm. Gini and the entropy metric are the most popular ways of selected predictors in the CART decision tree algorithm.

GUI Graphical User Interface.

H

Hebbian Learning: One of the simplest and oldest forms of training a neural network is Hebbian learning. It is loosely based on observations of the human brain. The neural net link weights are strengthened between any nodes that are active at the same time.

Hill Climbing Search: A simple optimization technique is Hill-climbing search that modifies a proposed solution by a small amount and then accepts it if it is better than the previous solution. The technique can be slow and suffers from being caught in local optima.

HOLAP: Hybrid Online Analytical Processing

Hypothesis Testing: The statistical process of proposing a hypothesis is to explain the existing data and then testing to see the likelihood of that hypothesis being the explanation.

Hidden Nodes: The nodes in the hidden layers in a neural net. Unlike input and output nodes, the number of hidden nodes is not predetermined. The accuracy of the resulting model is affected by the number of hidden nodes. Since the number of hidden nodes directly affects the number of parameters in the model, a neural net needs a sufficient number of hidden nodes to enable it to properly model the underlying behavior. On the other hand, a net with too many hidden nodes will overfit the data. Some neural net products include algorithms that search over a number of alternative neural nets by varying the number of hidden nodes, in the end choosing the model that gets the best results without overfitting.

I

ID3: One of the earliest decision tree algorithms.

Independence (statistical): The property of two events is displaying no causality or relationship of any kind. This can be quantitatively defined as occurring when the product of the probabilities of each event is equal to the probability of the both events occurring.

Independent Variable: The independent variables (inputs or predictors) of a model are the variables used in the equation or rules of the model to predict the output (dependent) variable.

Induction: A technique that infers generalizations from the information in the data.

Interaction: Two independent variables interact when changes in the value of one change the effect on the dependent variable of the other.

Internal Data: Data collected by an organization such as operating and customer data.

Intelligent Agent: A software application is in which assists a system or a user by automating a task. Intelligent agents must recognize events and use domain knowledge to take appropriate actions based on those events.

K

Kohonen Networks: A type of neural network where locality of the nodes learn as local neighborhoods and locality of the nodes is important in the training process. They are often used for clustering.

Kohonen Feature Map: A type of neural network that uses unsupervised learning to find patterns in data. In data mining it is employed for cluster analysis.

k-nearest Neighbor: A classification method that classifies a point by calculating the distances between the point and points in the training data set. Then it assigns the point to the class that is most common among its *k*-nearest neighbors (where *k* is an integer).

Knowledge Discovery: A term often used interchangeably with data mining.

L

Layer: Nodes in a neural net are usually grouped into layers, with each layer described as input, output or hidden. There are as many input nodes as there are input (independent) variables and as many output nodes as there are output (dependent) variables. Typically, there are one or two hidden layers.

Leaf: A node not further split — the terminal grouping — in a classification or decision tree.

Learning: Training models (estimating their parameters) based on existing data.

Least Squares: The most common method of training (estimating) the weights (parameters) of a model by choosing the weights that minimize the sum of the squared deviation of the predicted values of the model from the observed values of the data.

Left-hand Side: When an association between two variables is defined, the first item is called the left-hand side (or antecedent). For example, in the relationship "When a prospector buys a pick, he buys a shovel 14% of the time", "buys a pick" is the left-hand side.

Logistic Regression (Logistic Discriminant Analysis): A generalization of linear regression. It is used for predicting a binary variable (with values such as yes/no or 0/1). An example of its use is modeling the odds that a borrower will default on a loan based on the borrower's income, debt and age.

Lift: A number representing the increase in responses from a targeted marketing application using a predictive model over the response rate achieved when no model is used.

M

MARS: Multivariate Adaptive Regression Splines. MARS is a generalization of a decision tree.

Maximum Likelihood: Another training or estimation method. The maximum likelihood estimate of a parameter is the value of a parameter that maximizes the probability that the data came from the population defined by the parameter.

Machine Learning: A field of science and technology concerned with building machines that learn. In general it differs from Artificial Intelligence in that learning is considered to be just one of a number of ways of creating an artificial intelligence.

Memory-Based Reasoning (MBR): A technique for classifying records is in a database by comparing them with similar records that are already classified.

Mean: The arithmetic average value of a collection of numeric data.

Median: The value in the middle of a collection of ordered data is called Median. In other words, the value find with the same number of items above and below.

Minimum Description Length (MDL) Principle: The idea that the least complex predictive model (with acceptable accuracy) will be the one that best reflects the true underlying model and performs most accurately on new data.

Missing Data: Data values can be missing because they were not measured, not answered, were unknown or were lost. Data mining methods vary in the way they treat missing values. Typically, they ignore the missing values, or omit any records containing missing values, or replace missing values with the mode or mean, or infer missing values from existing values.

Model: A description is that adequately explains and predicts relevant data but is generally much smaller than the data itself.

Mode: The most common value in a data set. If more than one value occurs the same number of times, the data is multi-modal.

Model in Detail: An important function of data mining is the production of a model. A model can be descriptive or predictive. A descriptive model helps in understanding underlying processes or behavior. For example, an association model describes consumer behavior. A predictive model is an equation or set of rules that makes it possible to predict an unseen or unmeasured value (the dependent variable or output) from other, known values (independent variables or input). The form of the equation or rules is suggested by mining data collected from the process under study. Some training or estimation technique is used to estimate the parameters of the equation or rules.

MOLAP: Stands for Multidimensional Online Analytical Processing.

MPP: Massively parallel processing, a computer configuration that is able to use hundreds or thousands of CPUs simultaneously. In MPP each node may be a single CPU or a collection of SMP CPUs. An MPP collection of SMP nodes is sometimes called an SMP cluster. Each node has its own copy of the operating system, memory, and disk storage, and there is a data or process exchange mechanism so that each computer can work on a different part of a problem. Software must be written specifically to take advantage of this architecture.

N

Nearest Neighbor: A data mining technique is that performs prediction by finding the prediction value of records (near neighbors) similar to the record to be predicted.

Neural Network: A computing model based on the architecture of the brain. A neural network consists of multiple simple processing units connected by adaptive weights.

(or)

A complex nonlinear modeling technique based on a model of a human neuron. A neural net is used to predict outputs (dependent variables) from a set of inputs (independent variables) by taking linear combinations of the inputs and then making nonlinear transformations of the linear combinations using an activation function.

Nominal Categorical Predictor: A predictor is that categorical (finite cardinality) but where the values of the predictor have no particular order. For example, red, green, blue as values for the predictor "eye color".

Node: A decision point in a classification (*i.e.*, decision) tree. Also, a point in a neural net that combines input from other nodes and produces an output through application of an activation function.

Noise: The difference between a model and its predictions. Sometimes data is referred to as noisy when it contains errors such as many missing or incorrect values or when there are extraneous columns.

Non-applicable Data: Missing values that would be logically impossible (*e.g.*, pregnant males) or are obviously not relevant.

Normalize: A collection of numeric data is normalized by subtracting the minimum value from all values and dividing by the range of the data. This yields data with a similarly shaped histogram but with all values between 0 and 1. It is useful to do this for all inputs into neural nets and also for inputs into other regression models.

O

Occam's Razor: A rule of thumb used by many scientists that advocates favoring the simplest theory that adequately explains (or predicts) an event. This is more formally captured for machine learning and data mining as the minimum description length principle.

OLAP: On-Line Analytical Processing tools give the user the capability to perform multi-dimensional analysis of the data.

On-Line Analytical Processing (OLAP): Computer-based techniques used to analyze trends and perform business analysis using multidimensional views of business data.

Optimization Criterion: A positive function of the difference between predictions and data estimates that are chosen so as to optimize the function or criterion. Least squares and maximum likelihood are examples.

Ordinal Categorical Predictor: A categorical predictor (*i.e.*, has finite number of values) where the values have order but do not convey meaningful intervals or distances between them. For example the value of income is high, middle and low predictor.

Outlier Analysis: A type of data analysis that seeks to determine and report on records in the database that are significantly different from expectations. The technique is used for data cleansing, spotting emerging trends and recognizing unusually good or bad performers.

(or)

Technically, outliers are data items that did not (or are thought not to have) come from the assumed population of data — for example, a non-numeric when you are expecting only numeric values. A more casual usage refers to data items that fall outside the boundaries that enclose most other data items in the data set.

Overfitting: The effect in data analysis, data mining and biological learning is of training too closely on limited available data and building models that do not generalize well to new unseen data. At the limit, overfitting is synonymous with rote memorization where no generalized model of future situations is built.

Overlay: Data not collected by the organization, such as data from a proprietary database, that is combined with the organization's own data.

P

Parallel Processing: Several computers or CPUs linked together so that each can be computing simultaneously.

Pattern Analysts: and statisticians spend much of their time looking for patterns in data. A pattern can be a relationship between two variables. Data mining techniques include automatic pattern discovery that makes it possible to detect complicated non-linear relationships in data. Patterns are not the same as causality.

Predictor: The column or field in a database is that could be used to build a predictive model to predict the values in another field or column. Predictor is variable, independent variable, dimension, or feature.

Precision: The precision of an estimate of a parameter in a model is a measure of how variable the estimate would be over other similar data sets. A very precise estimate would be one that did not vary much over different data sets. Precision does not measure accuracy. Accuracy is a measure of how close the estimate is to the real value of the parameter. Accuracy is measured by the average distance over different data sets of the estimate from the real value. Estimates can be accurate but not precise, or precise but not accurate. A precise but inaccurate estimate is usually biased, with the bias equal to the average distance from the real value of the parameter.

Predictability: Some data mining vendors use predictability of associations or sequences to mean the same as confidence.

Prediction: A field in a database that currently has unknown value that will be assigned when a predictive model is run over other predictor values in the record. Also called dependent variable, target, classification.

The process is to applying a predictive model to a record. Generally prediction implies the generation of unknown values within time series though in this book prediction is used to mean any process for assigning values to previously unassigned fields including classification and regression.

Predictive Model: A model created or used to perform prediction. In contrast to models created solely for pattern detection, exploration or general organization of the data.

Prevalence: The measure of how often the collection of items in an association occur together as a percentage of all the transactions. For example, "In 2% of the purchases at the hardware store, both a pick and a shovel were bought."

Principle Components Analysis: A data analysis technique that seeks to weight the importance of a variety of predictors so that they optimally discriminate between various possible predicted outcomes.

Prior Probability: The probability of an event is occurring without dependence on (conditional to) some other event. It is in contrast to conditional probability.

Pruning: Eliminating lower level splits or entire sub-trees in a decision tree. This term is also used to describe algorithms that adjust the topology of a neural net by removing (*i.e.*, pruning) hidden nodes.

R

Radial Basis Function Networks: Neural networks that combine some of the advantages of neural networks with those of nearest neighbor techniques. In radial basis functions the hidden layer is made up of nodes that represent prototypes or clusters of records.

Range: The range of the data is the difference between the maximum value and the minimum value. Alternatively, range can include the minimum and maximum.

RDBMS: Relational Database Management System.

Record: The fundamental data structure is used for performing data analysis. It is also called a table row or example. A typical record would be the structure that contains all relevant information pertinent to one particular customer or account.

Regression: A data analysis technique is classically used in statistics for building predictive models for continuous prediction fields. The technique automatically determines a mathematical equation that minimizes some measure of the error between the prediction from the regression model and the actual data.

Regression Tree: A decision tree that predicts values of continuous variables.

Reinforcement Learning: A training model where an intelligence engine (*e.g.*, neural network) is presented with a sequence of input data followed by a reinforcement signal.

Relational Database (RDB): A database built to conform to the relational data model; includes the catalog and all the data described therein.

Response: A binary prediction field is that indicates response or non response to a variety of marketing interventions. The term is generally used when referring to models that predict response or to the response field itself.

Re-substitution Error: The estimate of error based on the differences between the predicted values of a trained model and the observed values in the training set.

Right-hand Side: When an association between two variables is defined, the second item is called the right-hand side (or consequent). For example, in the relationship "When a prospector buys a pick, he buys a shovel 14% of the time," "buys a shovel" is the right-handside.

ROLAP: It stands for Relational Online Analytical Processing.

RTDW: Real Time Data warehouse is an analytical component of an enterprise level data stream that supports continuous, asynchronous, multi-point delivery of data. RTDW data moves straight from the source systems to decision makers without form the staging.

R-squared: A number between 0 and 1 that measures how well a model fits its training data. One is a perfect fit; however, zero implies the model has no predictive ability. It is computed as the covariance between the predicted and observed values divided by the standard deviations of the predicted and observed values.

S

Sampling: The process is by which only a fraction of all available data is used to build a model or perform exploratory analysis. Sampling can provide relatively good models at much less computational expense than using the entire database.

(or)

Creating a subset of data is from the whole. Random sampling attempts to represent the whole by choosing the sample through a random mechanism.

Segmentation: The process or result of the process that creates mutually exclusive collections of records that share similar attributes either in unsupervised learning (such as clustering) or in supervised learning for a particular prediction field.

Sequence Discovery: The same as association, except that the time sequence of events is also considered. For example, "Twenty percent of the people who buy a VCR buy a camcorder within four months."

Sensitivity Analysis: The process is in which determines the sensitivity of a predictive model to small fluctuations in predictor value. Through this technique end users can gauge the effects of noise and environmental change on the accuracy of the model.

(or)

Varying the parameters of a model to assess the change in its output.

Significance: A probability measure of how strongly the data support a certain result (usually of a statistical test). If the significance of a result is said to be .05, it means that there is only a .05 probability that the result could have happened by chance alone. Very low significance (less than .05) is usually taken as evidence that the data mining model should be accepted since events with very low probability seldom occur. So if the estimate of a parameter in a model showed a significance of .01 that would be evidence that the parameter must be in the model.

Simulated Annealing: An optimization algorithm loosely based on the physical process of annealing metals through controlled heating and cooling.

SMP: Symmetric multi-processing is a computer configuration where many CPUs share a common operating system, main memory and disks. They can work on different parts of a problem at the same time.

Snowflake Schema: It contain normalized dimension tables in a tree like structure with many nesting levels.

Standardize: A collection of numeric data is standardized by subtracting a measure of central location (such as the mean or median) and by dividing by some measure of spread (such as the standard deviation, interquartile range or range). This yields data with a similarly shaped histogram with values centered around 0. It is sometimes useful to do this with inputs into neural nets and also inputs into other regression models.

Star Schema: It is a data warehouse schema where there is only one "fact table" and many denormalized dimensional table. Fact table contains primary keys from all the dimension tables and other numeric columns of additive numeric facts.

Structured Query Language (SQL): A standard language is for the access of data in a relational database.

Supervised Learning: A class of data mining and machine learning applications and techniques where the system builds a model based on the prediction of a well defined prediction field. This is in contrast to unsupervised learning where there is no particular goal aside from pattern detection.

Support: The relative frequency or number of times a rule produced by a rule induction system occurs within the database. The higher the support is the better the chance of the rule capturing a statistically significant pattern.

Surrogate Key: It is a substitution for the natural primary key. It is unique identifier or number for each record of a dimension table that can be used for the primary key to the table.

T

Targeted Marketing: The marketing of products to select groups of consumers those are more likely than average to be interested in the offer.

Test Data: A data set independent of the training data set, used to fine-tune the estimates of the model parameters (*i.e.*, weights).

Test Error: The estimate of error based on the difference between the predictions of a model on a test data set and the observed values in the test data set when the test data set was not used to train the model.

Time Series: A series of measurements taken at consecutive points in time. Data mining products which handle time series incorporate time-related operators such as moving average.

Time-series Forecasting: The process of using a data mining tool (e.g., neural networks) to learn to predict temporal sequences of patterns, so that, given a set of patterns, it can predict a future value.

Time Series Model: A model that forecasts future values of a time series based on past values. The model form and training of the model usually take into consideration the correlation between values as a function of their separation in time.

Topology: For a neural net, topology refers to the number of layers and the number of nodes in each layer.

Training: Another term for estimating a model's parameters based on the data set at hand.

Training Data: A data set used to estimate or train a model.

Transformation: A re-expression of the data such as aggregating it, normalizing it, changing its unit of measure, or taking the logarithm of each data item.

U

Unsupervised Learning: A data analysis technique is whereby a model is built without a well defined goal or prediction field. The systems are used for exploration and general data organization. Clustering is an example of an unsupervised learning system.

V

Validation: The process of testing the models with a data set different from the training data set.

Visualization: Graphical display of data and models which helps the user in understanding the structure and meaning of the information contained in them. Graphical capabilities range from simple scatter plots to complex multi-dimensional representations.

Variance: The most commonly used statistical measure of dispersion. The first step is to square the deviations of a data item from its average value. Then the average of the squared deviations is calculated to obtain an overall measure of variability.

W

Windowing: It is used when training a model with time series data. A window is the period of time used for each training case. For example, if we have weekly stock price data that covers fifty weeks, and we set the window to five weeks, then the first training case uses weeks one through five and compares its prediction to week six. The second case uses weeks two through six to predict week seven, and so on.

REFERENCES

1. Data Mining : Concepts and Techniques -Jaiwei Han, Macheline Kamber.
2. Introduction to Data Mining with Case Studies —K.Gupta.
3. Text Mining Application Programming —Manu Konchady.
4. Data Mining techniques —Arun K pujari.
5. Soft computing in information retrieval —Fabio Crestani, Gabridge pasi.
6. Introduction to Machine learning —Nils J Njlsson.
7. Soft computing methodologies and Applications —Frank Hoffman, Mario koppen, Frank.
8. Artificial Neural Networks —B. Yagnanaraya.
9. Cohen M, Grossberg S 1983 Absolute stability of global pattern formation and parallel storage by competitive neural networks. IEEE Trans. Syst, Man Cybern. SMC-13: 815-825.
10. Cole R, Fanty M, Muthuswamy Y, Gopalakrishna M 1992 Speaker-independent recognition of spoken English letters. Proc. Int. Joint ConJ Neural Networks, San Diego, CA.
11. Collins E, Ghosh S, Scotfield C L 1988 An application of a multiple neural network learning system to emulation of mortgage underwriting judgements. IEEE Int. Conf. Neural Networks (Piscataway, NJ: IEEE Press) 2: 459-466.
12. Cybenko G 1989 Continuous value neural networks with two hidden layers are sufficient. Math. Control. Signal Syst. 2: 303-314.
13. Artificial Neural Networks —Robert J.Schalkoff Mc Graw Hill.
14. Fausett, L., Fundamentals of Neural Networks, Prentice-Hall, Englewood Cliffs, NJ, 1994.
15. Haykin, S., Neural Networks: A Comprehensive Foundation, Prentice Hall, Upper Saddle River, NJ, 1999.
16. www.dataminninglab.com.

INDEX

T

U

V

W

Z